"There are few books that have touched, moved and inspired me as much as The Millionaire Fastlane. It has crystallized my thought processes in building, developing and implementing that 'formula' in my businesses and in life as a whole. It has also helped me in formulating AND creating multiple scalable revenue streams to the tune of nearly $2 million a year and growing. All without any formal education and a C student in high school. It isn't easy, but it is simple."

— R. RUDE, SPRINGFIELD, MISSOURI

"To say that your advice and the 'Fastlane principles' have changed my life is an understatement. I knew there was a better life out there, but I had become frustrated about how to reach it. After reading your advice, it all started coming together for me. I began to see why I was living paycheck to paycheck. I decided then that I was going to escape it. Four years later, I have almost quadrupled my net worth. I have saved and invested more in the past few years than many of my friends in their 30s."

— M. GOMEZ, WASHINGTON, NEW JERSEY

"I've owned my own business for 40 years and have read countless books... in the hundreds of business books I've read—NONE—I mean NONE are even close to delivering the humor, the clarity and the wisdom that MJ has demonstrated in his two books. If you are looking for a better way, this is your LAST STOP. You have arrived. Don't waste another moment. Get and read the books, NOW!"

— A. BERNADUCCI (USER, FASTLANE FORUM, NEW JERSEY)

"Before reading Fastlane, I was living the perfect suburban dream. Solid job, stockpiling money in a 401(k), mortgaging a house I couldn't afford, and drowning in student loan debt. That's when I learned about the Slowlane. I was going nowhere on that 40-year journey, hoping to retire on a shaky 401(k) that probably won't be worth much with inflation. Every page was a sucker punch to the gut. It shook my beliefs in what was expected of me as an American adult. But it uncovered something deep inside of me: the desire to control my own destiny and create a legacy. So, while I slaved away at my job, I joined MJ's community and learned. After a year of learning, trials and tribulations, I started my own business. Another year later, I have launched a health food company that is nationally distributed and on the verge of becoming a big player in my category. I'm no millionaire yet, but my blinker is ON and I'm merging into the Fastlane!"

— SCOTT WEST, TAMPA, FLORIDA

"It's one of the greatest books I've ever read. I know people say there aren't any shortcuts to success, but this book is literally the only shortcut that I truly think exists. Read it if you haven't already. And if you have, read it again, at least once a year. Every time you'll find a new golden nugget that you didn't notice before."

— AMINMO (USER, FASTLANE FORUM, TACOMA WASHINGTON)

"The Millionaire Fastlane is THE quintessential book for business. Consider it your business Bible."

— T. PHAM (USER, FASTLANE FORUM, SAN JOSE CALIFORNIA)

"Exceptional is the only word I have. The book woke me up so many times at night because of the impact it had."

— ECLS18 (USER, FASTLANE FORUM, BC, CANADA)

"If I had to trade in all my knowledge from self-development books and could keep only one, it would be Millionaire Fastlane. The amount of paradigm shifts in the book is stupefying. I feel that if we lived in more backwards times, this would be decreed forbidden knowledge to thwart social mobility and maintain the social hierarchy. Thanks MJ for giving us the manifesto of our age!"

— WAX COMICAL (USER, FASTLANE FORUM, NSW, AU)

Wow! Has to be one of the most fantastic business books I've read, and I've read many. It should be made compulsory reading for every young person once they turn 16, as a matter of government policy. The clarity at which MJ drives his points and examples he uses are exceptional. Thanks MJ for bringing such a book to the world. I'm sure it will remain a legend for several decades to come, if not centuries.

— GENIUS01 (USER, THE FASTLANE FORUM, VIRGINIA)

"The implications of this book are absolutely empowering and makes freedom in today's world 100 percent attainable. I thought I had the right conclusions about business and life, but this pulls everything together for a real paradigm shift."

— CHINGADING (USER, FASTLANE FORUM, SEATTLE WASHINGTON)

"I read every chapter twice. It was like waking from a 20 year coma to a spotlight in my face. The hard truth analogies did as intended, challenging and changing everything I knew about my financial path, or lack thereof. It put real perspective on my world of hourly wage limits and saving for decades as the value of a dollar diminishes. No more trading 5 for 2. MJ, thanks for waking me up."

— B. COLE (USER, FASTLANE FORUM, VIRGINIA)

To read more testimonials (over 5,000 of them!) about how Fastlane has changed lives, please visit: http://bit.ly/2ILqKQ6

the Millionaire FASTLANE

CRACK THE CODE TO WEALTH AND LIVE RICH FOR A LIFETIME

MJ DeMARCO

Published by
Viperion Publishing Corporation
PO Box 18151
Fountain Hills, AZ 85269

ISBN 978-0-9843581-0-6
Library of Congress Control Number: 2010934089

Printed in the USA

Additional Fastlane Resources

Advance Your Fastlane!

In 2007 I founded The Fastlane Forum,
a global community dedicated to the
advancement of Unscripted® Entrepreneurship.
Join over 40,000 entrepreneurs who are
transforming their dreams to reality.
(And YES, it is FREE.)
https://www.theFastlaneForum.com

MJDeMarco

https://www.MJDeMarco.com
https://twitter.com/MJDeMarco
https://instagram.com/MJ.Demarco
https://youtube.com/FastlaneMJ

The Millionaire Fastlane

http://www.theMillionaireFastlane.com

Unscripted: Life, Liberty, & the Pursuit of Entrepreneurship

http://www.getUnscripted.com

Language Translations Available

The Millionaire Fastlane is available
worldwide in the following languages:
French, Italian, Spanish, Chinese (Simplified and Complex)
Thai, Vietnamese Italian, Polish, Turkish, Russian,
Estonian, Korean, Hungarian, Japanese,
and more coming soon.

Preface

THE "LAMBORGHINI PROPHECY" COMPLETES

The Millionaire Fastlane is the echo of a chance encounter I had long ago when I was a pudgy teenager. It was a Fastlane spark of awareness, an enlightenment triggered by a stranger driving a mythic car—a Lamborghini Countach. The Fastlane was born, and with it the belief and resolution that wealth need not take 50 years of financial mediocrity devoured by decades of work, decades of saving, decades of mindless frugality, and decades of 8% stock market returns.

Often, this book references the Lamborghini brand, and it isn't to brag to say I've owned a few. The Lamborghini icon represents the fulfillment of a prophecy in my life. It innocently began when I saw my first Lamborghini and it kicked my ass out of my comfort zone. I confronted its young owner and asked a simple question: "How can you afford such an awesome car?"

The answer I received, unveiled in Chapter 2, was short and powerful, but I wish I had more. I wish that young man had taken an hour, a day, or a week to talk to me. I wish that stranger would have mentored me on how to get what I thought the Lamborghini represented: *wealth*.

I wish that man had reached into his car and given me a book.

Years later, I would relive that same moment in role reversal. To celebrate my burgeoning Fastlane success, I bought my first exotic car—a legendary beast known as a Lamborghini Diablo. If you've never had the opportunity to drive a car that costs more than most people's homes, let me tell you how it works: You can't be shy. People chase you in traffic. They tailgate, rubberneck, and cause accidents. Getting gas is an event: people snap photos, enraged environmentalists throw you an evil eye, and haters speculate about the length of your penis—as if owning a Hyundai implies being well endowed. Mostly, people ask questions.

The most frequent questions come from leering and inquisitive teenagers, as I was many years ago: "Wow, how can you afford one of these?" or "What do you do?" People associate Lamborghinis with wealth, and while that's an illusion (any dimwit can finance a ridiculously expensive car), it's indicative of a dream lifestyle that most people conceive as incomprehensible.

Now when I hear the same question I asked decades ago, I have the power to gift a book and perhaps, to gift a dream...

This book is my official answer.

Contents

Introduction

THE ROAD TO WEALTH HAS A SHORTCUT

There's a hidden road to wealth and financial freedom, a shortcut of blistering speed where you can achieve wealth in youthful exuberance over elder entropy. Yes, you don't have to settle for mediocrity. You can live rich, retire four decades early, and live a life that most can't. Sadly, the shortcut is cleverly camouflaged from your view. Instead of the shortcut, you're led down a paralyzing road to mediocrity—a dulled cornucopia of financial orthodoxy preened to the slumbering masses, a legion of mandates that sacrifices your wildest dreams in favor of numbed expectations.

That road? It's financial mediocrity, known as "Get Rich Slow," "The Slowlane," or "Wealth in a Wheelchair." That tedium sounds like this:

> *Go to college, get good grades, graduate, get a good job, save 10% of your paycheck, invest in the stock market, preferably in a low cost indexed-fund, max your 401(k), slash your credit cards, and clip coupons . . . then, someday, when you are, oh, 65 years old, you will be rich.*

This dictation is a decree to trade life, for life. It's the long way, and no, it isn't scenic. If wealth were an ocean voyage, "Get Rich Slow" would be sailing around the horn of South America, while the Fastlaner uses the shortcut—the Panama Canal.

The Millionaire Fastlane isn't a static strategy that preaches "go buy real estate," "think positively," or "start a business," but a complete psychological and mathematical formula that cracks wealth's code and unlocks the gateway to the shortcut. The Fastlane is a progression of distinctions that gives probability to the unspeakable: Live richly today while young, and decades before standard norms of retirement.

Yes, you can win a lifetime of freedom and prosperity, and it doesn't matter if you're 18 or 40. What "Get Rich Slow" tries to accomplish in 50 years, and I emphasize "try", the Fastlane shortcut does in five.

WHY CAN'T YOU DRIVE THE SHORTCUT?

If you're a typical wealth seeker, your approach can be predictably foretold by a timeless question: *What do I have to do to get rich?* The quest for the answer—wealth's Holy Grail—throws you into a frame of mind likened to hot pursuit. Sought and chased are a variety of strategies, theories, careers, and schemes that supposedly promise great wealth. Invest in real estate! Start an Amazon business! Trade cryptocurrencies! Play pro ball! "What do I have to do?" screams the wealth seeker!

No, please stop.

The answer is more about *what you've been doing than what you haven't.* There's an old proverb that has mutated a few times but the gist is this: If you want to keep getting what you're getting, keep doing what you're doing.

The translation? **STOP!** If you aren't wealthy, STOP doing what you're doing. STOP following the conventional wisdom. STOP following the crowd and using the wrong formula. STOP following the roadmap that forsakes dreams and leads to mediocrity. STOP traveling roads with punitive speed limits and endless detours. I call it "anti-advice," and much of this book follows this prescription.

This book lists nearly 300 wealth distinctions designed to crack the code to wealth and get you off your current road and onto a new one where you can expose wealth's shortcut. The distinctions are directional markers to "STOP" your old ways of action, thinking, and believing, and reorient you into a new direction. In essence, *you have to unlearn what you have learned.*

YOUR REALITY DOESN'T CHANGE MINE

This section is for the haters. I present the Fastlane with brash cynicism. This book contains a lot of "tough love," and while it is opinionated, you ultimately have to seek your own truth. The Fastlane might insult, offend, or challenge you because it will violate everything you've been taught. It will contradict the teachings of your parents, teachers, and financial planners. And since I violate all that society represents, you can bet mediocre minds will take issue.

Thankfully, your belief (or disbelief) of Fastlane strategy doesn't change my reality; it only changes yours. Let me repeat: Your opinion of the Fastlane doesn't change (and can't change) my reality; *its purpose is to change yours.*

So let me tell you about my reality. Everyday I pinch myself bruised in gratitude and happiness. My home is a big McMansion overlooking the mountains in beautiful Fountain Hills, Arizona. It has everything but the mortgage. There are rooms in my house that I don't visit for months. Yes, the home is too large, and that story is a horrifying epic best forgotten.

I can't remember the last time I set an alarm clock and jolted awake—everyday is a Saturday. I have no job and no boss. I don't own a suit or a tie. My cholesterol level confirms that I dine at Italian restaurants too often. I smoke cheap cigars. As of this edition, I drive a twelve year old Toyota Tacoma with over 120,000 miles. While I used to own a variety of exotic cars, mostly Lamborghinis, I traded in that ostentatiousness for eleven jaw-dropping acres in Sedona Arizona. The only "toy" I own is an off-road, rock-crawling UTV capable of scaling Mount Everest, but the Sedona red rocks will do just fine. I almost lost my life street racing a

750-horsepower Viper laced with nitrous oxide. I shop at Costco, Kohl's, and wherever store is convenient. Yes, that includes Wal-Mart, but only if the parking lot is empty . No, I didn't drive the Lamborghini to Wal-Mart; that might cause a disruption in the space-time-continuum. Trekkies know better.

I don't own a watch more expensive than $149. I enjoy tennis, biking, swimming, hiking, softball, poker, pool, art, travel, writing, and exploring the beautiful Arizona desert in my UTV. I travel whenever and wherever I want. I have no debt and paid cash for my homes. I also paid off mother's mortgage so she could enjoy retirement while not fretting about cost of living increases.

If you're looking to buy me a gift, good luck. I have everything I want so finding me a gift "I need or want" is akin to solving the Drake equation. Because prices for most things are inconsequential, I buy when the urge hits.

I made my first million when I was 31. Five years earlier, I was living with my mother and struggling. I retired when I was 37. Every month I earn thousands of dollars in income, interest and appreciation on investments working around the globe. No matter what I do on any day, one thing is sure: I get paid and I do not have to work. I have financial freedom because I cracked wealth's code and escaped financial mediocrity. I'm a normal guy living an abnormal life. It's a fantasy land but my reality, my normal, my deviation from ordinary where I can pursue my most implausible dreams in a life free of financial encumbrances. Had I chosen the preordained road, "Get Rich Slow," my dreams would be on life-support, likely replaced with a mortgage, a heavy morning commute, and a 50 MG prescription of Prozac.

How about your dreams? Do they need resuscitation? Is your life on a road that converges with a dream, or is one? If your dreams have lost probability it's possible "Get Rich Slow" has killed them. "Get Rich Slow" criminally asks you to barter your freedom for freedom. It's an insane trade which suffocates dreams.

Alternatively, if you travel the right roads and leverage the right roadmap, you can resurrect your dreams to realistic probabilities. Yes, as a Fastlane traveler you can create wealth fast, screw "Get Rich Slow," and win a lifetime of prosperity, freedom, and dream fulfillment . . . just as I did.

If this book hasn't found you early in life, don't worry. The Fastlane doesn't care about your age, your job experience, your race, or your gender. It doesn't care about your "F" in eighth grade gym class or your beer-drinking reputation in college. The Fastlane doesn't care about your Big-Ten college degree or your Harvard MBA. It doesn't ask you to be a famous athlete, actor, or a finalist on *American Idol*. The Fastlane is merciful on your past if you just unlock the gateway into its universe.

Finally, at the risk of sounding like a wannabe guru who proliferates your Facebook feed, let me clarify: I'm not a guru and don't want to be one. This is the book I wish I had when I was twenty—and it doesn't include a "free training" that funnels into $10,000 seminar.

Likewise, "guruness" implies "know-it-all" and that's not me. Twenty-plus years into this and I humbly admit, I have more to learn. If a label is sought, call me the "anti-guru" of "Get Rich Slow."

SORRY, NO FOUR-HOUR WORK WEEK HERE

First, let's get something clear: This isn't a "how-to" book. I'm not going to tell you every nuance about "how I did it" because how I did it isn't relevant. This book doesn't contain a list of websites that outline ways to "outsource" your life. Success is a journey, and it can't be outsourced to the Philippines in a four-hour work-week. The Millionaire Fastlane is like a yellow brick road paved in PSYCHOLOGY and MATHEMATICS that put the odds of massive wealth in your favor.

During my Fastlane journey of discovery, I always sought the absolute, infallible formula that would lead to wealth. What I found was ambiguity and subjective imperatives like "be determined" or "persistence pays" or "it's not what you know, but who." While these tidbits were pieces of the puzzle, they didn't guarantee wealth. A workable formula uses mathematical constructs, not ambiguous statements. Does wealth have a mathematical formula, a code that you could exploit to tilt the odds in your favor? Yes, and the Fastlane quantifies it.

Now for the bad news. Many wealth seekers have false expectations about "money" books and think that some fairy-guru will do the work. The road to wealth has no escort and is always under construction. No one drops millions on your lap; the road is yours to travel and yours alone. *I can open the door but I can't make you walk through it.*

I don't claim the Fastlane is easy; it's hard work. If you expect a four-hour work week here, you will be disappointed. All I can be is that creepy munchkin pointing off in the distance with a stern directive, "Follow the yellow brick road."

The Fastlane is that road.

COFFEE WITH A MULTIMILLIONAIRE

I've approached this book conversationally, as if you're my new friend and we're having coffee in a quaint neighborhood café. My sole intent is education—not to upsell you into some expensive seminar, membership website, or some backend marketing funnel. That's right—I'M SELLING NOTHING—but the wisdom I wished I had when I was struggling. While I will talk with you like a friend, let's face it: I don't have a clue who you are. I don't know about your past, your age, your biases, your spouse, or your education. Thus, I need to make some general assumptions to ensure that our conversation seems personal to you. My assumptions:

- You look around your life and think, "there's got to be more."
- You have big dreams, yet you're concerned that the road you're traveling will never converge with those dreams.

- You're college-bound, college-enrolled, or college-educated.
- You have a job you don't enjoy or isn't going to make you rich.
- You have little savings and carry a load of debt.
- You contribute regularly to a 401(k) or a low cost indexed mutual fund.
- You realize that at the rate your invested savings are growing, you'll be able to retire far beyond your life expectancy.
- You see rich people and wonder, "how did they do it?"
- You have bought a few "get rich quick" books and/or programs.
- You live in a free, democratic society where education and free choice are standards.
- Your parents subscribe to the old school: "Go to college and get a good job."
- You don't have any physical talent; your chances of becoming a professional athlete, singer, entertainer, or actor are zero.
- You are young and full of enthusiasm about the future, but unsure where to direct it.
- You are older and have been in the workforce for some time. After all these years, you don't have a lot to show for it and are tired of "starting over."
- You've put your heart and soul into a job only to be laid off due to a bad economy, corporate BS, or cutbacks.
- Your children are parented by an electronic device because you're too busy, too overworked, and too underpaid.
- You've lost money in the stock market or traditional investments championed by mainstream financial gurus.

If some of these assumptions reflect your situation, this book will have an impact.

HOW THIS BOOK IS ORGANIZED

At the conclusion of each chapter, there is a subsection titled "Chapter Summary: Fastlane Distinctions" which chronicles the critical distinctions to Fastlane strategy. Don't ignore these! They're the building blocks to engineering your Fastlane. Additionally, the stories and examples in this book come from the Fastlane Forum (TheFastlaneForum.com) and other personal finance forums. While the stories are real and come from real people with real problems, I've changed the names and edited the dialogue for clarity. And finally, feel free to discuss Fastlane strategy with thousands of others at the Fastlane Forum. When the Fastlane changes your life, stop by and tell us how!

It took me years to uncover and assemble the Fastlane strategies, learn them, use them, and ultimately make millions. Bored, retired, and yes, still young with hair, I give you *The Millionaire Fastlane: Crack the Code to Wealth and Live Rich for A Lifetime!* Fasten your seat belts, grab a ten-buck latte, and let's go on a road trip!

Part 1

Wealth in a Wheelchair: "Get Rich Slow" is Get Rich Old

The Great Deception

Normal is not something to aspire to,
it's something to get away from.

~ JODIE FOSTER

THE "MTV CRIBS" EPISODE THAT NEVER HAPPENED

Host: "Today we visit 22-year-old Big Daddyhoo and his 8,000-square-foot crib here on the beautiful Atlantic coastline live from sunny Palm Beach Florida . . . so, Big Daddyhoo, tell us about your rides!"

Big Daddyhoo: "Yo dawg, we gotz the Ferrari 488GTB over there with the 22-inch rims, the sick Lamborghini Huracan over there with the custom 12-speaker stereo, and for those nights when I just wanna chillax with the ladies, the Rolls Royce Arnage does my do."

Host: "So, Big Daddyhoo, how can you afford all these gorgeous rides? And this mansion on the beach? It must have cost more than $20 million!"

Big Daddyhoo: "Yo let me tell you dawg, Big Daddyhoo got rich chilling in low cost index-funds and popping phat money in my 401(k)s down at my Win-Go Wireless job."

Suddenly, you hear a record screech off the turntable.

Silence.

As you can imagine, this scenario would never happen. Big Daddy's answer is preposterous and laughable. We're smart enough to know that wealthy 22-year-olds aren't rich because they diligently saved their paycheck from a job and stashed it away in an index-fund. We know that people who get rich young fall into a unique subset of society: pro athletes, rappers, actors, entertainers, and famous people. Those of us outside this demography are stuck with the traditional advice showered upon us by financial experts.

It's called "Get Rich Slow" and sounds something like this: Go to school, get good grades, graduate, get a good job, invest in the stock market, max-out your 401(k), cut up your credit cards, and clip coupons . . . then someday, when you are, oh, 65 years old, you will be rich.

"GET RICH SLOW" IS A LOSING GAME

If you want to get rich and "Get Rich Slow" is your strategy, I have bad news. It's a losing game, with your time wagered as the gamble. Is the guy with the palatial beach estate and the $500,000 supercar on the driveway rich because he invested in mutual funds? Or clipped coupons from the local Super-Saver? Of course not. So why do we give credence to this advice as a legitimate road that leads to wealth and financial freedom? Because the government, a radio personality, and Goldman Sachs says so?

Show me a 22-year-old who got rich investing in indexed-funds. Show me the man who earned millions in three years by maximizing his 401(k). Show me the young twenty-something who got rich clipping coupons. Where are these people?

They don't exist. They're impossible fairy tales.

Yet, we continue to trust the same tired gang of financial sycophants who preach these doctrines of wealth. Yes sir, get a job, work 50 years, save, live mindlessly frugal, invest in the stock market, and soon, your day of freedom will arrive at age 70 . . . and if the stock market is kind and you're lucky, 60! Gee, doesn't this "wealth in a wheelchair" financial plan sound exciting?

In today's reckless financial climate of monetary debt and inflation, I am shocked people still believe these strategies even work. Wasn't it the 2008 recession that exposed "Get Rich Slow" for the fraud it is? Oh I get it, if you're employed for 40 years and avoid 40% market downturns, "Get Rich Slow" works; just sit back, work, and hope death don't meet you first because, golly-gee, you're going to be the richest guy in the retirement home!

The message of "Get Rich Slow" is clear: Sacrifice your today, your dreams, and your life for a plan that pays dividends after most of your life has evaporated.

Let me be blunt: If your road to wealth devours most of your active adult life and is not guaranteed, that road sucks. A "road to wealth" codependent on Wall Street and anchored by time with your life wagered as the gamble is a rotten alley.

Nonetheless, the preordained plan continues to wield power, lickspittled and enforced by a legion of hypocritical "financial experts" who aren't rich by their own advice, but by their own Millionaire Fastlane. The Slowlane prognosticators—people who make a fortune on investment management fees, seven-figure book deals, and ancillary financial programs and subscriptions— know something that they aren't telling you: *What they teach doesn't work, but selling it does.*

WEALTH YOUNG: IS IT BULLSHIT?

The Millionaire Fastlane isn't about being retired old with millions, but about redefining wealth to include youth, fun, freedom, and prosperity. Take this comment posted on the Fastlane Forum:

> *"Is it bullshit? You know, the dream to be young and live the life—to own the exotic cars, to own the dream house, to have free time to travel and pursue your dreams. Can you really get free of the rat race young? I'm a 23-year-old investment banker in Chicago, Illinois. I make a modest salary with modest commissions. By most people's standards, I have a good job. I hate it. I cruise Chicago's downtown and I see some guys living the life. Guys driving expensive exotic cars and I think to myself . . . They're all 50 or older with silver hair! One of them once told me, 'You know kid, when you finally can afford a toy like this, you're almost too old to enjoy it!' The guy was a 52-year-old real estate investor. I remember looking at him and thinking 'God . . . that can't be true! It's gotta be bullshit! It's gotta be!'"*

I can verify—it isn't bullshit. You can live "the life" and still be young. Old age is not a prerequisite to wealth or retirement. However, the real BS is thinking you can do it by the default "Get Rich Slow" construct, at least by the time you hit your 30th birthday. Believing that old age is a precondition to retirement is the real BS. The real BS is allowing "Get Rich Slow" to steal your dreams.

REINVENT RETIREMENT TO INCLUDE YOUTH

Say "retirement" and what do you see? I see a crotchety old man on a porch in a creaky rocking chair. I see pharmacies, doctor's offices, walkers, and unsightly urinary undergarments. I see nursing homes and overburdened loved ones. I see old and immobile. Heck, I even smell something musty circa 1971. People retire in their 60s or 70s. Even at that age, they struggle to make ends meet and have to rely on bankrupted government programs just to survive. Others work well into their "golden years" just to maintain their lifestyle. Some never make it and work until death.

How does this happen? Simple. "Get Rich Slow" takes a lifetime and its success is nefariously dependent on too many factors *you cannot control.* Invest 50 years into a job and miserly living, then, one day, you can retire rich alongside your wheelchair and prescription pillbox. How uninspiring.

Yet, millions undertake the 50-year gamble. Those who win the Wall Street lottery receive their reward of financial freedom with a stinking lump of turd: *old age.* Gee thanks.

But don't worry; patronization rains from the heavens: "These are the golden years!" Who they kidding? Golden to whom?

If the road to wealth and freedom devours 50 years of your life, is it worth it? A 50-year journey isn't compelling, and because of it, few succeed and those who do settle for financial freedom in life's twilight.

The problem with accepted norms of retirement is *what you do not see.*

You don't see youth, you don't see fun, and you don't see the realization of dreams. The golden years aren't golden at all but a waiting room for death. If you want financial freedom before the Grim Reaper hits the on-deck circle, "Get Rich Slow" isn't the answer.

If you want to retire young with health, vibrancy, and luxurious hair, the kind fit for a shampoo commercial, you need to ignore society's default "Get Rich Slow" roadmap and the mainstream gurus spoon-feeding you the slop in the trough. There is another way.

CHAPTER SUMMARY: FASTLANE DISTINCTIONS

- "Get Rich Slow" demands a long life of gainful employment.
- "Get Rich Slow" is a losing game because it is codependent on Wall Street and anchored by your time.
- The real golden years of life are when you're young, sentient, and vibrant.

How I Screwed "Get Rich Slow"

The object of life is not to be on the side of the masses, but to escape finding oneself in the ranks of the insane.

~ MARCUS AURELIUS

EXPOSING THE "GET RICH SLOW" DREAMKILLER

As a teenager, I never considered the idea of getting rich young. "Wealth + youth" was an equation that didn't compute simply because I didn't possess talent or physical capabilities. Common roads to wealth for the young are competitive and need talent; actor, musician, an entertainer or a pro athlete—all roads that had a big "ROAD CLOSED" sign that sneered, "Not a chance, MJ!"

So, early in life, I conceded. I gave up on my dreams. "Get Rich Slow" made it abundantly clear: Go to school, get a job, settle for less, sacrifice, be miserly and quit dreaming about financial freedom, mountainside homes, and exotic cars. But I still dreamed. It's what teenage boys do. For me, it was all about the cars—specifically, the Lamborghini Countach.

THE 90 SECONDS THAT CHANGED MY LIFE

I grew up in Chicago as a porky kid with few friends. I wasn't interested in teenage girls or sports, but lying around in a beanbag stuffing my face with doughnuts while watching Tom-n-Jerry reruns. Parental supervision was absent; Mom divorced Dad years earlier, which left my mother to raise my older siblings and I alone. Mom didn't have a college education or a career, unless a deep-frying job at Kentucky Fried Chicken qualified. That left me to my own indulgences, usually sweet-toothing and the latest episode of the *A-Team*. My exertions were characterized by a long broken broomstick: I used it as the TV's remote control since the real one was broken and I was too lazy to move. When I did move, the local ice cream shop was often my target; a sugary delight was a motive I could count on.

That day was like any other day: I sought ice cream. I plotted the flavor of my next indulgence and headed toward the ice cream parlor.

When I arrived, there IT was. I was face to face with my dream car; a Lamborghini Countach famous from the 80s hit movie *Cannonball Run*. Parked stoically like an omnipotent king, I gazed upon it like a worshiper beholden to its God. Awestruck, any thoughts of ice cream were ousted from my brain.

Posterized on my bedroom walls and drooled upon in my favorite car magazines, I was acutely familiar with the Lamborghini Countach: cunning, evil, obscenely fast, spaceship doors, and ungodly expensive. Yet, here it was just a few feet away, like Elvis resurrected. Its raw tangible grandeur was like an artisan coming face to face with an authentic Monet. The lines, the curves, the smell . . .

I gawked for a few minutes, until a young man left the ice cream parlor and headed toward the car. Could this be the owner? No way. He couldn't have been more than 25 years old. Dressed in blue jeans and an oversized flannel shirt with what I spied to be an *Iron Maiden* concert shirt underneath, I reasoned this couldn't be the owner. I expected an old guy: wrinkled, receding gray hairline, and dressed two seasons late. Not so.

"What the heck?" I mulled. How could a young guy afford such a kick-ass automobile? For God's sake, that car costs more than the house I live in! It's got to be a lottery winner, I speculated. Hmmm . . . or maybe some rich kid who inherited the family fortune. No, it's a pro athlete. Yes, that's it, I concluded.

Suddenly, a dare invaded my head: "Hey, why don't you ask the guy what he does for a living?" Could I? I stood on the sidewalk, dumbfounded while I argued with myself. Emboldened and washed with adrenaline, I found my legs moving toward the car as if my brain weren't agreeable. In the back of my mind, my brother taunted, "Danger, Will Robinson, danger!"

Sensing my approach, the owner quickly opened his door and hid his trepidation with a forced smile. Whoa. The car's door flung up into the sky, vertically, as opposed to swinging out sideways like a normal car. It threw me off what little game I had and I tried to maintain composure, as if cars with futuristic doors were standard. What couldn't have been more than 20 words seemed like a novel. My opportunity was here and I snatched it. "Excuse me, sir?" I nervously muttered, hoping he wouldn't ignore me. "May I ask what you do for a living?"

Relieved that I wasn't a teenage derelict, the owner kindly responded: "I'm an inventor." Perplexed that his answer didn't match my guesses; my prepared follow-up questions were nullified, paralyzing my next move. I stood there frozen like the ice cream I had sought minutes earlier. Sensing an escape opportunity, the young Lamborghini owner plunked into the driver's seat, closed the door, and started the engine. The loud roar of the exhaust swept through the parking lot, alerting all life forms to the Lamborghini's formidable presence. Whether I liked it or not, the conversation was over.

Knowing it might be years before I could enjoy a similar spectacle, I took mental inventory of the automotive unicorn before me. I left awakened and motivated as if a neural pathway suddenly smacked open in my brain.

THE LIBERATION FROM FAME AND TALENT

What changed that day? I was exposed to the Fastlane and a new truth. As for the sweets I pursued that day, I never made it into the store. I turned around and went home with a new reality. I wasn't athletic, I couldn't sing, and I couldn't act, but I could get rich as an entrepreneur.

From that point forward, things changed. The Lamborghini encounter lasted 90 seconds, but transcended a lifetime of new beliefs, new studies, and altered choices. I decided that someday I would own a Lamborghini and I would do it while I was young. I was not waiting until my next chance encounter or my next poster: I wanted it for myself. Yes, I retired the broomstick and got off my lazy ass.

THE SEARCH FOR THE MILLIONAIRE FASTLANE

After the Lamborghini encounter, I made a conscious effort to study young millionaires who weren't famous or physically talented. But I wasn't interested in all millionaires, just those who lived a rich, extravagant lifestyle. This examination led me to study a limited, obscure group of people: a small subset of fameless millionaires who met these criteria:

1) They were living a rich lifestyle or were capable of such. I wasn't interested in hearing from frugal millionaires who lived "next door" in the middle class.
2) They had to be relatively young (under 35) or they had to have acquired wealth fast. I wasn't interested in people who spent 40 years of their life jobbing and penny-pinching their way to millions. I wanted to be rich young, not old.
3) They had to be self-made. I was broke. Silver-spoon winners of the lucky sperm lottery weren't invited to my lab.
4) Their riches could NOT be from fame, physical talent, playing pro ball, acting, singing, or entertaining.

I sought millionaires who would have started like me, an average guy without any special skill or talent, who, somehow, made it big. Through high school and college, I religiously studied this millionaire divergence. I read magazines, books, and newspapers and watched documentaries of successful businessmen; anything that provided insight into this small subset of millionaires, I absorbed it.

Unfortunately, this zest to uncover the secret to fast wealth led me to disappointments. I was a late-night infomercial marketer's dream come true—gullible, willing, and armed with a credit card. I bought into countless opportunities, from "one tiny classified ad" to the Asian real estate mogul and his sexy bikini-clad yacht vixens. None of them delivered wealth, and despite the slick commercials and their claims, the large-breasted models never materialized.

As I fed my appetite for knowledge and endured one odd job after another, my research uncovered some remarkable common denominators. I was confident I had uncovered all the components to the Millionaire Fastlane and fameless wealth. I was determined to become rich young, and the journey would begin after college graduation. Little did I know what lay ahead—the roadblocks, the detours, and the mistakes.

RESISTANCE INTO MEDIOCRITY

I graduated from Northern Illinois University with two business degrees. For me, college seemed like a five-year brainwashing program for corporate homogenization. Nobody talked about entrepreneurship. All I heard from my teachers was "when you get hired" and "when you get a job" as if starting a business was a dirty thought. I resisted, but my friends didn't. They were hired for great jobs and bragged about it:

"I work for Motorola."
"I got a job at Northwestern Insurance!"
"Hertz Rental Cars hired me as a training manager!"

While I was happy for them, my friends bought into the lie what I affectionately call, "The Slowlane". Me? Thanks but no thanks. I wanted to avoid the Slowlane like a medieval plague. My idea was to find the Fastlane, retire rich, and retire young.

ROADBLOCKS, DETOURS, AND DEPRESSION

Despite the confidence, the next few years fell horribly short of my expectations. I lived with my mother as I bounced from one "opportunity" to another. Success was absent. Every month was a different business: vitamins, jewelry, some hot "turnkey" marketing program purchased from the back of a business magazine, or some goofy long-distance network marketing gig.

Despite the hard work, my record of failures grew, as did my mounting debts. Years passed and folly fermented as I was forced to take a series of ego-crippling jobs better suited for a Neanderthal: a busboy at a Chinese restaurant (yes, there are cockroaches in the back), a day laborer in the Chicago slums, pizza-delivery boy, flower-delivery boy, dispatcher, limo driver, early morning newspaper delivery for the *Chicago Tribune,* Subway sandwich restaurant salesman (WTF?), Sears stock clerk (in the freaking drapery department), charity can collector, and house painter.

The only thing worse than these shitty jobs and their pay? The hours. Most required a predawn start . . . 3 a.m., 4 a.m. . . . if any ungodly hour was involved you could bet my job required it. Five years of college and I graduated to live like a dairy farmer. Hell, money was so tight that I prostituted myself to an older woman to pay for my best friend's wedding gift. Yes, cougars preyed in the 1990s.

Meanwhile, my friends progressed in their careers: They got their 3% yearly pay increases. They bought their Mustangs and Acuras and their 1,200-square-foot townhouses. They appeared content and lived the expectant life prescribed by society. They were normal and I wasn't.

At 26 years old, I fell into depression; my businesses were not self-sufficient and neither was I. Seasonal depression gnawed at my fractured psyche. Chicago's rainy, dark, dreary weather made me crave the comfort of a warm bed and tasty pastries. Accomplishments were preceded by sunshine; so yes, I wasn't accomplishing much. Tired of the high-school dropout jobs, I struggled to get out of bed, and doubt became the daily affirmation. Physically, emotionally, and financially exhausted from failure, I knew my results weren't reflective of my true self. I knew the Fastlane way to wealth but just couldn't get it executed. What was I doing wrong? What was holding me back? After years of research and education, complete with a full closet of books, magazines, and "quick start" videos, I was further away from wealth. I sat stalled on the sidewalk with the Fastlane nowhere in sight.

My deep depression sunk me into escapes, but instead of drugs, sex, or alcohol, I lost myself in books and kept studying fameless millionaires. If I couldn't be successful, I'd escape into the lives of those who were by absorbing success stories and other rags-to-riches tales.

But it got worse.

The people in my life gave up on me. My long-time girlfriend proclaimed, "You have no resolve." She had a safe and secure job with a rental car agency, but we'd argue because she worked long hours for chump change, a whopping $28,000 a year. Of course, she rightly retorted with the facts: "You don't have a job, you make $27,000 less than me, and none of your businesses work." She was a smart cat. Our relationship ended as she found courtship with a corporate radio ad executive.

And then there was my mother. For the first years after college, she cut me slack, but then came the failures and the low-rent jobs. I begged patience. One of my pleads was a detailed commentary about Fastlane wealth creation for entrepreneurs—it operates under an *exponential* scale—those with jobs operate under a *linear* scale. Unfortunately, it didn't matter how great my charts and diagrams were; mom lost faith and I didn't blame her. Landing a man on Mars showed more promise.

Her directives dulled my drive. She'd shout, "Get a job, baby!" at least 20 times a week. Ugh, even today I shudder. That phrase, shouted in that voice, could exterminate cockroaches in a post-apocalyptic world. There were days I'd want to pound my head into a vise and crush my ears into deafness. "Get a job, baby!" bore into my soul; it was a motherly decree that ended the trial with the jury's unanimous verdict: "Failure, with a vote of no confidence."

Mom suggested, "The grocery store is hiring a deli manager, why don't you go down there and check it out?" As if my disaffected college education and next five years of struggle were to eclipse at the deli counter, cutting blocks of bologna and ladling potato salad to the neighborhood soccer moms. Thanks for the job tip, but I'll pass.

MY BLIZZARD OF AWAKENING

The agony of a cold Chicago blizzard flung me onto life's crossroads. It was a frigid night and I was dead tired working as a limo driver. Wet snow drenched my shoes while I fought a migraine headache. The four aspirins I chased hours earlier had no effect. As the intensity of the storm increased, it was clear: I wouldn't be getting home soon. My usual routes were snowed in. Frustrated, I pulled to the shoulder of a unlit road. I parked the limo and faced myself in darkened and dead silence.

I felt the cold chill of melted snow crawl up from my toes into my legs. Outside I saw a beautiful cascade of snowflakes, an ironic reminder about how much I hated the ugliness of winter. I dropped my head back into the seat and unleashed an epic groan. As I gazed at the cigarette-burned ceiling of the limousine, the reality hit me: "What the hell am I doing? Is this what my life has become?"

Sitting on an empty road in a blizzard in the dead of the night in the middle of nowhere, I'd had it. Sometimes clarity washes over you like a peaceful breeze and other times it hits you like a falling *Steinway* piano. For me, it was the latter. A sharp declaration clobbered my brain: "You cannot live another day like this!"

If I was going to survive, I needed to change.

THE DECISION TO CHANGE

The harsh winter shot me into swift action. I decided to change. I took control over something I thought was uncontrollable: my environment. I decided to relocate—to where, I didn't know, and at that moment, I didn't care.

In an instant, I felt powerful. The velocity of that choice infused my miserable existence with hope and a small drip of happiness. My failures evaporated and I felt reborn. *Suddenly a dead-end road converged with a dream.*

It wasn't about the decision to move; it was about taking control and knowing that I had a choice.

With this new power, I considered options that never seemed possible. I asked a simple question: "If I could live anywhere in the country without restraint, where would I live?" I thought about the things important to me, and circled five cities on a map. Within the next few weeks, I took a road trip and visited all of them. Weeks after that, I moved, or I should say, escaped.

I arrived in Phoenix with 900 bucks, no job, no friends, and no family—just 330 days of sun and a burning desire to hit the Fastlane. My possessions included an old mattress, a 10-year-old rusty Buick Skylark with no third gear, a few side businesses that made little cash, and several hundred books. Ground zero for my new life was a small studio apartment in central Phoenix that rented for $475 per month. I transformed my studio apartment into an office. No bedroom set, no furniture, just a mattress that invaded the kitchen. I slept with Pop Tart crumbs, a side effect of laying a mattress next to the kitchen counter.

I lived poor and without security, but I felt rich. I was in *control* of my life.

One of the many businesses I created was a website. While driving that limo in Chicago, sometimes I'd sit idle for hours and had plenty of downtime to read books. I didn't waste that time. While I waited for clients at the airport or while they got smashed at the local watering hole, I sat in the limo and read. And read. I studied everything from finance to Internet programming to more autobiographies of the rich.

The limo job did something special: it put me at the forefront of an unsolved need that needed a solution. One of my limo clients asked if I knew of any good limo companies in New York. I dropped the passenger off at the airport, but he left me with a seed of invention. If I lived in Chicago and needed prices and booking options for limo service in New York, where would I go to find it? I didn't have a New York Yellow Pages handy, and surely no one else outside of New York did either. Faced with this question, I concluded that other travelers would have the same challenge. So I built a website that would solve this problem.

Naturally because the Internet has no geographical limits, this venture traveled with me to Phoenix. But, like my prior businesses, it didn't make a lot of money.

However, now it was different.

I was debt-strapped and naked in a strange town with no money, job, or safety net. I had to focus.

I aggressively marketed my website. I sent out emails. Cold-called. Mailed letters. I learned search engine optimization (SEO). Because I couldn't afford books, I visited the Phoenix library daily and studied Internet programming languages. (This was before Wordpress and easy "drag and drop" content management systems.) I improved my website and learned about graphics and copywriting. Anything that could help me, I consumed.

Then one day I had a breakthrough; I received a call from a company in Kansas that raved about my website service and wanted me to design its website. While my focus wasn't web design, I obliged for a price of $400. They thought the price was a steal, and within 24 hours, I had built the company its website. I was ecstatic. In 24 hours, I had most of my rent payment. Then, coincidentally, not 24 hours later, I received another call from a company in New York asking for the same thing, a new website. I designed it for $600 and it took me two days to complete. I had another rent payment!

Now, I know this isn't a lot of money, but from poverty to $1,000 in three days felt like winning the 50-million-dollar Powerball. My first few months in Phoenix I gained traction and survived on my own for the first time in my life. No flower boy. No busboy. No pizza delivery. No sponging off Mom with cheap rent. I was purely self-employed! It was a momentous acceleration, a wind at my back that foreshadowed a directional change into a new universe of wealth generation.

But something still wasn't right. Something was missing and I knew it. Most of my income was attached to my website designs and not my website service portal. My income was tied to my time, website construction. More websites jobs meant more time spent, and if I didn't work, my income would stop.

My *time* was being sold off for money.

A NEW WEALTH EQUATION YIELDS WEALTH ACCELERATION

In the winter, a friend visited from Chicago. I showed him my web service and he was amazed at all the traffic my service received. I'd get ride arrangement inquiries from around the world, every minute of the day. How much for a limo from Boston to Worcester? How much from JFK to Manhattan? We'd scan my email inbox and it had 450 emails. Ten minutes passed, click refresh, and then there would be another 30 emails. Emails were pouring in several per minute. He suggested "Dude! Turn those emails into money somehow."

He was right, but how? And how can it solve a legitimate need while providing value? He left me with this challenge and I was intent to solve it.

Days later, I invented a risky, unproven solution and started working on it.

What was I going to do?

Instead of selling ad space, I was going to sell targeted, detailed leads and reservation inquiries.

There was a big problem though. Like, huge.

I had to convince my customers that this method of business was beneficial to them. At that time, this revenue model was new and ground-breaking. Because I had no predictive data (in any industry, much less the limo industry) I had to nail execution. As far as I know, I was one of the early pioneers of the lead generation model (if not the first) to adapt and succeed at it. Remember, this was the late nineties when databases and animated GIFs were considered technological marvels.

Despite having no roadmap or preemptive practices, I launched it.

In the short term, I expected the change to kill my income and it did. I predicted its success would take months, if it worked at all. The first month the new system generated $473. Yikes. I built more websites to fill my income gap. The second month's revenues were $694. Third month, $970. Then $1,832. $2,314. $3,733. And it continued and continued.

It worked.

My revenue, my income, and my assets grew exponentially but not without issue. As traffic grew, so did the complaints, the feedback, and the challenges. Improvements came directly from customer suggestions. Within days, sometimes hours, I'd implement customer ideas. My employees and I were known to answer clients' emails within minutes, if not an hour. I learned to be receptive to the consumer, and business exploded.

The workdays became long and challenging. Forty hours was a vacation; typical workweeks were 60 hours long. Days and weekends blurred together. While my new friends were out drinking and partying, I was hunkered down in my tiny apartment, regurgitating code. I didn't know if it was Thursday or Saturday, and it didn't matter. The glory of the hard work was this: *It didn't feel like work*; in fact, I enjoyed it. I didn't have a job; I had a passion to make a difference. Thousands of people benefited from something I created, which addicted me to the process. Although I had zero passion for the limo business, the passion came from making a profound difference!

I started to compile testimonials from clients.

"Because of you, my business grew tenfold."
"Your website led me to my biggest corporate client."
"Your company has been instrumental in growing my business."

This feedback was a different form of currency called happiness. I wasn't awash in riches quite yet, but I felt rich.

MY "FAKED" SHORTCUT TO WEALTH

In 2000, my telephone rang with a different type of inquiry. Technology startups called; they wanted to know if I would sell my business. In that year, the dot-com frenzy was in full force. Not a day went by without a tall tale about some dot-com millionaire who struck it rich by selling a tech property. Remember the fameless millionaires? This subset of the rich grew at a staggering rate, and the wave swelled my way.

So, did I want to sell my company? Hell yes! I had three offers to sell. Offer 1: $250,000. Offer 2: $550,000. Offer 3: $1,200,000. I accepted offer three and became a millionaire . . . instantly . . . well, almost.

It didn't last, as didn't the tech boom.

At the time, I thought $1.2 million dollars was a lot of money. It wasn't. Taxes. Worthless stock options. I made mistakes and invested poorly. I bought a Corvette, hoping it would make me look rich. I thought I was rich, but I really wasn't. By the time it was over, I had less than $300,000 left.

The tech implosion arrived with unforgiving consequences, at least for buyers of my company. Against my recommendations and domain knowledge, they made poor decisions; decisions that were good for short term revenue but horrific for long-term growth. They flushed money down the toilet as if there were an endless supply. Do we really need custom-branded water bottles? And logo T-shirts? Are these revenue-generating actions?

Decisions were made slowly and by committee. Customers were ignored. Incredulously, most of the company's executive management had Ivy League MBAs, proof that the business logic doesn't come with expensive initials after your name. Despite having $12 million in venture capital to buoy the storm, my website slowly started to die.

A few months later, near the cliff of bankruptcy, it was voted that my website would be dissolved, even though it was still profitable. Tech buyers dried up and stocks tanked. Everyone was on life support, including them.

Unwilling to watch my creation fade into oblivion, I offered to repurchase my company at a fire-sale price—a mere $250,000, financed by its own profit. The offer was accepted and I regained control of the same company I had just sold 18 months earlier. Essentially, I'd operate the business, take the profit and pay down the carry-back loan. What was left over I reinvested into the business.

With my company back in my control, a new motivation surfaced—to not only survive the dot-com crash, but to thrive.

THE BIRTH OF THE MONEY TREE

The next few years I was revitalized to take my service to the next level. In hindsight, I wanted to prove to myself that I wasn't just some lucky chap who got caught up in the dot-com boom. I continued to improve my website. I integrated new technologies and listened to customers. My new passion was automation and process.

As I streamlined my processes and systems, a slow and steady transformation took place. I worked less and less. Suddenly, I worked an hour a day instead of ten. Yet, the money rolled in. I'd go to Vegas on a gambling spree; the money rolled in. I'd be sick for four days; the money rolled in. I'd day trade for a month; the money rolled in. I'd take a month off; the money rolled in.

It dawned on me that I did it: *This was the Fastlane.*

I built myself a real, living, fruit-bearing *money tree.* It was a flourishing printing press that made money 24 hours a day, 7 days a week, and it didn't require my life for the trade. It required a few hours a month of water and sunshine, which I happily provided. Outside of routine attention, this money tree grew, produced fruit, and gave me the freedom to do whatever I wanted.

For the next few years I lived a life of laziness and gluttony. Sure, I worked a few hours a month, but mostly, I worked out, traveled, played video games, bought and raced fast cars, entertained myself with dating websites, gambled—I was free because I planted and cultivated a money tree that *surrogated* for my time. Its harvest, bountiful and monthly.

Since reclaiming my business, it grew meteorically. Some months I'd PROFIT more than $200,000. Yes, profit! A bad month was $100,000. I earned in two weeks what most people earned in an entire year. Wealth poured in and I was flying low on the radar . . . no fame. If you earned $200,000 every month, how would your life change?

- What would you drive?
- Where would you live and take vacations?
- What passions—art, writing, charity—would you pursue?
- What schools would your children attend?
- Would debt be a noose around your neck?
- How fast would you become a millionaire? Four months or forty years?
- Would you be cursing Sunday night and rejoicing Friday afternoon?
- Would grabbing a $6 coffee at Starbucks be an issue?

You see, when you generate this kind of income, millionaire status happens quickly. By age 33 I became a multimillionaire. If I didn't initially sell my business, I would have probably arrived faster, but when you're eating cardboard noodles and someone slaps $1.2 million dollars in your face, not many would say, "Nah, I'll pass."

I purchased my first Lamborghini and completed the prophecy dreamt in my teens. After owning a variety of exotic cars for years, I learned that the same question I asked years ago wasn't unusual. It was asked almost weekly. And now I had an answer that I can give, and an answer I would have loved to have read.

In 2007, I decided to sell my company again. It was time to retire and think about my wildest dreams, things like this book, writing fiction, and who knows, maybe screenwriting. However, this time I entertained a variety of offers, ranging from $3.3 million to $7.9 million. After making millions over and over in a few short years, I accepted one of the full-cash offers and repeated the Fastlane process . . . in a matter of minutes. That's how long it took to cash the six checks that amounted to millions.

CHAPTER SUMMARY: FASTLANE DISTINCTIONS

- Fame or physical talent is not a prerequisite to wealth.
- Fast wealth is created exponentially, not linearly.
- Change can happen in an instant.
- Don't fear taking roads that have not been paved by others.
- I wrote this book because it is something I wished I could have read when I was 20 years old.

Part 2

Wealth is Not a Road, But a Road Trip!

The Road Trip to Wealth

The journey of a thousand miles must begin with a single step.

~ LAO TZU

WEALTH IS A ROAD TRIP, NOT JUST A ROAD!

While in college, my friends and I embarked on a spring break road trip from Chicago to South Florida. As young men, we were drooling with anticipation. Captivated by the destination, a sun drenched beach crowded with scantily clad boozed-up college coeds, we failed to focus on the most important thing: the vehicle we depended on getting there.

Eight hours into the trip, our old Dodge Duster started billowing smoke and clanked to a stop. With a ruptured gasket and no oil, our trip stalled on some country road in the middle of southern Illinois. Cows, manure stink, and cornfields, light years away from the sandy beaches of South Florida.

Sadly, for most, the journey to wealth often ends like my spring break road trip: stalled on the side of the road in the middle of nowhere, left to ask, "How the hell did I get here?"

Like my spring break trip, to know and drive "the road to wealth" is not enough because the road itself is deficient in delivering wealth.

Your pursuit of wealth stalls when your focus is the road and its destination, and not the road trip. Sure, the Fastlane might *open* a rapid road to wealth, but a successful road trip will demand your respect for all of the trip's vital tools. My spring break stalled because we neglected the road trip and focused on the road. Oil? Roadmap? Engine tune-up? Screw it, just head south! When you disregard critical road trip components, your engine redlines, oil burns hot, gas is squandered, and decade-long detours are encountered. When your focus is only the road, your journey is likely to stall and dreamy destinations never arrive.

WEALTH'S ILLUSIONARY ROAD

If wealth has escaped you, it's probably because you are "road-focused" and not using the whole formula. Sure, you might have bits and pieces: an ingredient captured from a book or two, another seeded by some "get rich" seminar or a hot stock tip from your broke college buddy. Unfortunately, these isolated ingredients can't create wealth and are likened to a dead car on the interstate with an empty gas tank and a dead battery. You can't crack wealth's code with one variable in a multi-variable equation.

Wealth's road trip formula is like a recipe.

Imagine if I threw you into the kitchen with sugar and flour and ordered you to bake cookies. The feat is impossible because two ingredients alone don't make the entire formula. Forget the baking soda and the cookies won't rise. Remove the butter and the cookies taste awful. One forgotten or flawed ingredient and the process fails. Therein lies the fault with most wealth books: They are "road-focused." They specialize on the most titillating part of the formula—the sugar! They tell you:

- Import goods from China and sell them on Amazon!
- Buy a franchise and be your own boss!
- Learn the mystical secret law and think positive!
- Follow your passion and start a business!
- Invest in real estate for passive income!
- Trade your way to riches with cryptocurrencies!

These strategies highlight various roads to wealth: the real estate road, the trading road, and the business road. They address *nothing else.* The failure is within the "else" because the else is the rest of the formula.

MILLIONAIRES ARE FORGED BY PROCESS, NOT BY EVENTS

All self-made multimillionaires create their wealth by a carefully orchestrated process. They have and use the entire formula. Despite what you may have read or heard, wealth is not an event. Wealth doesn't drop from the sky or come from a game show. It doesn't ring the doorbell and stand on the front porch with balloons and a check the size of a refrigerator. Wealth does not chime from a machine with spinning bars, lemons, and cherries.

Wealth is a process, not an event. Ask any chef and they will confirm that the perfect dish is a series of ingredients and a well-engineered process of execution: a little this, a little that, done at the right time at the right place, and wham, you have a tasty meal. Wealth creation has the same method of execution—a mixed collection of many disassociated ingredients into a consolidated whole that has value and is worth millions.

Wealth eludes most people because they are preoccupied with events while disregarding process. Without process, there is no event. Take a moment and reread that. Process makes millionaires, and the events you see and hear are the results of that process. For our chef, the *cooking* is the process, while the *meal* is the event.

For example, an athlete who scores a $100-million-dollar contract to play pro basketball is an event from process. You see and hear about the big contract, the spectacular "get-rich" event, but you typically ignore the process that preceded it. The process was the long, arduous road you didn't witness: The daily four-hour practices, the midnight pickup basketball games, the torn ligaments, the surgery and rehabilitation, the rejection of being cut from the junior varsity team, and the resistance to the neighborhood gangs, all frame the journey that forms process.

When a 20-year-old sells his Internet company for $50 million dollars, you read about it on a tech blog. The event is lauded and showcased for all to admire. Sidelined is the process—you didn't hear about the long hours of coding the founder had to endure. You don't hear about the cold dark days working in the garage. You don't hear about how the company was founded on credit cards at 21.99% interest. You don't hear about the founder and his rusty P.O.S. Toyota with 174,000 miles.

When Kevin Plank founded Under Armour in 1996 and takes the company public in less than 10 years, the accomplishment makes headlines around the world. What doesn't? Subtle facts of process. Like Plank went broke one year after founding the company. To carry the business forward, he blew through $20,000 in his personal savings and later $40,000 in credit card debt. The billion dollar "get rich" outcome is the event—the process is the struggle and the backstory.

The sale of my company (twice) climaxed in an event, but its progress was carved by process. Outsiders see the nice house and the expensive cars and might think, "Wow, if I only could be so lucky." Such a belief is a mirage of event over process.

All events of wealth are preceded by process, a backstory of trial, risk, hard work, and sacrifice. If you try to skip process, you'll never experience events.

Unfortunately, as a media-driven, "I want it now" society, we spotlight and glorify the event, but usher the process behind the woodshed, carefully drying its sweat from the public cognition. However, if you search long and hard, you can always find the process, buried in another story or in the trailing paragraphs that glorify the event.

When you make your first million, it will be because of process and not some clandestine happenstance that just happened to waltz across your path. Process is the road trip to wealth: The destination shines as an event, but it's found by process. Yes, the elevator to success is out-of-order—you will need to climb the stairs.

WEALTH'S ROAD TRIP FORMULA

The formula for wealth is like a cross-country road trip. Success demands your focused discipline into the journey and the journey's tools (process) as opposed to the destination (event). There are four ingredients that make up the winning formula. They are:

Your Roadmap (Parts 3, 4, and 5)

The compass for the trip—your roadmap—is the guiding force behind your actions. Your roadmap pens your financial belief system and your preconceived convictions about wealth and money. There are three roadmaps that will chart your course to wealth:

1) The Sidewalk
2) The Slowlane
3) The Fastlane

Much like a recipe, your roadmap will outline why, where, how, and what.

Your Vehicle (Part 6)

Your vehicle is you. No one can drive the journey but you. Your vehicle is a complicated system composed of oil, gas, an engine, a steering wheel, a windshield, horsepower, and an accelerator—all needing frequent tuning and maintenance to ensure peak efficiency during the road trip.

Your Roads (Part 7)

Your roads are the career pathways you travel. For example, you can travel the job road, and within that road you have unlimited choices: You can be an engineer, a project manager, a physician, a plumber, a truck driver. Then there are entrepreneurial roads: You can be a real estate investor, a retail store owner, a franchiser, a freelancer, or an inventor. Just like a cross-country road trip, roads are plentiful with millions of permutations. Each carries with it a mathematical equation.

Your Speed (Part 8)

Speed is execution and your ability to go from idea to implementation. You could sit in a Ferrari on an empty, straight road, but if you fail to hit the accelerator, you fail to move. Without speed, your roadmap has no direction, your vehicle stands idle, and your road mutates into a dead end.

THE ROAD TRIP IS PAVED WITH TOLL ROADS

Successful Fastlaners are warriors who live and die on rough roads. Toll roads pave the road to wealth, and that toll can't be paid on Easy Street. For some of us, this is good news because the toll weeds out the weak and escorts them to the land of normal. If you resist the toll, wealth will resist you. Unfortunately, some feel that wealth's toll can be paid by entitlements or certain "prerequisites," such as:

- A functional family/good childhood
- "Hard work" versus "smart work"
- Educational accomplishments and credentials after your name
- A stellar business plan
- Venture capital
- Being a certain sex, color, or age
- Wishing, dreaming, and thinking positively
- Knowing the right people in the right places
- Attending the right schools
- Being passionate or "doing what you love"

Nothing is further from the truth. The Millionaire Fastlane doesn't care about these things. The Fastlane isn't a straight tree-lined street with white picket fences and children swinging on tires hanging from oak trees. It's a dark, deserted, unpaved road strewn with potholes that forces change and evolution. If the road trip to wealth were easy, wouldn't everyone be wealthy?

Expect a price to be paid. Expect risk and sacrifice. Expect bumps in the road. When you hit the first pothole (and yes, it will happen) know that you are forging the process of your unfolding story. *The Fastlane process demands sacrifices that few make, to resolve to live like few can.*

THE ROAD TRIP CAN'T BE OUTSOURCED TO A CHAUFFEUR

We live in a society that wants to outsource everything, from our household chores to raising our kids. Outsourcing might work for a dirty bathroom, but it doesn't work for wealth. Wealth's road trip has no chauffeur and the toll can't be outsourced to a virtual assistant in the Philippines.

Had someone gifted a Lamborghini to me (or any dream) when I was 16 years old, I wouldn't be where I am today. When you are granted gifts without any effort, you effectively handicap process. The person I needed to become would have been dwarfed because process would have been outsourced. There is no wisdom or personal growth gained in a journey that someone else does for you. The journey is yours. And unless you find like-minded Fastlaners, you will walk it alone.

CHAPTER SUMMARY: FASTLANE DISTINCTIONS

- Wealth is a formula, not an ingredient.
- Process makes millionaires. Events are residual by-products of process.
- To seek a "wealth chauffeur" is to seek a surrogate for process. Process cannot be outsourced, because process dawns wisdom, personal growth, strength, and ultimately, events.

The Roadmaps to Wealth

If you don't know where you are going, any road will get you there.

~ LEWIS CARROLL

THE COMPASS FOR WEALTH

If you don't know where you are going, how will you know if you get there? An undefined destination means an undefined arrival. More than likely, you'll end up where you don't want to go. You find wealth with a roadmap, not a dartboard.

Self-made millionaires don't become millionaires by stumbling into money. Likewise, financial failures don't become failures by stumbling into poorness. Both are residual outcomes of the chosen financial roadmap and the actions and beliefs evolving from that roadmap. Your financial roadmap is definitive to process, and it's the first tool for your road trip to wealth.

Whether you know it or not, your current financial status is the aftermath of your financial roadmap. It guides your actions which renders consequences which renders your financial life.

Ultimately your choices determine how your life unfolds.

But where do these choices come from?

They bud from your belief systems which are defined within your roadmap.

To change your choices it has to start from your roadmap because it is there where your beliefs lie, both literally and figuratively. Radical life disruption comes from a radical disruption in your roadmap. Change that, and you change everything.

For instance, here's how roadmaps and their bound beliefs affect finances: if you believe "rich people got rich investing in S&P index funds" your actions will reflect that belief. If some financial guru tells you to cancel your credit cards because "all debt is bad," you do it. If an author says, "$50 invested today will be worth $10 million in 40 years," and you believe it, your actions spring from that belief.

Beliefs are powerful mechanisms that drive action, whether true or not. Our parents said Santa Claus was real and we believed it. We left cookies, looked out the window for the flying reindeer, and wondered how he got his big butt down the chimney. We believe what we're taught, even when evidence appears to the contrary!

Your belief system acts like a compass that, if errant, can lead you to a lifetime of detours. Fictitious beliefs are lying roadmaps; they escort you down dead-end roads where "Wealth: Next Exit" never happens.

THE THREE FINANCIAL ROADMAPS TO WEALTH

Plotting your course to wealth and building your process starts with an examination of your current financial roadmap and the alternatives. There are three financial roadmaps:

The Sidewalk Roadmap
The Slowlane Roadmap
The Fastlane Roadmap

Within these three roadmaps lies a psychology, a belief system that dictates actions relative to each roadmap. More importantly, each roadmap operates within a "universe" governed by a mathematical "wealth equation." Whatever roadmap you choose, your universe for wealth creation will abide by each map's respective wealth equation. Additionally, each roadmap is naturally predisposed toward a specific destination. Those predispositions are:

The Sidewalk >— Poverty
The Slowlane >— Mediocrity
The Fastlane >— Wealth

Whichever financial roadmap you follow will predispose you to the destination inherent in the roadmap—the roadmap's "true essence."

What is true essence?

If you play blackjack and win 15 consecutive hands, you violate the true essence of randomness. The natural state of randomness is to not deliver 15 wins in a row.

When a wild African lion is tamed to perform in a Las Vegas magic act, the lion is trained to violate its true essence. The lion naturally wants to be wild, to hunt, to kill, to feed, to mate. The lion wants to revert to its natural self, which is why some flamboyant magicians get their heads bitten off. You have to be special to bend the laws of true essence.

Likewise, the roadmaps each possess a true essence that leads either to poverty, mediocrity, or wealth. For example, if you follow the Sidewalk, you'll likely end poor. While wealth is possible with any of the maps, divergence from the map's essence is like defying odds: gambling for six hours at the roulette table and winning.

Each roadmap contains key mindsets that act as signposts, or "mindposts," that provide direction and guide actions, just like a roadmap. Those mindposts are:

Debt Perception: Does debt control you or do you control your debt? Or, do you even have debt?

Time Perception: How is your time valued and treated? Abundant? Fleeting? Inconsequential? Do you work for time? Or does time work for you?

Education Perception: What role does education have in your life? Does it have a role at all?

Money Perception: What is money's default position in your life? Is money a tool or a toy? Plentiful or scarce?

Primary Income Source: What is your primary means of creating income?

Primary Wealth Accelerator: How are you accelerating your net worth and creating wealth? Or are you?

Wealth Perception: How do you define wealth?

Wealth Equation: What is your mathematical plan for accumulating wealth? What wealth equation defines the physics of your wealth universe?

Destination: Is there a destination? If so, what does it look like?

Responsibility & Control: Are you in control of your life and your financial plan?

Life Perception: How do you live your life? Do you plan for the future? Forsake today for tomorrow? Or tomorrow for today?

THE ROADMAPS OPERATE WITHIN DISTINCT UNIVERSES

Each roadmap operates under a specific set of mathematical formulas, *the wealth equation* that determines the speed at which you can create wealth. Like Einstein's $E=MC^2$, these formulas govern your wealth universe much like physics governs our universe. And because physics is bound by mathematical absolutes, so are your equations (and probabilities) to wealth.

The velocity of wealth acceleration evolves from your chosen roadmap's "universe," and it is within these universes that your financial plan accelerates or stalls. Think of it as a railroad track, with each track having its own set of speeds, rules, and laws. You can hop aboard a track that allows speeds of 20 mph or speeds of 200 mph.

If you're unhappy in your financial situation, you can change your universe immediately by switching roadmaps. However, before you can swap the roadmaps, you have to understand them. Let's dissect the roadmaps in the next three parts of the Millionaire Fastlane: the Sidewalk, the Slowlane, and the Fastlane.

CHAPTER SUMMARY: FASTLANE DISTINCTIONS

- To force change, change must come from your beliefs, and your roadmap circumscribes those beliefs.
- Each roadmap is governed by a wealth equation and predisposed to a financial destination—Sidewalk to poverty, Slowlane to mediocrity, and the Fastlane to wealth.

Part 3

Poverty:
The Sidewalk Roadmap

The Road Most Traveled: The Sidewalk

When you're the first person whose beliefs are different from what everyone else believes, you're basically saying, "I'm right, and everyone else is wrong." That's a very unpleasant position to be in. It's at once exhilarating and at the same time, an invitation to be attacked.

~ LARRY ELLISON

THE SIDEWALK ROADMAP

Most people are lifelong Sidewalkers, followers of the Sidewalk Roadmap. The Sidewalk is the plan most followed, a contract for a pleasurable today in lieu of a more secure tomorrow.

A Sidewalker exists in a state of one-something-from-broke: One album failure from broke. One business deal from broke. One gig from broke. One layoff from broke. On the Sidewalk, you're always "one something" from being homeless, bankrupt, or back living in your parent's basement.

Yes, some Sidewalkers actually earn large incomes, but none of them ever obtains true wealth. Don't let the contradiction fool you. The Sidewalk doesn't have an exit ramp to wealth—only a "DEAD END" sign signaling impending doom. The Sidewalker's road trip is a financial treadmill with a destination that typically ceases at bankruptcy or a crisis of reckoning.

WHAT IS A SIDEWALKER?

A Sidewalker's financial destination doesn't exist. *The plan is to have no plan.* Surplus money is immediately spent on the next great gadget, the next trip, the next newer car, the next fashionable styles, or the next hot fad. Sidewalkers are carelessly trapped in a "Lifestyle Servitude" fed by an urgent, insatiable need for pleasure, image, and instant gratification. This perpetuates an accelerating cycle of consumption, increasing the velocity of the burden, forever enslaving the Sidewalker to their job or their business.

The Sidewalk is the road most traveled because it's the path of least resistance. Its siren song is instant gratification, and money is a hot potato that's quickly exchanged for the latest fix of the week. Want to witness how Sidewalkers live and think? Watch the television show *Judge Judy* for a few hours. Daughters suing moms for $100, people denying responsibility, consequence ignorance, people wanting rent for free. Seriously, the show should be renamed *Life from the Sidewalk.*

THE MINDPOSTS OF A SIDEWALKER

The Sidewalker's roadmap contains behavioral characteristics that drive the Sidewalker's actions. These mindsets are signposts, or "mindposts" that guide the Sidewalker through life.

Debt Perception: *Credit allows me to buy things now! Credit cards, consolidation loans, car payments—these supplement my income and help me enjoy life today! If I want it now, I'm going to get it now.*

Time Perception: *Time is abundant and I spend money like there's no tomorrow. Heck, I could be dead in two weeks, and you can't take it with you!*

Education Perception: *I finished school when I graduated, hooray!*

Money Perception: *If you got it, flaunt it! Why save for a rainy day? I spend every dime I earn and most of my bills are paid on time; isn't that being fiscally responsible?*

Primary Income Source: *Whatever gig pays the most is what I will do. I chase money baby! It's all about the Benjamins!*

Primary Wealth Accelerator: *Net worth? I hit the casino, I buy lottery tickets, and I have an active lawsuit against an insurance company . . . does that count?*

Wealth Perception: *He who dies with the most toys wins!*

Wealth Equation: *My formula for wealth is (Wealth = Income + Debt).*

Destination: *Destination? I live for today and I can't be bothered about tomorrow.*

Responsibility & Control: *Everything bad happens to me. The man is keeping me down. The system is against me. I am a victim. It's someone else's fault.*

Life Perception: *Live today, to hell with tomorrow. Life is too short to plan any further than 30 days out. You can't take it with you! You're only young once! Besides, I'll hit it big someday.*

THE DISTURBING SIDEWALKING FACTS

While these hypothetical mindposts and their commentary might sound ridiculous, they aren't. Just look at the data. Read the reports. According to a US Census Bureau study released in 2017 and conducted in 2014 (for 2013, years after the recovery of both the 2001 and 2008 bubbles), here are the disturbing facts:

- A person under the age of 55 is 69.7% likely to have zero net worth, or negative net worth.
- An estimated 54% of all households in the United States have less than $100,000 in net worth.
- 83% of all "under 35" households had a net worth less than $100,000.
- A person in the 35–44 age range has a median net worth of $18,197 excluding home equity.
- A person in the age 45–54 group has a median net worth of $38,626, excluding home equity.

According to 2016 Census Bureau data, 61% of all people who earned income earned less than $75,000/year. This data unmasks the ugliness behind the Botox injections and the luxury German sedans: Sidewalkers are the majority. An estimated 60% of adults live their lives on the sidewalk. Yes, the world is full of financial illusionists. And this is after the recoveries of the most recent financial bubbles. Immediately after the 2008 financial meltdown, it wouldn't surprise me if 85% of American families would have had zero or negative net worth. But you can bet they have 650 cable channels streaming into their five flat-screen HDTVs. If you're older than 35 and you have less than $19,000 in net worth let me be blunt: What you are doing isn't working. You need a new roadmap.

THE STANDARD SIDEWALKER: INCOME POOR

"Income-Poor" Sidewalkers are the mainstream populous and reflect the lower to middle class. These Sidewalkers work for modest salaries and possess all the toys to show for it, but have little savings and no retirement plan. Their future is mortgaged to the hilt in favor of a lifestyle, with purchase affordability of any extravagance determined by the monthly payment. Every dime is spoken for: car payments, clothes, or is sent off to stall the credit reaper.

If you live this way, you are driving at the financial redline on a narrow road bordering a cliff. There is little hope for Sidewalkers because their roadmap is corrupted by gratification, selfishness, and irresponsibility. This problematic disposition repels wealth and thrusts codependency on overburdened hosts: taxpayers, employers, friends, parents, and loved ones. Income-Poor Sidewalkers rationalize, "Life is short. Get out of my way or get run over!"

SIDEWALKING SYMPTOMS: ARE YOU ON IT?

You haven't learned much since graduating from high school or college.
"I'm done with school, hooray!"

You change jobs frequently.
"C'mon, MJ, I left because this other job pays more."

You think people with money have it because they had rich parents, luck, or easier life circumstances than you.
"I've had it hard. If my parents would have paid for college I could have had a good job. I had a rough childhood. Those people with money have no idea."

You are easily impressed and seek to impress.
"I love designer purses, German cars, Italian clothes, and purebred dogs. I work hard for my money and I deserve it!"

You have poor credit.
"I pay my bills most of the time . . . it's just that I can't always pay on time because of situations outside of my control. Besides, the banks and utility companies are big, rich companies—they are the enemy."

You put faith into politicians and government to change the system, instead of focusing on how you can change yourself.
"A bigger government is the solution. More regulation, more programs, and more services. The government should serve the people. Rich people should pay more in taxes for their good fortune—they can afford it and I can't!"

You view pawnshops, payday loan stores, and credit cards as a means of supplemental income.
"Groceries can't wait until the next paycheck—my family has to eat! Besides, there's a sale on crab legs for only $22 a pound."

You have filed for bankruptcy at least once.
"It wasn't my fault—I overextended myself and didn't expect to lose my job. I didn't expect a recession. I don't feel bad about bankruptcy because it wipes my slate clean and I can start over fresh. I'm already pre-approved for another credit card."

You live paycheck to paycheck.
"Wait, doesn't everyone?"

You don't alert a business when they give you incorrect change in your favor.
"Are you crazy? If a business makes a money mistake, I'm keeping it. It's not my fault their employee screwed up."

You have a negative net worth and little, if no savings.
"What's the point? You only make 1% on a savings account anyhow, and look at all those people who invested in the stock market and lost nearly everything in 2008. Suckers! At least if I spend every dime I can't lose it!"

You have no car insurance, no health insurance, and you have unprotected sex with uncommitted partners.
"What can I say, I'm a risk taker. I know that insurance and birth control are important, it's just not a priority."

You regularly gamble at the casino or buy lottery tickets.
"You gotta play to win right? Forget the odds—this time's different, I just feel it."

You immerse yourself in alternate realities, including website celebrity gossip blogs, television, sports, video games, or soap operas.
"*I just love* American Idol, The Walking Dead, *and* Law and Order. *Monday through Friday from* 6 *p.m. to* 11 *p.m., I know exactly where I will be."*

You've lost money on "get rich" schemes.
"There's got to be an easy way to wealth. If I just buy this crypto-coin, program/DVD series/late-night infomercial product, I'll have the secret! Get rich easy is out there!

Your family cringes when you ask for money or you quit asking because you know a lecture follows.
"Geez, it's just $500. My parents should take care of me until I die. Don't they see how hard I have it? I mean, look at this apartment! The granite countertops need to be replaced!

Can you identify a behavioral pattern? These mindsets are indicative to the Sidewalk. Hopefully you're not feeling angry or defensive because that might hint your beliefs are bred from the Sidewalk.

THE SIDEWALK'S GRAVITATIONAL PULL: POVERTY

A recession is a bump in the road. How many people lost their homes due to the last economic bubble? Their savings, their jobs, or their 401(k)s?

The Sidewalk offers no protection, because you're naked and you can't absorb the hits. If you're hit by traffic, you're roadkill. If you want to be unshakable on your financial road trip, you have to get tough and strap on a bulletproof vest. Your plan must transcend years of change and variability, not days.

A life on the Sidewalk naturally pulls you to poverty.

Because the Sidewalk is about the short term, it never works for the long term. Your future becomes a mortgage for a comfortable present. Unfortunately, any bump in the road causes the loans of the Sidewalk to be called in: a recession, a job loss, an interest rate hike, a mortgage reset. Living on the Sidewalk can literally end in living on the sidewalk.

If you ask any derailed Sidewalker what spun his financial life out of control, he will quickly blame some external factor: I was laid off! My car broke down! I had no health insurance when I broke my foot! The judge ordered a 20% increase in alimony! When you rev your financial engine at the redline you're guaranteed to burnout. And then, ironically, your pleasant todays turn into horrible tomorrows: more work, more debt, and more stress.

I don't know your age, but let's be honest and ask the uncomfortable question: Can you seriously expect to retire on $19,000 in net worth? Or $119,000? Is it rational to think you can live off your home equity refinance? Have you thought beyond next week's paycheck? At what threshold do you realize that it's time to shift gears and reevaluate? Is there a threshold? Why would something that you've been doing for 5, 10, 20 years suddenly start working?

Yes, insanity is doing the same things repeatedly and expecting different results.

The Sidewalk is not a road to wealth unless your strategy is casinos, lottery tickets, or some poison-your-spouse insurance scheme. Government aid, social security, charity, and "my parents will soon die and leave me a fortune" inheritance is not a financial plan! If you don't want to retire under a bridge in a cardboard box or work at Wendy's until you're 75 years old, you have to have a plan.

Should life grant you another 50 years, what the heck is the plan?!

The first step to escape the Sidewalk is recognizing that you might be on it . . . then replace it with something that works!

MONEY DOESN'T SOLVE MONEY PROBLEMS

Newsflash: The Sidewalk is money blind. It doesn't care how much money you make. *You can't medicate poor money management with more money.* Yes, you can look filthy rich and still be riding the Sidewalk dirty.

Sidewalkers come from all walks, even those with conspicuous wealth. They own businesses, work high-paying careers like medicine or law, or live as successful actors or musicians and earn big incomes. The common denominator is consistent: There is no plan and no savings—spend more than you earn and trade a secure tomorrow for a "living large" lifestyle of today. A Sidewalker's wealth equation is determined by income plus debt, determined by available credit.

Wealth = Income + Debt

Sidewalkers peg their lifestyle in direct proportion to their income and supplement that lifestyle with extensive use of debt. All Sidewalkers stress about paying their mortgage or rent, paying the utility bills, meeting the minimum payments on their credit cards—it's just what happens when there is no thought given past the happy hour after payday.

THE AFFLUENT SIDEWALKER: INCOME-RICH

When an income-rich Sidewalker goes broke it makes big news. Have you ever wondered how a rich rapper can go broke three years after his last album? Or why a famous actor needs to file bankruptcy a few years removed from the public spotlight? How does one transform an $80-million NBA contract into the oblivion of bankruptcy? I'll tell you: The Sidewalk where wealth equals income plus debt.

You don't have to look hard to find an "Income-Rich" Sidewalker. These are people who look rich, but in reality are one paycheck, one album, or one movie failure from broke. They make large incomes, with every dime spent on the next lavish accoutrement. Their lifestyle is accelerated by a big income and a big credit line. Yes, after their big income is spent, they buy more things they don't need with money they haven't yet earned, trusting fully that their large incomes will go on forever.

I call these Sidewalkers "all credit cards." They drive nice cars and wear expensive clothes, but are one blown gasket from a total financial meltdown.

A member of the Fastlane Forum (TheFastlaneForum.com) posted this slice of Sidewalking overhead from a friend who works at a lending agency:

> *"A famous rapper was denied a loan for $60,000 . . . despite putting on his application that he was making $400,000 per month . . . yet, after having two hits in the past year, he must be broke. He also had a terrible credit score. Goes to show you, money management skills and having good credit are very important, even when you are having a ton of success."*

Since Income-Rich Sidewalkers earn big incomes, their extravagances are commensurate with their earnings. For example, if an Income-Rich Sidewalker earns $20,000 a month, they feel justified in buying a pair of $400 jeans. The problem is that, just like Income-Poor Sidewalkers, an Income-Rich Sidewalker's spending isn't satisfied until they've burned through their entire monthly income plus some. It's an irrational way to live, as if these people fear that not spending the money will cause it to disappear. Earn $50,000 a month? Spend $60,000. Earn $250,000? Spend $350,000.

The money outflow always outpaces the money inflow.

Someone who earns $2 million a year is susceptible to the same Sidewalking pitfalls as someone who earns $20,000! *Financial discipline is blind to income.* Lack of financial discipline resides on the Sidewalk and it doesn't care what you earn or drive.

THE INCOME/WEALTH MIRAGE OF THE SIDEWALK

Notice how both income-poor and income-rich sidewalkers share the same problems but different scenery. *The reason is, more money is not a solution to poor financial management.* Poor money management is like gambling at a casino, because, over time, the house always wins. Tossing more money at the deficiency is like trying to plug a hole in a dam with more water. More money doesn't buy financial discipline.

Those lacking financial discipline misuse money to delay the inevitable. If you can't live on $40,000 a year, you won't be able to live on $400,000 a year. While you might fret about your $900 mortgage payment, the income-rich Sidewalker frets about his $9,000 mortgage payment. The fretting is alike; the problems are the same, only the amounts differ.

Only a mindset change regarding money is a solution to money problems. To change your mindset, you must change your roadmap. Get off the Sidewalk and stop equating wealth to income and debt.

CHAPTER SUMMARY: FASTLANE DISTINCTIONS

- A first-class ticket to the Sidewalk is to have no financial plan.
- The Sidewalk's natural gravitational pull is poverty, both in time and money.
- You cannot solve poor financial management with more money.
- You can be income rich and still ride the Sidewalk dirty.
- If wealth is defined by income and debt, wealth is an illusion, because it is vulnerable to potholes, detours, and "bumps in the road." When the income disappears, so does the illusion of wealth.
- Poor financial management is like gambling; the house eventually wins.

Is Your Wealth Poisoned?

Wealth is the ability to fully experience life.

~ HENRY DAVID THOREAU

SOCIETY'S TOXIC DEFINITION OF WEALTH

The lure of the Sidewalk evolves from society's poisonous and toxic corruption of wealth. Society has resolutely declared wealth's definition for you: "Wealth" is a chauffeur-driven Rolls Royce, chartered jets, exotic trips to the South Pacific, a mansion on the bay, and a Las Vegas penthouse. Society says wealth is six-carat diamond earrings, Aston Martins, and watches that cost more than most people's homes. Society says wealth is an *Indecent Proposal* to buy a romp in the sack with Demi Moore for $1 million based on the argument "the night will come and go, but the money will last a lifetime." How am I doing? Sound like wealth?

Ask 10 people "what is wealth?" and you'll hear 10 different answers. Your "wealth" might be symbolized by a Lamborghini like it was for me, or it might be a farm on 70 acres in Montana and a stable full of race horses. If you think like most, "wealth" is instinctively defined by lavish luxury lifestyles.

Society has us believing that wealth is an absolute perfected by material possessions and reckless consumption. In fact, I've had to tailor the "hook" of this book to society's definition of wealth's real definition. Why the misdirection? Like Pavlov's dogs, you've been trained to respond to it. You see, society has done a fabulous job of defining wealth for you, and unfortunately, they (again) have misled you. But don't worry; if you want luxury, the Fastlane can deliver.

THE WEALTH TRINITY: WHAT IS WEALTH?

Wealth isn't as ambiguous as it may seem. The happiest moments in my life were when I felt true wealth. And guess what? It wasn't the day I bought my first

Lamborghini. It wasn't the day I moved into a big house on a mountain or sold my company for millions. Wealth is not authored by material possessions, money, or "stuff," but by what I call the three fundamental "F's": *family (relationships), fitness (health), and freedom (choice).* Within this wealth trinity is where you will find true wealth and, yes, happiness.

Wealth is strong-spirited familial relationships with people. Not just your family, but with people, your community, your God or spirituality, and your friends. At the end of the iconic movie *It's A Wonderful Life* we're given the final lesson: "Remember, no man is a failure who has friends." This reflects on the importance of having your life shared with friends, family, and loved ones. Wealth is making a difference. Wealth is community and impacting the lives of others. Wealth cannot be experienced alone in a vacuum. Believe me, the richest moments of my life occurred when I was surrounded by friends or loved ones.

Second, wealth is fitness: health, vibrancy, passion, and boundless energy. If you don't have health, you lack wealth. Ask any terminally ill person what they value. Ask any cancer survivor how they suddenly feel reborn and happiness is displaced from "stuff" to people and experiences. There is no price on health and vibrancy.

And finally, wealth is freedom and choice: freedom to live how you want to live, what, when, and where. Freedom from bosses, morning alarms, and the pressures of money. Freedom to passionately pursue dreams. Freedom to raise your children as you see fit. And freedom from the five-day drudgery of doing things you hate. Freedom is the liberty to live your life as you please.

WEALTH CAN'T BE BOUGHT FOR 60 EASY PAYMENTS

I vividly remember the day. After I sold my company in 2000, my attorney handed me my first installment payment, a check for $250,000.

"Yippee, $250,000! I'm rich! I made it!" I mistakenly gleamed. And now it was time to announce it the world. I immediately envisioned fast cars, designer clothes, speedboats, and an entourage of bikini-clad women. I thought I was wealthy and I was going to flaunt it.

Unfortunately, that fantasy was miles from the reality. Yet, I tried. I bought a candy-apple red convertible Corvette. Sports car? Check. Designer clothes from Nordstrom? Check. I researched buying a speedboat until the Internet crash interrupted my silly fantasy. I invested my newfound wealth in tech stocks and lost thousands of dollars. Within months, more than half of my "wealth" evaporated, and after a conversation with my accountant, another third was soon to be parted with, thanks to taxes.

Ironically, *in my attempt to look wealthy, real wealth slid further away.* With no job, no business, no income, and a small sum of money, I couldn't support my life forever, nor the wealthy lifestyle I envisioned for someone rich.

I wasn't rich at all.

THE ILLUSION OF WEALTH: LOOKING RICH

In pop culture, master illusionists of wealth are called "30K millionaires." If you haven't heard this phrase, it characterizes someone who maintains a millionaire image, yet has no net worth. These folks aren't hard to find. They drive entry-level BMWs with custom chrome rims, they wear fancy designer clothes with Gothic cursive lettering from some faux French guy, and they congregate in the VIP section of the club ordering bottle service, of course, on credit. These folks broadcast like dashing debutantes with an extraordinary A-game, but behind all the flash-and-cash they're miserable magicians of the Sidewalk.

The problem with *looking* wealthy versus *being* wealthy is that the former is easy while the latter is not. Easy credit and long-term monthly financing options (make no payments for one year!) are tempting conduits to help you purchase the illusion of wealth. Society has led you to believe that wealth can be bought at a mall, at a car dealership, or on an infomercial. Like my initial spending spree when I cashed my first check, these appearances of wealth are supposed announcements to the world: "I'm rich!"

But are you? When you finance an $90,000 Mercedes Benz over six years because that's all you could afford, that isn't wealth, but impersonation of wealth. You're fooling yourself, and it's a Fastlane detour. But don't jump the bandwagon yet; this isn't a sermon about how you can't spend money on pricey German sedans. Not at all.

Wealth isn't embodied in a car but in the freedom to know that you can buy it. Freedom to walk into the dealership, know your price, pay cash, and drive away.

For a gift, I bought my brother a new Lexus. It was the easiest transaction I ever did. I researched the car and determined the price I wanted to pay. I walked into the dealership with a cashier's check and told the salesman, "I have a cashier's check for $44,000 and I want to buy that car. I need a YES or a NO." Twenty minutes later, I owned a Lexus. This is wealth, not an impersonation of wealth.

When I drive to the gym, I pass a dilapidated apartment complex near the expressway. In the parking lot I always see the same car parked: a shiny black Cadillac Escalade with 22-inch chrome custom rims. See the incongruity? You live in a crappy apartment but drive a $60,000 car with $10,000 rims? Do I see monitors in those headrests and hear a 24-speaker stereo? Geez, 90 grand of image and two bucks of common sense. Wouldn't it be smarter if your priority was owning a nice house in a nice neighborhood instead of leasing the tightest car in the Marbella Gardens apartment complex? *Priorities: Some want to look rich, others want to be rich.*

FAUX WEALTH DESTROYS REAL WEALTH

"Faux wealth" is the illusion of wealth without having it. It believes society's definition of wealth. It's not realizing that the pursuit of "faux wealth" does something terribly destructive: *It destroys real wealth.*

And as the chasm between real wealth and faux wealth expands, expectations are violated and misery creeps in. Like a Chinese finger-cuff, the more you try to look rich, the tighter the grip of poorness becomes. Wealth cannot be purchased at a Mercedes dealership, but the destruction of your freedom can.

Lost in wealth's translation is freedom. People flaunt the icons of wealth yet they don't have freedom. And when you don't have freedom, it assiduously gnaws at wealth's other elements, health and relationships.

Henry Sukarano buys his dream house in the Baltimore suburbs for $2.2 million. As a pharmaceutical representative for one of the leading drug makers, Henry's career is on the fast-track. His big home has everything he wants, including a pool, horse stables, and an impressive five-car garage. The purchase gives Henry a feeling of "I've made it!" . . . for about eight weeks.

Corporate politics and job cuts invade Henry's career, forcing him to work longer hours. He assumes other territories once covered by recently laid-off workers. Henry commutes two hours daily and is mandated to cover the entire Eastern seaboard. He's either on the road, in a plane, or sleeping. The long hours have disturbing clarity: Henry rarely "lives" at his dream home, and when he does, he spends it sleeping or recharging from the hustle of the work week. His relationship with his wife and kids suffers. His health declines as the stress of responsibility mount.

Henry comes to a moment of truth: "I'm not living a dream, but my dream is living me." Feeling trapped to the lifestyle illusion, Henry continues to work believing the ideology that wealth has its price.

Notice how the destruction of freedom attacks the other sibling wealth components. Unaffordable material possessions have consequences to our health and relationships. The irony of looking wealthy is that it is an enemy to real wealth: *It destroys freedom, it destroys health, and it destroys relationships.*

Foremost, The Millionaire Fastlane addresses the FREEDOM portion of the wealth trinity, because freedom offers protection to health and relationships. Only you can define your freedom and how you see your life. If you want the freedom to fly private jets, that's it. If you want to live a minimalist lifestyle in Thailand, then that is it. Everyone's freedom is different! Within your personal definition, you'll find a big piece of your wealth puzzle, as opposed to society's version, which leads to Sidewalking purgatory.

CHAPTER SUMMARY: FASTLANE DISTINCTIONS

- Wealth is authored by strong familial relationships, fitness and health, and freedom—not by material possessions.
- Unaffordable material possessions are destructive to the wealth trinity.

Misuse Money and Money Will Misuse You

Money can't buy happiness,
but it can make you awfully comfortable while you're being miserable.

~ CLARE BOOTHE LUCE

MONEY DOESN'T BUY HAPPINESS . . . DOES POVERTY?

People who declare, "Money doesn't buy happiness" have already concluded they will never have money. This old equivocation becomes the torchbearer to their poorness. And since money doesn't buy happiness, why save it? And then logic begs, if money doesn't buy happiness, does poverty? Does the guy who owns a Ferrari automatically have a small penis while the guy driving a Honda must be well hung?

Go to Google and search the phrase "Money doesn't buy happiness." Page after page concludes that money has no bearing on happiness. Should you be shocked that a Connecticut businessman earning a six-figure salary might be unhappier than a cattle-herder in Kenya? Absolutely not.

That fact is, these analyses fall short because they don't isolate the real thief of happiness: *servitude,* the antithesis of freedom. The irony is that when most people earn "more money," it doesn't add freedom, it detracts. By creating *Lifestyle Servitude,* more money becomes destructive to the wealth trinity: family, fitness, and freedom.

According to Creighton University's Center for Marriage and Family, debt is the leading cause of strife for the newly married. Debt and Lifestyle Servitude keeps people bound to work and unbound to relationships. A 2003 World Value Survey (worldvaluessurvey.org) as well as the 2018 Happiness Report (http://worldhappiness.report) found that the happiest people in the world have a tight sense of community, social support, and strong family bonds. After basic needs are met (security, shelter, health, food), our happiness quotient is most significantly impacted by the quality of our relationships with our partners, our family, our friends, our spirituality, and ourselves. If we are too busy chasing the next greatest gadget to strike down the competitive opulence of the Joneses, we finance our misery. Numerous studies, including The World Value Survey, concluded that "consumerism" is the leading obstacle to happiness.

The fact is, there are many millionaires and well paid career folks who are absolutely miserable, and it has nothing to do with the money.

It has to do with their freedom.

Money owns them, instead of them owning their money. The well-salaried workaholic who is never home to strengthen the relationship with his wife and kids is likely to be less happier than the poor farmer in Vietnam who spends half his day tending to his fields and the other half with his family.

In 2009, the popular American talk show host David Letterman went public with an extortion plot by a producer from another CBS show. The men who perpetrated the alleged $2 million blackmail scam reportedly earned $214,000 a year. Yet the man claimed to be in severe financial ruin, partly due to spousal alimony payments of nearly $6,000 per month. Was this extortionist trying to blackmail a celebrity because he wanted to "buy happiness?" What was his real motive? I contend that he was trying to buy freedom because his debts kept him contained in servitude. Would $2 million have made a difference? Perhaps in the short term, but not in the long term because his relationship with money was already corrupted. A source close to the investigation said, "He just didn't want to work anymore." In other words, he craved freedom.

NORMALCY IS THE RAT RACE, A MODERN-DAY SLAVERY

Why am I wealthy, versus the guy stuck in morning traffic driving to work? I have freedom. I wake up and do what I want. I pursue dreams. I write this book without worrying about how many will sell. I hop a plane to Las Vegas for two weeks without worrying about jobs, bosses, or unpaid electric bills. Freedom is fantastic.

Yet my lifestyle is not "normal." Like wealth, society, through its "Get Rich Slow" mandates, has defined "normal" for you. Normal is waking at 6 a.m., working eight hours at a tolerated job Monday through Friday, save 10%, and repeat for 50 years. Normal is to buy everything on credit. Normal is to believe the illusion that trusting Wall Street and their cohorts will make you rich. Normal is to believe that a faster car and a bigger house will make you happy. You're conditioned to accept normal based on society's corrupted definition of wealth, and because of it, normal itself is corrupted. *Normal is modern-day slavery.*

I'm amazed that most people perilously operate one crisis away from financial ruin. We have become a nation of undisciplined spenders and consumers. We have become a nation where unfettered spending and material extravagance write our obituaries in the ink of stress. If you're held hostage to your lifestyle, you aren't wealthy, because you lack freedom.

THE PROPER USE OF MONEY

Money doesn't buy happiness when it's misused. Instead of money buying freedom, it buys bondage. "Wealth" and "happiness" are interchangeable, but only if your definition of wealth hasn't been corrupted by society's definition. Society says wealth is "stuff," and because of this flawed definition, the bridge between wealth and happiness collapses.

When you don't feel wealthy, you'll try to manufacture that feeling. You buy icons of wealth to feel rich. You crave feelings, respect, pride, and joy. You want admiration, love, and acceptance. And what are these feelings supposed to do for you? You expect happiness.

And that's the bait. We equate wealth's corrupted version of happiness, and when it doesn't deliver, expectations are violated and unhappiness is left behind.

Used properly, money buys freedom, and freedom is one parcel in the wealth trinity. Freedom buys choices. The fact is, there are plenty of poor people who live richer than their overworked upper-middle-class counterparts because the latter lack freedom, they lack solid relationships, and they lack health—all deleterious effects of working a hated job five days a week for 50 years.

Money secures one agent of the wealth formula, freedom, which is a powerful guardian to wealth's sibling ingredients: health and relationships.

1) Money buys the freedom to watch your kids grow up.
2) Money buys the freedom to pursue your craziest dreams.
3) Money buys the freedom to make a difference in the world.
4) Money buys the freedom to build and strengthen relationships.
5) Money buys the freedom to do what you love, with financial validation removed from the equation.

Are any of the above likely to make you happy? I bet they will. They certainly won't make you unhappy.

LIFESTYLE SERVITUDE: THE TRAP OF THE SIDEWALK

Sidewalkers are engulfed in Lifestyle Servitude, where life is forced into a rat race, a constant tug-of-war between lifestyle extravagances and work, a self-perpetuating merry-go-round of work for income, income for lifestyle, and lifestyle for work. Wherever there's Lifestyle Servitude, there's a systematic erosion of freedom.

1) Work creates income.
2) Income creates lifestyle and debt (cars, boats, designer clothes).
3) Lifestyle creates comfortable expectations and the desire for more, better, etc.
4) Repeat . . .

I learned about Lifestyle Servitude in my early 20s. After college graduation, I took a hellacious job as a construction laborer in Chicago and fought city traffic daily. The pay was more than I had ever earned at my young age, and with my increase in income, I felt wealthy.

So what did I do?

I elevated my lifestyle and financed the illusion of wealth. I bought my first sports car, a Mitsubishi 3000GT. It didn't take long for me to realize that my dream car wasn't a wealth icon, but a parasite that fed on my freedom. I hated my job: it was stressful, drained my energy, and left my entrepreneurial dreams tethered. I couldn't quit. I had responsibilities: car payments, gas, and insurance. Because of my obligations to "stuff," I imprisoned myself into a job I loathed.

Yet, this type of servitude is normal. We're taught to strive for the latest and greatest regardless of consequence. It leaves us indentured for years, condemning us to lifestyle imprisonment... and the more stuff you buy that you can't afford, the longer your jail sentence becomes.

IF YOU THINK YOU CAN AFFORD IT—YOU CAN'T

Think about the last time you bought a pack of gum. Did you fret over the price? Did you ask, "Hmmm, can I afford this?" Probably not. You bought the gum and it's done. The purchase had no impact on your lifestyle or future choices. To a rich man who walks into a dealership and buys a six-figure Bentley without thought, the acts are the same.

Affordability is when you don't have to think about it.

If you have to think about "affordability," you can't afford it because affordability carries conditions and consequences. If you buy a boat and resort to mental gymnastics over affordability, YOU CAN'T AFFORD IT. Sure you can assuage affordability and make outlandish arguments, often starting with "I can afford this as long as . . .

. . . I get that promotion."
. . . my mortgage doesn't adjust."
. . . my stock portfolio makes another 10% this month!"
. . . my sales forecasts are double."
. . . my wife finds a job."
. . . I cancel my health insurance."
. . . my cryptocurrency portfolio doesn't lose money."

This self-talk is a warning that you can't afford it. Affordability doesn't have strings attached. You can bluff yourself but you can't bluff the consequences.

So how do you know if you can afford it? If you pay cash and your lifestyle doesn't change regardless of future circumstances, you can afford it. In other words, if you buy a boat, pay cash, and are NOT be affected by unexpected "bumps in the road," you can afford it. Would you regret a gum purchase if you lost your job a week later? Or if your sales forecast was slashed by 50%? Nope, it wouldn't make a difference. This is how affordability is measured against your level of wealth.

To overcome wealth impersonation, know what you can and can't afford. There is nothing wrong with buying boats and Lamborghinis if you can truly afford them. There is a time and a place to indulge. *The Millionaire Fastlane is designed to bring you to that place.*

THE BAIT OF LIFESTYLE SERVITUDE

The siren call of Lifestyle Servitude is the false prophet of feel-good—instant gratification and immediate pleasure. Wouldn't it be nice if everything that felt good were good? Chocolate? That super-sized fast-food combo meal? Sunbathing? Smoking? Unfortunately, short-term feel-good is often long-term bad. Instant gratification is a populous plague and its predominant side effects are easily spotted: debt and obesity.

Most Americans are obese because the easiest (and cheapest) instant gratification comes from food. When you plop your butt on the recliner and maul through a can of Pringles, you choose pleasure now in lieu of pain later. If you live with your parents and you finance $45,000 over 72 months for a new Mustang based on a $31,000-a-year bartender's wage, you let instant gratification win, and Lifestyle Servitude ensues.

Wealth, like health, isn't easy. Both are cut from the same fabric with identical processes. They require discipline, sacrifice, persistence, commitment, and yes, delayed gratification. If you can't immunize yourself from the temptations of instant gratification, you'll be hard pressed to find success in either health or wealth. Both demand a lifestyle shift from short-term thinking (instant gratification) to long-term thinking (delayed gratification). This is the only defense to Lifestyle Servitude.

LOOK FOR THE HOOK!

Instant gratification is the bait and Lifestyle Servitude is the hook. The advertising industry is on a great fishing expedition, and their goal is to hook you. Their juicy bait? That shiny new car, the bigger house, the latest tech gadget, the "got-to-have-it-now" product.

Every day you are bombarded with instant gratification's bait . . .

"You can't compete unless you subscribe now!"
"Buy this drug and you will be so much healthier and happier!"
"Your new iPhoneX will make you that much more productive!"
"You are not a serious gamer until you own this graphic card!"
"Imagine the neighbor's envy when you roll in with that new Audi!"

These messages share one commonality: You're their prey and the peddlers don't care if you can afford it or not. Defend yourself by exposing the hook beneath the bait: the bucket of bondage which is Lifestyle Servitude.

When instant gratification entices you to bite the bait, you become a casualty of the hook: Lifestyle Servitude. *Instead of you owning your stuff, your stuff owns you.*

Know wealth's enemies and the actions inviting those enemies into your life. Wait until you can truly afford your lifestyle luxuries ... and in the Fastlane, that day can come sooner rather than later.

CHAPTER SUMMARY: FASTLANE DISTINCTIONS

- Money doesn't buy happiness because money is used for consumer pursuits destructive to freedom. Anything destructive to freedom is destructive to the wealth trinity.
- Money, properly used, can buy freedom, which can lead to happiness.
- Happiness stems from good health, freedom, and strong interpersonal relationships, not necessarily money.
- Lifestyle Servitude steals freedom, and what steals freedom, steals wealth.
- If you think you can afford it, you can't.
- The consequence of instant gratification is the destruction of freedom, health, and choice.

Lucky Bastards Play The Game

I'm a great believer in luck,
and I find the harder I work, the more I have of it.

~ THOMAS JEFFERSON

PSST . . . WANNA GET LUCKY?

I once overheard someone call me a "lucky bastard." What a sad, delusional Sidewalking belief. I'm not lucky; *I'm a player of the game.* While Mr. Lucky-Bastard-Hater uttered that under his breath and sat his ass in the dugout, I was at the plate taking swings.

Joe is a Sidewalker and believes luck is required to get rich. He spends his days working construction and his evenings commenting on gossip blogs, playing video games, and watching TV. He has given up on his dreams of financial independence based on his ideas of luck. "I'm just not a lucky guy," he laments. Joe's brother Bill also has a job in construction, except Bill spends his evenings surfing the Internet, researching the newest practices of inventing and engineering. Bill's dream is to be an inventor and has created four prototypes of inventions in various fields. Bill also spends his vacation time at trade shows and marketing seminars. While Joe is killing ogres and wizards in the latest dungeon of doom, Bill is out of the box of nothingness and exposing himself and his inventions to the world.

Who's going to "get lucky"?

SELF-MADE MILLIONS ARISE FROM SELF-MADE LUCK

Mark Cuban, billionaire entrepreneur and owner of the Dallas Mavericks NBA team (http://www.blogmaverick) told a telling tale of luck in regards to his success. Mark recalls the struggles of his early successes before his big sale to Yahoo for

$5.9 billion. In each story, Mark remembers how people attributed his success to luck . . . lucky to sell his first company, MicroSolutions . . . lucky to make money trading in the technology boom . . . and lucky to sell his company to Yahoo for a few billion. Notice how events are quickly reasoned to be luck and process is swept underneath the rug.

Cuban understands the dichotomy that most don't: *Process creates events that others see as luck.* He goes on to comment how nobody mentioned luck when it came time to reading complicated software texts or Cisco router manuals or sitting in his house testing and experimenting with new technologies. Where was luck then?

"Rich people got lucky" is a Sidewalker's creed and a disempowering belief that strips you of your free will. While luck can create riches by way of lotteries, casinos, and rich parents, it rarely creates long-lasting wealth. To take advantage of The Millionaire Fastlane understand that luck is a *product of process*, action, work, and being "out there." And when you are "out there" you stand a chance at being in the right place at the right time.

There are right places and wrong places. The right place isn't on your sofa watching *The Voice* or slapping greenbacks into thongs at Betty's Booty Cabaret, or down at the neighborhood bar getting jacked-up on Bud Light while watching the Dodgers lose another game. If you want to be at the right place at the right time you indeed have to be at the right place—and the right place knows which places are the wrong places.

If you aren't off the Sidewalk taking action and engaging in process, you will never realize luck. Luck is always perceived to be a matter of event: you win the lottery, a sweepstakes, or find a 200-year-old painting in the attic worth millions. Again, more falsities. Like wealth, luck is not an event but *the residue of process.*

Sidewalkers love events but hate process. It's only natural for Sidewalkers to assume wealth is luck, because they believe wealth is an event. A member of the Fastlane Forum (TheFastlaneForum.com) recently posted that Bill Gates got lucky. I had to disagree. Luck didn't create Windows. Luck didn't create a company. Luck didn't create repetitive, concerted action toward a specified purpose. When you consistently act and bombard the world with your efforts, interacting with the waves of others, stuff happens. And that stuff? Sidewalkers interpret it as luck, when it is nothing more than action interacting with *better probabilities.*

Luck occurs when probability moves from impossible to likely. For our two brothers in construction, who is going to get lucky? The brother who exposes his inventions to the world bends probability into a real number. His lazy brother does not and is operating on zero probability. Force your process out into the world and you can defy the odds of "being in the right place at the right time."

When I think of luck, I think about poker players. Mistakenly, their craft is construed as luck, while career poker players will affirm it isn't luck, but systematic analytics and player psychology. The best poker players in the world are superior statisticians and interpreters of human behavior. Does luck play a role? Sure, but the role is minor, while player competency siphons the majority's bankroll. To tell a great poker player "you're lucky" is to hurl an insult. Likewise, to ascribe luck to a self-made millionaire's success is to perform the same insult.

To create luck, engage in processes so probabilities move from NOTHING, to SOMETHING. *Luck is introduced when you play.* If you don't play, you can't win. Unfortunately, Sidewalkers assign luck to events of mystical chance. They don't see the manipulated probabilities imbued by process which makes the chance possible. If you want luck, dive into process, because process raises events from the ashes.

RENOUNCE THE "BIG HIT" AS YOUR FINANCIAL PLAN

Sidewalkers loathe process, so their financial plan omits standard process (such as saving or budgeting) and relies on events. If you believe luck precedes wealth, you'll gravitate toward events needing luck—a diligent quest to finding "the big hit."

What's a big hit? Big hits are sudden miracles that create wealth fast. Lotteries, casinos, poker tournaments, heck, even frivolous lawsuits and defrauding the government are considered avenues to "the big hit." In effect, "big hits" are attempts to bypass the wealth journey and start at the finish line. It's the removal of your yellow brick road and the sharpening lessons that come from it.

Sidewalkers seek "big hits" because their belief system tells them wealth is an event. Unfortunately, big hits are long shots and violations of true essence. Do you believe in miracles? Sidewalkers do.

Why do reality TV competitions such as *American Idol* attract so many people when most of the contestants suck? These people are searching for that elusive "big hit." While the talented make it through (they have talent because they have process), the disqualified bemoan off the set, blaming Simon Cowell, the microphone, or some other insignificant factor for their failures. Singing *Someday Over the Rainbow* a few times in the shower doesn't make a process.

GETTING SWINDLED: A SIDEWALKER'S TEMPTATION

Order now for just three easy payments of $39.95 and I'll teach you how to make millions working just 40 minutes a week while hanging upside down on a trapeze in your basement. Yes folks, it's that easy. But wait, there's more! Order today and, as a bonus, you'll receive photos of this buxom woman right here next to me. Doesn't she look great? When you start making money like me, ladies like her will be ringing your doorbell at all hours of the day. Yes, folks, this system is awesome and it won't be here for long. Act now!

The infomercial guru knows exactly what he's doing. He targets Sidewalkers, who are magnetized to events and the big hit. Why advertise at 2 a.m.? That's when Sidewalkers congregate, because they're either unemployed or watching reruns of *Seinfeld*. Believe me, Fastlane drivers aren't up at 2 a.m. because of some boob tube rerun; they're forging process and muscling toward their destination.

Sidewalkers are ripe for swindling because they seek events (shortcuts) and want to avoid process. When this becomes etched into your mindset, infomercial pitches suddenly become the evening's entertainment.

DISEMBARKING THE SIDEWALK: THE THREE ANCHORS

Use logic. Think for a moment. If you came across a magic system that easily made millions in months, what's the first thing you'd do? Of course you know, and I know! You'd hire a web design firm, package your secret into a landing page and a super-slick marketing funnel, and start placing ads on Facebook. Yes, that's the first thing I'd do if I had the billion-dollar secret! Screw traveling the world, forget charity, and dump the idea of making more millions. Nope! Let's package this baby and tell the world it can be theirs for one easy payment of $197!

Do people believe the pitch or do they desperately seek the easy event? The art of selling moneymaking "systems" on the internet and TV infomercials is a strong Fastlane. Unfortunately, the systems being sold aren't Fastlane or as profitable as the act of selling the system itself. How do gurus get away with this madness? Easy. A Sidewalker's mindset is anchored in three beliefs that keep them trapped there and vulnerable to moneymaking scams:

Belief 1: Luck is needed for wealth.
Belief 2: Wealth is an event, or an easy 1-2-3 system.
Belief 3: Others can give wealth to me.

Here is where these beliefs fail. First, wealth is not about luck but about process improving probabilities. Second, events of wealth (lotteries/casinos) are long shots and not process. Process is rarely defined by a 1-2-3 system. And finally, only you can deliver yourself to true wealth. There is no chauffeur and no moneymaking program advertised on your Instagram feed that will escort you. These deceptions keep Sidewalkers anchored in good company with the majority, swiping away at 2 a.m. on the couch thinking they're one click away from making millions because the Instagram dude with 500,000 followers says so.

CHAPTER SUMMARY: FASTLANE DISTINCTIONS

- Like wealth, luck is created by process, not by event.
- Luck is created by increased probabilities that are improved with the process of action.
- If you find yourself playing the odds of "big hits," you are event-driven, not process-driven. This mindset is conducive to the Sidewalk, not the Fastlane.
- "Get Rich Quick" marketing is a Fastlane because savvy marketers know that Sidewalkers place faith in events over process.
- Moneymaking "systems" are rarely as profitable as the act of selling them to Sidewalkers.

Wealth Demands Accountability

Responsibility is the price of greatness.

~ WINSTON CHURCHILL

HITCHHIKERS DON'T DRIVE!

The biggest anchor to the Sidewalk is to entrust your financial plan to others, or worse, no one. Another anchor is to seek a wealth chauffeur; someone else that can drive the journey for you. Unfortunately, this mindset makes you vulnerable to victimhood.

Imagine if you hitchhiked across the country. There's a chance you won't make it to your destination. You could climb into a psycho's car who takes you on an unannounced and unexpected detour. You could encounter a murderer who slashes your throat and dumps you in a roadside ditch.

Hitchhiking is inefficient and dangerous.

Yet, the Sidewalker's manifesto is predicated on hitchhiking: faith unto others, and when things don't work out as intended, blame unto others. After faith in lucky events, blame is the third anchor to the Sidewalk.

Back in the late 80s, when I was a teenager, my mother chummed with friends at a local restaurant. Within that friendship circle several of them put their life savings into an investment innocuously named "The Fund." These folks—some respected businessmen—raved about this investment, claiming impressive monthly returns. These friends encouraged my mother, as a struggling single mom, to invest. Mom was no dumb cookie. She asked questions and didn't like the answers. Something didn't "feel" right. Logic tickled her inner brain. Ultimately, she passed on the investment and it remained outside her world.

Years later "The Fund" made headline news. An investment company had bilked millions of dollars from investors. The investment company was exposed as a Ponzi scheme, and several swindled investors committed suicide, including the perpetrator. This investment company was none other than that great investment mother declined years earlier—"The Fund."

THE LAW OF VICTIMS

The Law of Victims says *you can't be a victim if you don't relinquish power to someone capable of making you a victim.* When you abdicate control to others, you essentially become a hitchhiker with no seat belt. You take the passenger seat in a stranger's car, which could be murderous to your financial plan. And when that happens, you're vulnerable to joining the ranks of victims.

The road to victimhood is through denial: First responsibility, then accountability. People who don't take responsibility are victims. Some of them are born victims and, instead of trying to improve their hand, they fold and give up. For them, everyone has the solution to their problems but them. And their problems? Not their fault. Nope, someone else is to blame. Instead of looking within, they look outward and project responsibility to some other entity. Victims are Sidewalkers who refuse to take the driver's seat of their own lives and live under a dark cloud of "theys" reflective of a "me against them" attitude.

"They laid me off."
"They changed the terms."
"They cheated me."
"They didn't tell me."
"They raised my rent."
"They raised my interest rate."

Invariably, all these "theys" are self-imposed. If the landlord raised your rent, is it his fault you decided to live there and didn't read the lease agreement? If the company laid you off, is it their fault you chose to work there? Was it my fault that I was a broke 25-year-old stuck in a blizzard in a limo on the side of the road? It was.

In psychological parlance, this mental defect to assign blame externally is a condition known as an "external locus of control," penned by American psychologist, Julian Rotter.

In another example of blame and an external locus, there was a recent labor union rally against Wal-Mart. Employees were protesting the retailer's poor wages. A 33-year-old employee named Eugene complained about his employer arguing that he spent three years unloading trucks for $11.15 an hour, which was below the retail industry average of $12.95 an hour. His grievance? He can't afford a car or Wal-Mart's health insurance.

Wow, how disturbing. Was someone arrested? Seriously, someone should arrest the man who put the loaded gun to Eugene's head forcing him to work at Wal-Mart for a below-market wage! Give this guy a bitch-slap. No one forced him to work at Wal-Mart; he works there *because he chose* to work there. Hey, Eugene and to anyone else reading, if you're tired of making $11 an hour, raise your value to society. Get your butt over to the library or take an online class at uDemy. Wal-Mart can't offer low wages if they don't have an endless supply of victims like you.

You see, when a financial adviser promises you 14% guaranteed income from a bank certificate of deposit and you later discover that he scammed you, it's your fault. You didn't do the diligence. You didn't investigate. You ignored the tickle of logic in your brain. You are a victim of your own malfeasance.

THE POLITICS OF HITCHHIKING

Sidewalking hitchhikers are a major constituency in all countries. These people seek the easy life yet want someone else to pay for it. They're lifetime hitchhikers. They believe the government (or some other entity) should do more for them. They are victims of the system. They are life's victims because they were dealt a bad hand. They vote for whatever politician promises them the world at no cost. Free health care. Free education. Free gas. Free mortgages. Wow, give me a ballot!

John F. Kennedy's "Ask not what your country can do for you, but what you can do for your country" has maligned into "What can my country do for me?" While I can't comment on the societal deterioration outside of the United States within the last 20 years, Sidewalking has become the American way to the point they are now a political constituency. Americans once loyally proclaimed, "Give me liberty or give me death." Now we just say, "Give me."

As I wrote this in 2008, the economy was in a tailspin. The housing market crashed, lending dried up, and millions lost their savings.

How did that happen?

It isn't complicated: We relied on "others" to make financial decisions for us. We ignored the fine print. We didn't read the contract. We didn't read the legislation. We made government an insurance policy. As a society, history is doomed to repeat if we continue to repeat the same behavior.

I was a minor participant in the 2008 recession. Sure, my home declined in value but that's OK because I never used my home as a wealth tool! Yet the gurus say "your home is your greatest investment!" Baloney! When the markets crashed, I didn't lose money because the markets weren't my wealth acceleration vehicle! The Fastlane is about control, and if you live like a Sidewalking hitchhiker, you have no control.

On a public forum in August 2005, I predicted the forthcoming housing bust and outlined my theory with seven reasons I thought so. As it turns out, I was correct, and that truth crystallized because *I chose to make financial decisions for myself.* I didn't rely on CNBC pontificators who rapaciously declared that housing was safe. I didn't rely on the mainstream media. I didn't rely on others. *I relied on me.* I was driving, not hitchhiking. And the beauty of driving is something that escapes most people: *responsibility.*

WEALTH DEMANDS RESPONSIBILITY, FOLLOWED BY ACCOUNTABILITY

Responsibility is the forefather to accountability, but one doesn't evidence the other. When you admit responsibility to overdrafting your checking account yet do it again next week, you're not accountable. When you admit responsibility to fathering a child out of wedlock, yet continue that behavior, you're not accountable. When you take responsibility for having your purse stolen but flaunt it on the table in open view, you're not accountable.

Accountability is culpability to consequences and modifying your behavior to prevent those consequences. You can be responsible while not being accountable. A Fastlane Forum user does a great job distinguishing between responsibility and accountability:

> *"What kills me is when people make the same piss-poor choice multiple times but then claim to be responsible. It's easy to be "responsible" when responsible means just walking away. I've seen single parents who pledge to be "responsible" for the wild oats they've sown, only to occasionally send a check in the mail. I've seen people walk away from homes, claiming to be "responsible" for their actions, only to buy another home they can't afford. I've seen people being "responsible" for the actions their drinking and driving caused only to do it again! I am sick and tired of people being "responsible!" I want people to be accountable. People need to think before they act. Own their choices before they make them. I am okay with people making mistakes—but freaking own that you made a mistake and learn from it. That's what true accountability and responsibility is all about."*

A friend of mine recently had her identity stolen. As we dined at a restaurant she bellyached about the nightmarish ordeal. Determined to find the cause of her problem, I stopped her contempt midstream and asked a few questions. I wondered, was she a victim, or not being accountable?

I asked, "How did your identity get stolen?"

"My purse was stolen in Mexico."

"How did that happen?" I probed.

"I was at a restaurant and someone swiped it"

"Oh? Was your purse laid out, wide-open on the table, like it is now?"

She glanced at her purse and got my point. As we dined, her purse sat on the tabletop in open view of everyone. Any thief could easily snatch her purse and run. She looked at me, scoffed, and then grabbed her purse and secured it to her lap.

A victim? Or not holding herself accountable? Her problem was caused by a bad choice—the choice to not safeguard her purse. And even after this costly lesson, she still didn't understand the power of being accountable. If she were accountable to the error, her purse wouldn't lie exposed on the table as a beacon of opportunity to thieves, but safe in her lap.

IMMUNIZE YOURSELF FROM VICTIMIZATION

Stop being a victim by taking responsibility, followed by accountability.

In 2006, I bought my dream home in Phoenix, Arizona, overlooking a gorgeous mountain range. The home had one of the best views in Phoenix but needed a substantial remodel. A new friend recommended a general contractor whom I hired without investigation; no diligence, no reference check, no license investigation, nothing.

Duh.

What should have taken eight months rotted into a three-year ordeal, a nightmare that framed the worst decision of my life. The contractor was grossly incompetent and an idiot.

Yet, I was to blame.

I accepted both responsibility and accountability because I hired the contractor. To plunder a line from *Star Wars*, slightly modified, "Who's the idiot, the idiot himself or the idiot that hires the idiot?"

But I wasn't a victim because I first was responsible: *It was my fault.*

I allowed it to happen.

Then, second, I became accountable: Now when I hire house workers, I do an investigation. Or, I could sink my teeth into being a victim and play the pity violin like everyone else.

For my friend with the stolen purse, the Fastlane mindset is to take responsibility followed by accountability.

Responsibility: It was my fault that my purse was stolen.

Accountability: In the future, I will take precautions to ensure it doesn't happen again.

Immunization for victimitis occurs when you are both responsible for AND accountable to your actions and the action's possible poor consequences. Own your mistakes, failures, and triumphs. Reflect on your choices. Are you in a situation because you put yourself there? Did you error in the process? Were you lazy? Most bad situations are consequences of bad choices. *Own them and you own your life.*

No one can steer you off course, because you are in the driver's seat. And when you own your decisions, something miraculous happens. Failure doesn't become the badge of victimhood—*it becomes wisdom.*

Deny accountability and responsibility and the keys of your life are given to someone else. In other words, take the damn driver's seat to your life!

YOU DESERVE! YOU DESERVE! YOU DESERVE!

The other day I heard successive radio commercials that were utterly disturbing. You don't need to be a nuclear physicist to know their target . . . Sidewalking victims.

The first commercial was for a mortgage loan modification company. The sales pitch went like this: "Modify your loan and get the lower payments you deserve." The next commercial was from an attorney. "Been in an accident? Get the money you deserve." The final commercial was from a credit repair company. "Let us negotiate your debts down to nothing so you can live the life you deserve!"

Notice the common phrase?

You deserve.

Seriously, what do these people really deserve?

Your credit sucks, you don't pay your bills on time, and you deserve a better life? Grandma rear-ends your car and suddenly you deserve a large cash award from some rich insurance company? You buy a house you can't afford and now you deserve a lower rate? How does "deserving" suddenly come so easy with no particular effort, like an event raining from the heavens?

We're being methodically brainwashed to believe that we deserve everything without obedience to process, or accountability.

You deserve what your actions earned, or haven't earned.

Being responsible is one thing; being accountable is another.

When you're accountable to your choices, you alter your behavior in the future and take the driver's seat of your life.

CHAPTER SUMMARY: FASTLANE DISTINCTIONS

- Hitchhikers assign control over their financial plans to others, which effectively introduces probabilities to victimhood.
- The Law of Victims: You can't be a victim if you don't relinquish power to someone capable of making you a victim.
- Responsibility owns your choices.
- Taking responsibility is the first step to taking the driver's seat of your life. Accountability is the final.

Part 4

Mediocrity: The Slowlane Roadmap

The Lie You've Been Sold: The Slowlane

What if I told you 'insane' was working fifty hours a week in some office for fifty years at the end of which they tell you to piss off; ending up in some retirement village hoping to die before suffering the indignity of trying to make it to the toilet on time? Wouldn't you consider ***that*** *to be insane?*

~ STEVE BUSCEMI (*CON AIR*, PARAMOUNT PICTURES, 2003)

NEXT EXIT: "SLOWLANE" MEDIOCRITY AHEAD

In the previous chapter, we highlighted that a Sidewalker has no financial plan and is only focused on today's pleasures, often governed by instant gratification. While the Sidewalk is a lifestyle that mortgages the future for a comfortable today, the Slowlane is the antithesis: a sacrificial today in the hopes of a more comfortable tomorrow.

As a Slowlane traveler, you're besieged by a hodgepodge of doctrines that plead discipline to the trade-off. Get a job and waste five days a week toiling at the office. Bag a lunch and stop drinking $10 coffee. Faithfully entrust 10% of your paycheck to the stock market and your 401(k). Quit dreaming about that sports car in the window because you can't buy it! Eat cheaply and buy everything on clearance. Delay gratification until you're 65 years old. Save, save, save because compound interest is powerful: $10,000 invested today will be with 10 gazillion in 50 years!

Surprisingly, the Slowlane is the Sidewalk's first convenient exit and evolves from maturity and increased adult responsibilities. Most college graduates begin their post-schooling life on the Sidewalk. I certainly did. Graduation sanctioned a license to buy stuff that yielded instant pleasure: trips to Cancun, a flashy car with a booming stereo, nightly drinking binges, a massive music collection. Life was all about *now*, regardless of future consequences. Sidewalkers (and people in general) instinctively regard a better future: "I'll be making more money," "I'll hit the lottery," "After my father dies I'll inherit thousands." Future crutches justify pleasurable nows and, behind the scenes, Lifestyle Servitude swells.

However, with increased responsibilities, perhaps a growing family, mounting debts, and future expectations not matching reality, the Sidewalker comes to terms with the uncertainty of the Sidewalk. He does the seemingly responsible lane change: He off-ramps and graduates to the Slowlane roadmap, a strategy touted and praised by credible sources. While the Sidewalk is typified by undisciplined behavior, the Slowlane's financial plan introduces responsibility and accountability into the wealth formula. That can't be bad right?

Unfortunately, the Slowlane is like bad directions given at a gas station, except these directions aren't given by strangers, but by people you trust: teachers, television and radio personalities, financial advisers, and yes, even our parents. These ostensible sources reinforce the strategy's fraudulent strength when its efficacy is a sucker's bet. The Slowlane is a lifetime wager that a sacrificial today will yield a wealthier tomorrow.

THE PROMISE OF WEALTH . . . THE PRICE? YOUR LIFE

The Slowlane is rarely challenged. It's a lie so deceiving that when the ruse comes to light, decades of life have passed . . . meanwhile, millions more are being newly indoctrinated to the deception.

If you buy the lie, you sell off today in hopes of a glorious tomorrow. And when does this glorious tomorrow happen? When can you splurge, spend your millions, and enjoy life? When? The driving force behind Get Rich Slow is *time*—time employed at the job and time invested in the markets. Your glorious tomorrow might arrive after 40 years, when you're living your last presidential administration and on your second hip replacement. Your glorious tomorrow might arrive when you're 83 years old and soaked in urine and strapped to a stinking bed because you've lost your mind to Alzheimer's. Seriously, when does this Slowlane plan of retiring rich actually become real so you can enjoy your millions?

As a teenager, Joe reads several personal finance books about getting rich. They tell him to save, get a career, clip coupons, and live below your means. After graduating with a law degree, Joe follows this advice. While it is difficult, Joe follows this plan for wealth diligently. He works 60 hours weekly at his law firm, often neglecting his family and children. His weekdays are consumed at the office, while his weekends are spent home "recharging" from the rigors of the workweek.

After 12 years in law, Joe decides his profession is no longer enjoyable. Yet, he decides to endure, as he is just one promotion away from making partner and a base $250,000 salary. As Joe's life progresses, he never loses sight of his goal: Retire by age 55 because, after all, financial guru David says, "The smart people finish rich."

Joe saves, works overtime, invests in mutual funds, and participates in his firm's 401(k). He continues to endure his job for the sake of the plan. No one said it'd be easy. That "one day" was coming, the day when he'd retire with millions. He justifies that five miserable days in a hated job is worth the sacrifice for the future. Then, one hot summer day while mowing the lawn, Joe has a heart attack and dies at age 51 . . . four years before his destination.

You can either *live rich young* or *live rich old* while risking death along the way. The choice is yours and it shouldn't be a contest. Rich at 25 years old beats the snot out of rich at 65 years old. Ask a youngster how to get rich young. Will coupons, mutual funds, and 401(k)s be the answer? Comedic, I know.

Wealth is best lived young and enjoyed while you have health, vibrancy, energy, and yes, maybe even some hair. Wealth is best lived in the prime of your life, not in its twilight after 40 years of 50-hour workweeks have pulverized your dreams into surrender. Deep in our soul we know this, yet we continue to faithfully pledge obedience to a financial roadmap that *promises* wealth after four or five decades.

And the bigger concern you should have is, does it even work?

The 2008 global recession exposed the Slowlane for the fraud it is. With no job, the plan fails. When the stock market loses 50% of your savings, the plan fails. When a housing crisis erases 40% of your illiquid net worth in one year, the plan fails. *The plan is a failure because the plan is based on time and factors you can't control.*

Unfortunately, millions of people have loyally entrusted decades into the plan only to discover the ugly truth: The Slowlane is risky and insufferably impotent.

A strategy that requires your life and dreams as penance is a sucker's bet. The Slowlane arrogantly assumes that you will live forever and, of course, be gainfully employed forever. Unfortunately, wheelchairs don't fit in the trunks of Lamborghinis.

SLOWLANE MINDPOSTS AND MISSIVES

Over time, the Slowlaner collects and then endures a series of mindposts reinforced by credible sources. Mom and Dad say go to college, graduate, and get a job. Best-selling author David says, "Stop drinking expensive lattes." Suze says, "Open a Roth IRA and contribute 10% of your paycheck." Ramsey says, "Snowball that debt." CNBC proudly proclaims that the secret to wealth is simply explained on handwritten index card promoting 50 years of indexed-funds. All these missives formulate the Slowlaner's mindposts, a journey to wealth that consumes a lifetime.

Debt Perception: *Debt is evil. It must be religiously attacked, even if that means working overtime for life.*

Time Perception: *My time is abundant and I will gladly trade my time for more dollars. The more hours I can work, the more I can pay off my debt and save money for retirement at 65.*

Education Perception: *Education is important because it helps me earn a bigger salary.*

Money Perception: *Money is scarce and every dime and dollar must be accounted for, budgeted, and rigorously saved. If I want to retire by 65 with millions, I have to ensure I don't squander my hard-earned money.*

Primary Income Source: *My job is my sole source of income.*

Primary Wealth Accelerator: *Compound interest is powerful because $10 invested today will be worth $300,000 in 50 years. Oh yes, and don't forget about mutual funds, home appreciation, and my employer's 401(k).*

Wealth Perception: *Work, save, and invest. Work, save, and invest. Repeat for 40 years until retirement age . . . 65 years old or, if I'm lucky and the markets return 12% yearly, maybe 55!*

Wealth Equation: *Wealth = job + market investments.*

Destination: *A comfortable retirement in my twilight years.*

Responsibility & Control: *It's my responsibility to provide for my family although for that plan to work I have to rely on others, including Wall Street, my employer, my financial adviser, the government, and a good economy.*

Life Perception: *Settle for less. Give up on big dreams. Save, live frugal, don't take unnecessary risks, and one day I will retire with millions.*

So how do you know you're being sold the Slowlane? The following lists the primary munitions indigenous to the Slowlane roadmap.

Slowlane Weapons

- Go to school
- Get good grades
- Graduate
- Pay yourself first
- Overtime
- Corporate ladder
- Save X% of your paycheck
- Contribute to your 401(k)
- Invest in mutual funds
- Buy and hold
- Paychecks, pensions, benefits
- Diversify
- Raise your insurance deductible
- The stock market, preferably index-funds
- Say "no" to expensive lattes
- Be frugal
- Get out of debt
- Clip coupons
- Cancel your credit cards
- Dollar cost averaging
- Get an advanced degree
- Pay off your house early
- Your home is an asset
- Individual retirement accounts (IRAs)
- Live below your means
- Understand compound interest

When you encounter these "buzz phrases," be wary—someone is selling you the Slowlane as a total plan to wealth. While coupons and other Slowlane strategies aren't worthless *IN* a plan, they shouldn't be *THE* plan. *The Slowlane as a <u>total plan</u> is the problem, not the Slowlane being <u>a piece</u> of the plan.* This distinction is critical because financial discipline must accompany any wealth campaign.

THE SLOWLANE ROADMAP: A MATHEMATICAL INTRODUCTION

How is wealth created in the Slowlane? To expose its method (and its weakness) you need to reverse engineer and deconstruct the strategy down to its mathematical roots, or its wealth equation. In other words, you want to expose the plan's theoretical speed limits for wealth, which is always determined by two variables: your primary income source (a job) and your wealth acceleration vehicle (market investments). These two variables formulate the Slowlane's wealth equation and governs its wealth creation power or, in this case, futility.

Wealth = (Primary Income Source: Job) + (Wealth Accelerator: Market Investments)

This equation factored looks like this:

Wealth = Intrinsic Value + Compound Interest

The primary income variable, *intrinsic value* has two variables itself dependent on how you are paid within your job. It could be either:

Intrinsic Value = Hourly Wage × Hours Worked

~ or ~

Intrinsic Value = Yearly Salary

Compound interest is derived from "market investments," which is the universal concept that $x invested in the stock market today will be worth $x millions decades from now. In Chapter 12, we will examine the Slowlane's mathematical constructs and exploit their true deficiency. Therein, you'll discover why society's plan, your parent's plan, the mainstream media's plan, and the guru's plan are horrific strategies for wealth.

HAVE YOU SOLD YOUR SOUL FOR A WEEKEND?

Your soul is worth more than a weekend. The side effect of Slowlane institutionalization is numbed blindness, followed by ignorance.

In 2007 on a cold January morning, a violinist stationed himself in a Washington, DC, train station and played six classical pieces from Bach. Except this was no ordinary violinist and it was no ordinary violin. This was an incognito Joshua Bell, one of the greatest musicians in the world, who nights earlier had played to a sold-out concert hall in Boston for nearly $100 a ticket. As Joshua played his $3.5 million violin in the midst of the morning commuter rush, approximately 2,000 people passed through the station, most of them on their way to work.

He played continuously for 45 minutes.

Only six people stopped to listen briefly. No crowd formed. About 20 folks gave money but continued onward at a brisk pace. When he finished, there was silence except for the rhythmic hustle of a busy train station. No applause. No crowd. No recognition.

This experiment, conducted by the *Washington Post*, uncovers something incredibly powerful—and disturbing. Not even the greatest musician in the world can illuminate the blinding depths of the rat race and those suffocating by its indifference.

Has making a living made you so apathetic that the living has been sucked out of you? Are you so deadened by Monday through Friday that the beauty in front of you has become blind and its melody muted?

The train commuters come and go like zombies—they're oblivious to the splendor of Monday through Friday. Yet, what if this experiment occurred on Saturday; would its outcome be any different?

This story exposes the Slowlane for its contempt: When you trade your life mindlessly for a paycheck, you risk being blinded to life itself as you cursively walk by it in a busy train station. *Life does not begin on Friday night and end Monday morning.*

"THANK GOD IT'S FRIDAY": BORN AND BRED IN THE SLOWLANE

A friend recently berated me because I declined to go out on a Saturday night. "Are you crazy? It's Saturday night!" he wailed. I told him something a Slowlaner doesn't understand: For me, every day is a Saturday because I haven't sold off Monday through Friday.

Wealth's provenance evolves from the three Fs: family, fitness, and freedom. Freedom's value to wealth is evidenced on Friday evenings, which just so happened to be the setting for an epic conversation I had with my friend during happy hour. While we sat on the bar's patio, we heard a chattering cacophony of patrons immersed in spirited conversation. The bar was "happening" and within the rustling soundtrack, you'd never guess a recession was ongoing.

Over the noise, I asked "What do you hear?"

"I hear people having a great time, a celebration," she said.

I asked further, "Why?"

"Why what? It's Friday!" she declared.

I probed further. "What's so special about Friday? If we came here on Monday, this place would be empty and the sound of celebration would be absent. What makes Friday so special as opposed to Monday or Wednesday?"

Knowing that she was trapped into one of my paradoxical interrogations, she humored me.

"Uhh . . . people get paid on Friday?"

I levied the verdict: Friday evening is celebrated because people are rejoicing over the dividends of their trade: five days of work-bondage exchanged for two days of unadulterated freedom. Saturday and Sunday is the payment for Monday through Friday. Friday evening symbolizes the emergence of that payment, freedom for two days. The prostitution of Monday through Friday is the reason "Thank God it's Friday" exists. On Friday, people are paid FREEDOM in the currency of Saturday and Sunday!

NEGATIVE 60%: THE DISMAL RETURN OF THE SLOWLANE

The ultimate insanity is to sell your soul Monday through Friday for the paycheck of Saturday and Sunday. Yes, give me $5 today and in return I'll give you $2 back tomorrow.

5-for-2. No?

How about five loaves of bread today and in return, I'll give you two back tomorrow. No again? Why? This is a smoking deal!

Hopefully you recognize that five of anything in exchange for two is a bad return. The 5-for-2 return on investment is a negative 60%. If you make consistent negative 60% return on investments, you'd go bankrupt quick. What logical person would accept such a horrific deal?

Most likely, you already do. When you accept the Slowlane roadmap as your strategy, you accept 5-for-2. You give five days of work servitude in exchange for two days of weekend freedom. Yes, Monday through Friday is prostituted for Saturday and Sunday. While people easily recognize and reject a negative 60% return on their money, they do it willingly with their time.

If you have children you have to question this normality. Kids grow on Mondays and Tuesdays. I've heard they grow on Wednesdays, Thursdays, and Fridays too. Yes, they don't wait for the weekend to grow up. When little Miranda speaks her first word, walks her first walk, dances the first dance, she doesn't care if you're in Houston for the quarterly manager's meeting. Kids and relationships don't wait for the weekend to grow, and while you're out trading 5-for-2, guess what—the kids get older and so do you.

People who are bankrupt with time see their freedom, their families and their relationships disintegrate. Time is mismanaged because the Slowlane is predicated on time. Five days of servitude for two days of freedom is not a good trade unless you trade time into a system that can give you a better return on your time.

Instead of 5-for-2 for life, how about a 5-for-2 trade that has the potential to blossom into a better ratio? Like 1-for-2 or 3-for-10? Would you make a 5-for-2 trade knowing that it could transform into a 1-for-10? Would that be a something to invest in?

While I worked my plan, I gave 7-for-0 (I worked seven days and didn't take a day off) because I knew the roads within my roadmap converged with dreams. I worked for a better ratio in the near future, not in 40 years. I controlled my destiny and eventually my time trade investment yielded a dividend of 40 years.

Now I do 0-for-7. I work zero days and get seven days of freedom.

Sadly, if you are Slowlane grinding, your options to shatter this negative 60% return for your freedom is restricted. Remember, wealth is defined by freedom. If you want proof, look to Friday night when people celebrate freedom as the Slowlane dictatorship takes a weekend furlough.

NORMAL IS CONDEMNATION TO MEDIOCRITY

Revolutionary Road, the 2008 movie starring Leonardo DiCaprio and Kate Winslet, does an excellent job portraying the Slowlane's death grip. A young couple find themselves living in suburbia, going through life's motions: The husband (DiCaprio) goes to work every morning and immerses himself in a crowd of his peers while his wife (Winslet) fills the role of the good housewife.

Both instinctively know that something is wrong. They're settling. They've accepted normal. They've forsaken their dreams for the insane plan of everyone. Throughout the movie we witness their attempts to escape, and with precarious consequences.

The problem is, we've been brainwashed to accept the Slowlane roadmap as normal. The defective roadmap gains traction early in life and is sanctified as the "commoners" only probable means to wealth. Sounds logical right? Folks like us just don't get rich playing pro ball, rapping, acting, or entertaining, so we're left with the Slowlane. And for some, that just might be OK. But for the rest of us with big dreams, big goals, and big ideas, it just doesn't cut the mustard.

Here's a Slowlane story pulled from the pages of the Fastlane Forum (TheFastlaneForum.com):

In the quest for becoming wealthy, my life has become quite uncomfortable. It all started five years ago when I had nothing. I had turned 30 years old and I thought that living paycheck to paycheck was no way to live at all.

I made a vow to myself that I would become wealthy.

In order to do this I took on a second job and saved all of the money from that job while I used the money from the first job to pay for my living expenses. Basically, the last five years of my life have been as such in order for me to save money:

- *living and paying relatively cheap rent for an 8×13 foot room*
- *using public transportation and a motorcycle for transportation.*
- *working almost every day with no days off during the week*
- *rarely eating out*
- *never buying "toys" or nice things for myself or wife*
- *almost never going out and having a good time*

With the second job and my economical lifestyle I have managed to save about $50,000 in five years. It would have been more, but I lost a good $30,000 when I invested right before the Dow hit its peak in October of 2007.

I've reached a breaking point.

Five years is a long time to live in a room no bigger than a jail cell. The jobs are mind numbing. I feel like my life is a prison. I have a good lifestyle for saving money, but at the expense of my mental sanity and happiness as a human being. I just feel like I can't live like this any longer.

The Slowlaner accepts an existence of frugality and sacrifice to a tipping-point where life feels like incarceration.

Does this guy's life seem awesome or mediocre? Will it merge with a dream? The Slowlane plan forsakes *the now* for a faint promise of a wealthy future.

I don't consider "settle for less" a strategy, which is why the Slowlane is predisposed to mediocrity. Life isn't great, but it isn't so bad either. No, it could be better . . . but you've got to swap the Slowlane for a new plan.

CHAPTER SUMMARY: FASTLANE DISTINCTIONS

- The Slowlane is a natural course-correction from the Sidewalk evolving from responsibility and accountability.
- Wealth is best experienced when you're young, vibrant, and able, not in the twilight of your life.
- The Slowlane is a plan that takes decades to succeed, requiring masterful political prowess in a corporate environment, frugality, and Wall-Street wizardry.
- For the Slowlaner, Saturday and Sunday is the paycheck for Monday through Friday.
- The default return on your time in the Slowlane is negative 60%—5-for-2.
- The 5-for-2 trade inherent in the Slowlane is generally fixed and cannot be manipulated, because job standards are five days a week.
- The predisposed destination of the Slowlane is mediocrity. Life isn't great, but it isn't so bad either.

The Criminal Trade: Your Job

By working faithfully 8 hours a day, you may eventually get to be the boss and work 12 hours a day.

~ ROBERT FROST

I SPENT FIVE YEARS IN COLLEGE . . . FOR A PHONEBOOK?

Before college graduation, I humored myself and attended a few job workshops. I remember one vividly: an entry-level position at a big insurance firm in Chicago. During our introduction at the corporate facility, the company recruiters told us exactly what to expect:

> *"Over there* [pointing to a sea of cubicles] *is where our new hires sit. I won't be coy; in the beginning this job is difficult. We give you three things: a desk, a telephone, and a telephone book. You will spend 10 hours a day cold-calling to build your clientele. I know, not glamorous, but the rewards . . ."*

At that point I didn't give a shit about the "rewards". I immediately went into acting mode. I acted interested. I acted grateful for the opportunity. I acted like it was acceptable.

It wasn't.

So lemme get this straight: I spent five years and $40K+ in college just so I can sit in a 6×6 cubicle and cold-call people out of a damn telephone book? Are you kidding me? I could have done this without the college degree, without the mountainous pile of debt, and yes, without that five years lost!

Yet, my peers salivated at the opportunity of having a nice base salary, a great 401(k), and a top-tier health plan. No thanks. If I'm cold-calling a stranger and interrupting their supper, it won't be for my boss, but for me.

JOBS: DOMESTICATION INTO NORMALCY

If you want to escape the Slowlane, find wealth and freedom fast, you've got to dump the job. Let me repeat. Dump the damn job!

Jobs suck. I mean that generically, not targeted toward a specific job. Whether you're an electrician or a store manager, you hold a job. Jobs suck because they're rooted in *limited leverage* and *limited control.* Sure, you can have great job (and a fun one too!) but in the scope of wealth, they limit both LEVERAGE and CONTROL—two things desperately needed if you want wealth.

Here are six sucky reasons your financial plan shouldn't revolve around a job, the nucleus to the Slowlane.

SUCKAGE #1: TO TRADE TIME IS TO TRADE LIFE

Who taught us that trading time in exchange for money was a great idea? Why does this normalcy consistently translate into unrivaled suckage? If you're shackled to a job, you're married to a glorified time trade (your life) for pieces of paper that grant you freedom. *You sell your freedom to get freedom.* Pretty stupid, huh?

Jobs suck because they ravenously consume TIME. At a job, TIME TRADE is central to how you make money. A job is the basis for that horrific 5-for-2 exchange. But let me translate that word, TIME, differently: LIFE.

In a job, you sell your life for money. If you work, you get paid. If you don't work, you don't get paid. Who officiated this bloodsucking marriage?

Assuming a 20% income tax, here is a list of common jobs and how long it takes to earn (and then pocket) $1 million in after-tax dollars. If you diligently save 10% of your after-tax earnings and stuff it under a mattress, your time to $1 million multiplies by a factor of 10. Do you have 250 years to save your way to $1 million?

Career/Job	Average Annual Salary	Years to EARN $1 MM	Years to SAVE $1 MM
Architect	$85,000	15 years	147 years
Auto Mechanic	$43,000	29 years	291 years
Bartender	$26,000	48 years	481 years
Carpenter	$50,000	25 years	250 years
Software Engineer	$102,000	12 years	123 years
Secretary	$37,000	34 years	338 years
Hairdresser	$30,000	42 years	417 years
Teacher	$61,000	21 years	205 years
Pharmacist	$121,000	10 years	103 years
Police Officer	$64,000	20 years	195 years
Physical Therapist	$88,000	14 years	142 years
Veterinarian	$101,000	12 years	124 years

Source: US Bureau of Labor Statistics, May 2017 Occupational Wage Estimates. Figures rounded for simplicity.

Wouldn't it make sense to get paid regardless of what you're doing? Get paid while you sleep, while you have fun, while you poop, while you sit on the beach? Why not get paid with the simple passage of time and make time work for you instead of against you? Does that exist? It does, but it doesn't come from a Slowlane.

SUCKAGE #2: LIMITATION ON EXPERIENCE

I learned more as an entrepreneur in two months than I did working 10 years at dozens of dead-end jobs. The problem with a specialized skill set is, it narrows your useful value to a confined set of marketplace needs. You become one of many cogs in a wheel. And if that cog becomes obsolete or expendable? Guess what, you're out of luck.

For example, thousands of auto workers have been displaced because their jobs have been outsourced or replaced by robotics. Experience doesn't help them, it hinders them. Remember typewriters? How is the typewriter repairman doing these days? How about stockbrokers and travel agents? With the advent of ride-sharing apps like Uber and Lyft, how are taxi drivers faring? Dying breeds of jobs move out of favor like fashion fads. One year your skill set has value, the next, it doesn't.

Second, job experience is usually organized into a core group of activities that is routinely repeated over and over again, day after day. After the initial learning experience, the job becomes regimented and accumulation of new knowledge creeps to a crawl. A job limits learning and mutates into life's death knell: a trade of life force for money.

Experience comes from what you do in life, not from what you do in a job. *You don't need a job to get experience.*

Ask yourself this: Which experience is more important? The experience of a menial job designed to pay your bills? Or the experience (and failures) of creating something that could provide you financial freedom for a lifetime without ever having to hold a job again?

SUCKAGE #3: NO CONTROL

A job is like sitting in the bed of a pickup truck. You're exposed to the harsh elements while the driver of the truck sits comfortably in the driver's seat. And if the ride gets rough? You get jacked around or worse, tossed overboard. There is no control sitting in the back of a pickup truck, and to have this "strategy" at the core of your financial plan is insanely foolish.

If you don't control your income, you don't control your financial plan.

If you don't control your financial plan, you don't control your freedom.

Millions obediently sing the employee *Kumbaya*, believing that a job is central to supporting themselves. Sure, a job can support you, but is your goal only "support"? Do you want wealth or mediocrity? If your financial road trip can be derailed by a pink slip, you're gambling. You aren't being real; you're being stupid. There is neither safety nor security in a job.

SUCKAGE #4: LINDA'S BAD BREATH

I know people who are life-long employees. I hear about their trials and toils. Despite two dozen different jobs over the years, I noticed nothing changes when it comes to office politics. It's the same story, different people, different day, in a different office. So-and-so is sleeping with the boss and courting favor. Jim is lazy but takes credit for the work. Linda has bad breath and everyone is afraid to tell her. Lacey arrives late and leaves early. Horace steals food and wears the same sport jacket every day. Lazy Lester never replaces the copier paper.

Same stories, different people.

No matter where you work, office politics play a part. The stage is different but the actors are the same. And, unfortunately, as an employee immersed in the work environment, you have to play the game. You have to be obedient or face retribution from coworkers or your boss.

I can remember my friend's after-work rants as she toiled at a high-fat corporate environment. Everything had a process. Got an idea? Great, send it to the boss, the boss sends it to his boss, who then hands it off to legal, who then sends it back to her boss's boss for revisions, who sends it back, blah blah blah! By the time the "idea" gets anywhere it's either stale or four other people have staked a claim to it.

Who needs this entangled web destroying your sanity?

The only defense to office politics is to control the playing field, and to do that, you have to be the boss. And to be the boss, you not only need to run the show, you need to own it.

SUCKAGE #5: A SUBSCRIPTION TO "PAY YOURSELF LAST"

"Pay yourself first" is a Slowlane doctrine. The problem is that it's near impossible in a job.

Local, state, and federal governments heavily tax earned income and your options to shield that income from taxation is limited to contributions to 401(k)s and IRAs—which are also limited—10% of your income or a maximum of $16,500, whichever is less (as of publication). If you diligently trade your life and ascend into corporate management, expect 50% of your money to disappear before it touches your hands.

As an employee, you immediately receive a subscription to "pay yourself last," and yes, that subscription arrives even if you don't subscribe. If you are paying yourself last and everyone gets your money first, don't expect to build wealth fast.

SUCKAGE #6: A DICTATORSHIP ON INCOME

Ever get hit with a 1,000% pay raise from your boss? Imagine this: Impressed at the obvious returns you've provided at your job, you confidently stroll into your boss's office and demand a raise. "I bring value to this company," you argue. "I'm reliable and rarely call in sick."

Your boss takes a defensive posture, crosses his arms, tilts his head skyward, and leisurely reclines in his big, red executive chair. You take a deep breath and let it loose. "Therefore, sir, I'd like a 1,000% pay raise."

Your boss unleashes a guttural groan. He lurches forward, ends his recline and hammers his hands to the desk. "OK, what's the joke? I'm busy" he snipes.

You reply, "No joke. I'm serious. I make $9 an hour. I want a raise to $90 an hour."

"How about this? You'll get nothing and like it. Get out of my office, quit wasting my time, and if you do it fast, I won't fire you. How's that for an offer?"

You stammer out. I guess the boss didn't think the 1,000% pay raise was doable.

This scenario would never happen. As an employee, you can't demand a pay raise greater than 10%, let alone 1,000%. Yet, as an employee of any company, this is your playing field. This is the road you've put yourself on. *Your value is dictated, diminished, and delimited.* Therefore the job becomes a delimiter on what's important: wealth, freedom, and self-growth. And their limitations cannot be subverted.

A job seals your fate into a criminal time trade: five days of life traded for two days of freedom. A job chains you to a set grade of experience. A job takes away your control. A job forces you to work with people you can't stand. A job forces you to get paid last. A job imposes a dictatorship on your income. These limitations are counter-insurgencies to wealth.

Still want a job?

CHAPTER SUMMARY: FASTLANE DISTINCTIONS

- In a job, you sell your freedom (in the form of time) for freedom (in the form of money).
- Experience is gained in action. The environment of that action is irrelevant.
- Wealth accumulation is thwarted when you don't control your primary income source.

The Slowlane: Why You Aren't Rich

Somebody should tell us, right at the start of our lives, that we are dying. Then we might live life to the limit, every minute of every day. Do it! I say. Whatever you want to do, do it now. There are only so many tomorrows.

~ MICHAEL LANDON

EXPOSING SLOWLANE INEPTITUDE

If the Slowlane is your "get rich" strategy I can make a likely assumption: You're not rich and you never will be. Wow, how could I be so sure? Simple. The Slowlane strategy is rooted in *Uncontrollable Limited Leverage*, or ULL (pronounced "yule"). If you need help remembering this important concept, just think, "If the Slowlane is your plan, 'ULL' never get rich."

Uncontrollable Limited Leverage is the disturbing evidence that proves the Slowlane's futility. How do you get rich in the Slowlane? You get a great-paying job, save money, live frugal, invest in the stock market, and repeat for 50 years. If you mine this strategy into its mathematical constructs, you'll find that the variables that define the plan cannot be controlled or leveraged.

UNCONTROLLABLE LIMITED LEVERAGE (ULL) – PART 1

Why is ULL so important? To accumulate financial wealth, you need to attract and earn a large sum of money, relative to the average person. To attract a large sum of money, two things are absolutely required:

1) Control
2) Leverage

The Slowlane has NEITHER and that truth is exposed when you reverse engineer the strategy into its mathematical equivalent, or its wealth universe. Uncover the mathematics behind the plan and you uncover its weakness!

When the Slowlane is deconstructed, you find two variables:

1) The "primary income source" (defines how income is earned)
2) The "wealth accelerator" (defines how wealth is accumulated)

The Slowlaner's primary income source comes from "a job," while the wealth acceleration vehicle comes from "market investments" like 401(k)s and indexed-funds. Put it together and you arrive at the Slowlaner's wealth equation:

WEALTH = (Job) + (Market Investments)

The primary income source   The wealth accelerator

Under this plan, income from a job funds both lifestyle and market investments. However, to uncover the prohibitive ULL within the plan, we have to factor these variables further, starting with the job variable.

THE WARDEN OF WEALTH: INTRINSIC VALUE

How is money earned in a job? *Intrinsic value.*

Intrinsic value is determined by the marketplace and is the price at which you can trade your time for money. Intrinsic value is what you earn working a job. How much is someone willing to pay you for what you offer to society?

Intrinsic value is measured in units of time, either *hourly* or *annually.*

If you're paid $10/hour to flip burgers at the neighborhood grill, your intrinsic value is $10 per HOUR. If you're an accountant and earn a $120,000 annual salary, your intrinsic value is $120,000 per YEAR.

JOB [Intrinsic Value] = Hourly Rate of Pay × Hours Worked

~ or ~

JOB [Intrinsic Value] = Annual Salary

Notice that intrinsic value is measured in units of TIME. This "time attachment" introduces the Slowlane's first punitive element of wealth creation.

Can you control time? Can you leverage time?

You can't.

Your time is limited to 24 hours of exchange. If you earn $200/hour, you can't miraculously demand to work 400 hours in one day. If you earn $50,000/year, you can't miraculously demand to work 400 years in your life. *Time has no leverage.*

For the hourly worker, your maximum upper limit is 24 hours, and guess what. There's nothing you can do to change this limit. In theory, you can trade 24 hours of your day for income, but you can't trade more. Of course, working 24 hours a day is humanly impossible, so 8 to 12 hours per day are traded.

For the salaried worker, the prohibition is the same. You can't work more years than your normal life expectancy. What is the upper limit of this exchange? Forty, fifty years? In all of recorded history, no human has ever worked 10,000 years of his or her life. Whether you're paid hourly or annually—it doesn't matter—you can't leverage time!

Consider this. Is 12 a large number? Or 50? Are these numbers predisposed to create millionaires? They aren't, and it exposes why the mathematics of a job are wealth punitive: Your time is limited to small numbers and cannot be leveraged. "Hours worked" or "annual salary" are mathematically inept because they're based on time measurements that cannot be controlled or manipulated.

Mathematics doesn't lie; 12 will always be less than 10,000,000. If leverage is limited, so is wealth creation. *Small numbers do not make millionaires.*

Behind limited leverage is another corrosive wealth killer—no control. Can you control your employer? Can you control your salary? Can you control the economy? Can you earn $50,000 one year and next year bank $50 million? Can you control anything about your job, including your measly 4% pay raise?

You might think you can by job-hopping, but you can't.

Control is weak, if not absent.

COMPOUND INTEREST: WHAT "THEY" DON'T TELL YOU

The second variable in the Slowlane wealth equation is the "primary wealth accelerator," which comes from market investments like index-funds, 401(k)s, and other traditional investments touted by gurus and financial advisers.

These investments use the financial strategy known as "compound interest," which is a mathematical construct that outlines the power of interest accumulation over great periods of time.

The fundamental sell of compound interest is the old guru swan song regurgitated *ad nauseam*: $10,000 invested today will be worth gazillions in 50 years. Invest $250 a month for 50 years and you will retire rich!

Used correctly, "compound interest" is a powerful ally to wealth; used for Slowlane purposes and it bogs the wealth road trip to a crawl.

Why? Again, the puzzle is solved if you exploit the math—the answer plays sibling to why a job won't make you rich: *time.*

Wealth creation via compound interest requires the passing of time and lots of it. Like a job, compound interest, or market investments such as stocks and indexed-funds can't be leveraged nor can they be controlled. They rely on deficient math to create wealth.

Inasmuch as job income is measured in an hourly rate or an annual salary, the wealth acceleration process of "compound interest" is also measured in TIME (years) multiplied by a yearly yield. Let's again review the physics, the mathematical formula for the Slowlane pathology to wealth:

$$WEALTH = (Job) + (Market\ Investments)$$

The primary income source — The wealth accelerator

Or factored:

$$WEALTH = [Intrinsic\ Value\ (Yearly)] + [Compound\ Interest\ (Yearly)]$$

The primary income source — The wealth accelerator

Factored further:

$$WEALTH = (Time \times Hourly\ or\ Salaried\ Value) + Invested\ Sum \times (1 + Yield)^{time}$$

The primary income source — The wealth accelerator

Like a job, the flaw in "compound interest" lies in the same mathematical restrictions in which numbers work AGAINST you instead of FOR you. Take a look at this chart, which highlights the effect of compound interest and that $10,000 investment.

$10,000 Investment

Time (Years)	Rate of Growth			
	5%	10%	15%	20%
5	$12,763	$16,105	$20,114	$24,883
10	$16,289	$25,937	$40,456	$61.917
15	$20,789	$41,772	$81,371	$154.070
20	$26,553	$67,275	$163,665	$383,376
25	$33,864	$108,347	$329,190	$953,962
30	$43,219	$174,494	$662,118	$2,373,763
35	$55,160	$281,024	$1,331,755	$5,906,682
40	$70,400	$452,593	$2,678,635	$14,697,716

A Slowlane guru preaches that a $10,000 investment grown at 15% will be worth over $2.5 million dollars in 40 years!!! Hooray!!!

What don't they tell you?

They don't tell you that a 15% return year-after-year is impossible unless you invest with Bernie Madoff or Charles Ponzi. They don't tell you that in 40 years you'll be dead, and if you're not, you'll be close. They don't tell you that in 40 years, your $2.5 million will likely be worth $250,000 in today's dollars and that a pack of gum will cost $6.00. They don't tell you that this method of wealth acceleration is NOT what they use. They don't tell you plenty, and yet you're supposed to believe it without question.

UNCONTROLLABLE LIMITED LEVERAGE (ULL) - PART 2

For compound interest to be effective, you need three things:

1) TIME, as measured in years.
2) A favorable YEARLY INVESTMENT YIELD within those years.
3) An INVESTED SUM, repeatedly invested.

These three variables make up the latter portion of our Slowlane wealth equation:

$$\textit{Compound Interest} = \textit{Invested Sum} \times (1 + \textit{Yield})^{\textit{time}}$$

Although this is a simplified version of a more complicated equation, the point of this analysis is its variable components.

Compound interest demands that your investments yield a predictable 10% return per year. Good luck with that 40-year gamble. Have the markets ever lost 20% in one year? Or 40%? They have, and when they do, your hard-earned savings evaporate.

You see, wealth acceleration via *compound interest is deficient because its variables are deficient*. Neither time nor yield can be leveraged or controlled. Again, meet my friend Uncontrollable Limited Leverage.

Can you demand a 2,000% return on your money this year? Can you demand your investment time horizon increase from the standard 40 years to 400 years? Again, the numbers can't be leveraged. Your upper limit of time investment horizon is 50 years. Yield is worse—6%, 8%, or 10% yearly investment returns are typical standards. Time is restrained by the years in your life, yield is restrained by the average yield of typical market investments, and sum is limited because your means of creating income comes from a job—also limited! The only way to subvert the mathematical weakness of compound interest is to *start with a large number, and large numbers require leverage!*

Additionally, like a job, you can't control compound interest.

Can you demand your bank pay 25% interest on your savings? Hey, Mr. Slowlane Bank, I demand a 25% yield on my savings account!

Can you control the economy? Hey, Mr. Economy, can you guarantee me low unemployment and a business-friendly tax environment?

Can you control the average yield of the stock market? Hey, Mr. Stock Market, I'm tired of 8% returns, can you give me 250% this year? Funny stuff!

Can you control anything in this equation other than a furious, labor-intensive search for the best investments to ensure you eek out another marginal 1%?

You can't.

WHY INDEXED-FUNDS AND 401(K)S WON'T MAKE YOU RICH

In 2008, I went to a fixed-income investment seminar given by a major brokerage house. Fixed-income investments are instruments like municipal and corporate bonds. Approximately 50 people attended the standing-room-only seminar. I sat in the back and surveyed the crowd. Remove the gray hair, the socks-n-sandals combos, the canes, and the wheelchairs and what was left?

Just me.

I was the youngest person in the room (and I'm not even that young anymore). How does a thirty-something get in a room full of retirees?

The people in the room were Slowlane success stories. They used time to accelerate wealth, and what it got them was old age. I don't say that to be mean-spirited to older folks, but to cast light on the point: Compound interest (indexed-funds, mutual funds, the stock market) cannot accelerate wealth fast.

According to research and marketing firm The Harrison Group (HarrisonGroupInc.com), only 10% of penta-millionaires (net worth $5 million) report that their wealth came from passive investments. Age data was not provided but you can guess that none of the 10% were under 30.

Think about it. Have you ever met a college student who got rich investing in indexed-funds or his employer's juicy retirement program? How about the guy who bought municipal bonds in 2014 and retired in 2018? I wonder if that guy driving a $1.2-million car can because of his well-balanced portfolio of mutual funds?

These people don't exist because the youthful rich are not leveraging 8% returns but 800%! Has your wealth ever grown by 800% in one year? Probably not, but guess what? MINE HAS because I'm not shackled to the Slowlane wealth equation. My wealth acceleration vehicle isn't dependent on Wall Street.

Yet, you've been domesticated to believe that these tools accelerate wealth. Index-funds, stocks, bonds, 401(k)s, dollar cost averaging, and compound interest are perfunctory orthodoxy for Slowlane wealth acceleration.

Unfortunately, without control or leverage, they're impotent wealth accelerators.

BUY-AND-HOLD IS DEAD

In college, I was taught "buy and hold" was the safe investment strategy that made millions. Buy stocks in solid companies, sit back and wait decades, and voilà, I'd be awash with millions. They'd shove that graph in your face and say "A $10,000 Investment in XYZ Company in 1955 would be worth $5 million today!" *Thankfully, I ignored it.*

In 1997, I opened a Roth IRA with $1,000 and invested the monies in a growth mutual fund at a major investment firm. Yes, I let the "professionals" manage it for me. For the next decade, I didn't touch it. Essentially, I forgot about the account.

In the 10 years that followed, I made over $10 million dollars by following a Fastlane roadmap and leveraging Fastlane strategy. And what about that Roth IRA opened years ago? I never touched it and let it ride the ebbs-and-flow of the Slowlane. When I finished this book in 2010, that account was worth $698. *$698!*

With inflation, the real purchasing power is $500. My spare change bucket on my kitchen table was a better investment. Had I invested $1 million, I'd have lost more than $400,000.

And this is the Slowlaner's anointed weapon of wealth? Hilarious!

Millions worship the Slowlane roadmap with "buy and hold" as Main Street, a Main Street that is decades long, imperiled by uncontrollable hazards, and rarely leads to wealth.

I recently heard a Slowlane prognosticator proclaim the effectiveness of "Get Rich Slow" by citing this syrupy factoid: *If at the end of 1940 you had invested $1,000 in the stocks of the S&P500 you would now have $1,341,513.* So let's examine this fact, assuming it is fact.

1) It's 1940 and assume you are 21 years old.
2) It's 1940 and you somehow got your hands on $1,000, which in today's dollars is about $15,000.
3) You took that $1,000 in 1940s money and did as above.

Congratulations! It is NOW 2011 and you are 91 years old, rich with $1,341,513. Or if you were lucky to get your $1,000 ON BIRTH, you'd now be 71 years old! Yes, folks, it's time to get excited! "Get Rich Slow" is going to make you rich! Just ignore your 74-year life expectancy and make sure your wheelchair comes equipped with chrome rims.

Seriously, how does anyone get excited over this crap?

THE SLOWLANE'S TRAITOROUS RELATIONSHIP WITH TIME

Compound interest and a job have the same disease: the sinful and gluttonous consumption of your time while forsaking control. Both variables within the Slowlane wealth equation are anchored by time—time traded in a job and time traded in market investments. Time becomes the linchpin for wealth that congenitally ties to the mathematical handicaps of mortality: 24 hours in a day and a 50-year work-life expectancy.

Yes, "getting rich" is a function of time.

Unless you plan on living forever, this relationship is dubiously foolhardy. Why? *Because to trade your time away is to trade your wealth away.*

Examine these pathetically common examples. Assume a 5% savings rate on gross salary and an annual investment yield of 8% per year. We'll exclude taxes and inflation.

Salary @ $25,000/yr, save $1,250/year, invested over 40 yrs @ 8% = $362,895
Salary @ $50,000/yr, save $2,500/year, invested over 40 yrs @ 8% = $725,791
Salary @ $75,000/yr, save $3,750/year, invested over 40 yrs @ 8% = $1,088,686
Salary @ $100,000/yr, save $5,000/year, invested over 40 yrs @ 8% = $1,451,581
Salary @ $150,000/yr, save $7,500/year, invested over 40 yrs @ 8% = $2,177,132

Don't get enamored with the numbers. Keep in mind this is 40 YEARS from now. If you are 20 years old, you will be 60 years old. If you are 30 years old, you will be 70 years old. If you are 40 years old, you'll be dead. Sorry, but that's beyond life expectancy.

So at these ages, does this money and the freedom it buys sound appealing? Also, do you realize that this money will have 50% of today's buying power? Forty years ago you could buy a car for $5,000 and a loaf of bread for 50 cents. Lest we not forget the other lofty assumptions, gainful employment and a robust economy that behests a safe 8% per year. In 2008 the markets lost 50%. I guess the gurus forgot to mention these anomalies.

Folks, you don't want millions to accompany your cane, you want it to accompany your youth.

Every day, people sacrifice their time for tiny nuggets of wealth, where time is the liability and not the asset. Anything that steals time and doesn't have the power to free time is a liability.

Within the Slowlane, time is mistreated like an effervescent fountain that runs forever. Unfortunately, the mortality rate is 100% and life's prognosis is death. Some day you will die, and, hopefully, 60% of your time wasn't squandered in a cubicle while your children grew up and your spouse cheated with the yoga instructor.

THE SLOWLANE IS A PLAN OF HOPE

The Slowlane dilutes your control. You're reading this book because you want to control your financial destiny, NOT put it in the hands Wall Street or some corporation.

If you want to get rich, *you have to control and leverage the variables in your financial plan*—any financial plan without control immediately disintegrates into a plan of hope.

Hope I don't get laid off!

Hope my stocks rebound!

Hope I get that promotion!

Hope my hours aren't cut!

Hope my company doesn't go bankrupt!

Hope, hope, and hope!

Sorry, hope isn't a plan!

The Slowlane plan rests in a mathematical prison, with time as the warden. To create explosive wealth fast, you must abandon the Slowlane formula and its lecherous relationship to time. *Wealth is built with time as an asset, not as a liability!*

Yet, the Slowlaner's reaction to Uncontrollable Limited Leverage is predictable: They embark on an errant fight against the one variable they perceive as controllable—their intrinsic value. The Slowlaner argues, "I must make more money!" And that fight is fought futilely with an expensive education.

CHAPTER SUMMARY: FASTLANE DISTINCTIONS

- Slowlane wealth is improbable due to Uncontrollable Limited Leverage (ULL).
- The first variable in the Slowlane wealth equation stems from a job that factors to intrinsic value which is your nominal value for each unit of your life traded.
- Intrinsic value is the value of your time set by the marketplace and is measured in units of time, either hourly or yearly.
- In the Slowlane, intrinsic value (regardless of its time measurement) is numerically inhibited because there are only 24 hours in the day (for the hourly worker), and the average lifespan is 74 years (for the salaried worker).
- Like the Slowlaner's primary income source (a job), the Slowlaner's wealth acceleration vehicle (compound interest) is also pegged to time.
- Like a job, compound interest is mathematically futile and cannot be manipulated. You cannot force-feed the market (or the economy) to give you phenomenal returns, year after year.
- Wealth cannot be accelerated when pegged to mathematics based on time.
- Time is your primordial fuel and it should not be traded for money.
- Your time should not be an expendable resource for wealth because wealth itself is composed of time.
- Your mortality makes time mathematically retarded for wealth creation.
- If you don't control the variables inherent in your wealth universe, you don't control your financial plan.

The Futile Fight: Education

The only thing that interferes with my learning is my education.

~ ALBERT EINSTEIN

THE FIGHT AGAINST UNCONTROLLABLE LIMITED LEVERAGE: EDUCATION

The Slowlaner's natural reaction to the Uncontrollable Limited Leverage (ULL) genetically innate in their wealth equation is to wage war with intrinsic value by deploying the education weapon.

Since ULL defines the Slowlane, the Slowlaner rationalizes that the only variable worth escalating is their pay rate. I need to make six figures! I need to make more money! So, predictably, they go back to school and get an MBA or some certification. They'll argue, "MBA grads earn 15% more!" or "The starting salary of a certified PMP is $120,000 year!"

For example, Steve Debois enrolls into an MBA program to sweeten his credentials. The cost of the MBA is $55,000 and 800 hours. Steve justifies this twofold expense (time and money) because he anticipates his intrinsic value to rise. Upon completion, Steve expects to be worth more to his company and worth more in the competitive marketplace. Unfortunately, he still trades his time for money—just at a higher rate, yet still uncontrolled and unleveraged.

Another example is my friend who enrolled in a project management certification class that ate five eight-hour Saturdays from her life and cost $2,700. Her goal? A project management credential that would raise her intrinsic value in the marketplace. As a certified project manager, she exposes herself to new opportunities at higher grades of pay. But still, a trade of time for money.

Whether consciously or not, the Slowlaner believes that elevating intrinsic value can create wealth. Want to be highly paid right out of college? Go to medical school and become a doctor. As a physician, your intrinsic value is now worth $500 per hour. Become an engineer, a lawyer, or an accountant—all highly paid, professional, salaried positions. Typically, a formal college education is used to serve Slowlane purposes—an explicit attempt to raise intrinsic value. Fight that intrinsic value variable!

NOT ALL EDUCATION IS VIRTUOUS

The problem with formal education used to raise intrinsic value is that it's ungodly expensive in time and money. Not a week goes by when I don't hear about a freshly minted MBA grad who struggles to pay his student loans while working a job he could have secured out of high school. Debt that traps you to a job is not good debt. A preoccupation to become "highly educated" could be a Trojan horse to your freedom.

Not all education is equal or virtuous. Some education can deter wealth. If an education entombs you under a mountain of debt and shackles you to a job for the rest of your life, is it really a good education? If an MBA increases your salary by 15% but takes 15 years to pay, was it a good investment?

It's a great myth: To get rich you need an expensive college degree. Hogwash. A degree isn't a prerequisite to Fastlane wealth. Some of the richest Fastlaners are people who never finished either high school or college. Bill Gates, Steven Spielberg, Richard Branson, Michael Dell, Felix Dennis, David Geffen, and John Paul DeJoria all dropped out of school to pursue Fastlane objectives. How dare they get rich and not be "educated"?

SLOWLANE ENTRAPMENT

Financing expensive college tuition for an education is a dangerous game that can lead to Slowlane entrapment: *conformity and education servitude.*

A typical collegiate study progresses from general knowledge to very specific skill sets. For example, while studying finance I learned complex mathematical formulas that aided in financial decision-making, things like "lease or buy" and "return on investment." These concepts are specific trade tools that can hinder your future options. The prescribed path for finance graduates was a job in the financial sector, an insurance company, an accounting firm, or an investment house.

My education had the indirect and unintended consequence of restricting my options to specific disciplines based on an educative skill set. The result? *Conformity and limited choice.* If there aren't opportunities in my field, my education becomes marginalized and devalued. If the opportunities available require less education (say, a BS) than I have (MBA), I become overqualified and unemployable. If my skills erode in practicality based on technological evolution, my education becomes deprecated and my value to society plummets accordingly.

The second educational entrapment danger is "education servitude." While the Sidewalker deals with "Lifestyle Servitude," the Slowlaner wrestles with "Education Servitude" (freedom eroded by education) that traps the victim to a job. Has your education indentured you to a job? Advanced degrees are not cheap. According to The College Board the average college degree at a public university in 2017, including room and board, now costs over $100,000. Prefer the prestige of a private school? That tab will set you back $200,000+, the cost of a used Ferrari. This kind of debt will bury your dreams, not enliven them. It will permanently bind you to the Slowlane or worse, the Sidewalk.

Consider the statistics. In 2007, the *Washington Post* reported that, according to Nellie Mae, the big student loan service provider, by the time college students are seniors, 56% of them will have four or more credit cards with an average balance of $2,864. According to a research report by Demos-USA.org, a public policy research and advocacy organization, people in the 18–24 age bracket spend nearly 30% of their monthly income on debt repayment. This is double from 20 years ago. A survey of college borrowers found that the average college senior graduated with nearly $19,000 in student loan debts, and graduate degree pursuers more than $45,000. A 2007 Charles Schwab survey revealed that teenagers believe when they get older they will earn an average salary of $145,000. The reality? Adults with a college degree earned an average of $54,000. Unfortunately, the future isn't so bright that you have to wear shades. The truth behind reality and expectation is about a $100,000 chasm. This disparity might explain why the debts of our youth have exploded as they bridge reality to expectation. *If I can't make* $145,000, *I can look like I make* $145,000*!*

The best excuse people have for not having wealth is "I don't have time." Well, why don't you have time? Because you have a job. Why do you have a job? Because you need one. Why do you need one? Because you have bills to pay. Why do you have bills to pay? Because you have debt. Why do you have debt? Oh yes, because you went to school for six years and have six figures in student loans.

If you financed your advanced education with debt, the debt automatically becomes parasitic and traps you into forced job servitude, and that destroys freedom. While you might earn more, work is forced to feed the debt. The debt is parasitic because it fails to free time and instead creates indentured time. Sadly, the parasitic debt is unforgiving and isn't sympathetic to the source. Whether you owe $45,000 for your awesome BMW or for student loans, debt steals freedom and forces indentured time.

CHAPTER SUMMARY: FASTLANE DISTINCTIONS

- Slowlaners attempt to manipulate intrinsic value by education.
- Indentured time is time you spend earning a living. It is the opposite of free time.
- Parasitic debt is debt that creates indentured time and forces work.

The Hypocrisy of the Gurus

There was a time when a fool and his money were soon parted,
but now it happens to everybody.

~ ADLAI STEVENSON

YOU'VE BEEN DUPED

Suppose after college you're getting a bit pudgy around the middle and decide it's time to put yourself in cover-model shape. You enroll in a community college class called "Mega-Gains: How to Build Yourself the Body of a Spartan."

On the first day of class, you arrive early, seat yourself, and anxiously await the class instructor. After a few minutes, an obese man walks into the room and waddles to the front of the class. You think, "Wow, he's fat . . . but he's here to change that . . . good for him!" As the man profusely sweats while fumbling with a stack of papers, you glance at the student chair near the man and wonder if he can fit on it . . . he's twice the size of the chair!

Then suddenly you're hit with the paradox.

This isn't a student but the instructor!

Are you kidding me?

How can this man effectively teach a class called "Mega-Gains: How to Build Yourself the Body of a Spartan" when he clearly doesn't have the body of a Spartan?

How can anyone take him seriously?

Bewildered at the hypocrisy, you exit the class and hit-up the college for a tuition refund.

When it comes to gurus and financial advisers this is what you must do: leave class and request a refund because they're guilty of a PARADOX OF PRACTICE.

THE PARADOX OF PRACTICE

The Paradox of Practice asks, "Do you practice what you preach? Are you a model, an exemplification of what you teach?"

Would you take skin care advice from a butterface?
Would you take financial advice from a bankrupt bum?
Would you take medical advice from a sanitation worker?
Would you take bodybuilding advice from a 90-lb. weakling?

The Paradox of Practice is a heated debate in my forum. Some feel it's perfectly acceptable to preach a strategy for wealth yet never use it.

DO AS I SAY, NOT AS I DO

A Paradox of Practice exists when someone promotes a moneymaking strategy but that strategy is not what made him or her rich. In other words, *they're not practitioners of their own advice.*

These people effectively teach one wealth equation (the Slowlane) while they get rich leveraging another (the Fastlane).

When I see financial powerhouse "Suze" instructing people to "dollar-cost-average" their mutual fund portfolios, do I listen to her? Hell no. I laugh. When "Cramer" advocates stock in Lehman Brothers because he says it's a good buy, do I listen? No way.

I feel sorry for anyone who follows the investment advice of these people. I consider these people to be better entertainers than investment advisors. I have no love lost for the poor sap who lost his retirement savings because he listened to some CNBC pundit peddling some hot stock tip or investment advice.

What is wrong with people?

How do you not take responsibility for your financial plan?

And then there's your uncle. You know the guy—the well-educated elder in your life who knows everything, including the molecular structure of dark matter in the Horsehead Nebula. His army of factoids is always ready for deployment: stock tips, the latest and greatest investments, money trends. Yet, lest you forget, he lives paycheck to paycheck.

I call these people "Broke Know-It-Alls"—people who dispense financial, moneymaking advice, and yet are dirt poor. These blabber-mouthed imposters are 300-LB walking hypocrisies on how to live a life of health and fitness. Listen to these folks for entertainment, not advice. Good advice comes from the guy who scores touchdowns—not the guy who can't even get on the field! Yes, the best quarterbacking advice comes from Tom Brady, not MJ DeMarco.

IS A PARADOX OF PRACTICE IN PLAY?

In the game of money, money is the scorecard. If someone tells you how they "scored," make sure they disclose their real wealth methods, not the illusion concealing the real culprit.

Sadly, it's virtually impossible to get good, practical money advice, because most gurus live a Paradox of Practice. Yes, gurus are rarely rich because of their advice, but rich because they're successful Fastlaners who covertly hide their Paradox of Practice.

These paradoxical metaphors described earlier befit the hypocrisy of the people who you've entrusted with your financial roadmap. You're sold blindly down the river by a ride they've never completed. Meanwhile, they comfortably gaze at you above in their corporate jet, drinking champagne. No one tells you the real, unadulterated story behind their road to wealth, but I will.

The Slowlane roadmap is sanctimoniously trumpeted by best-selling book authors who dispense financial advice through TV, radio, and books. The strategies they sell are a travesty of grand illusions. Do you seriously think these people are rich from their preachings? *Or, are they selling you the Slowlane while they get rich in the Fastlane?*

Let me hypothesize about the probable wizardry behind their charade.

First is "Suze." Suze preaches mutual funds, dollar-cost averaging, and retirement accounts. We can absorb Suze in many media: radio, TV, and in any of her half-dozen books. Her grille is everywhere. She's the wretched Slowlane poster child, a high-volume producer of Slowlane junkets spewed to millions. So what's the problem? Ask yourself this: Is Suze rich because she followed her own advice like municipal bonds, dollar-cost-averaging and stock market investing? The probable hypocrisy—the Paradox of Practice—is that Suze's method of creating wealth doesn't appear to be the road she travels, nor teaches. Is Suze Fastlane rich because she leverages the Fastlane roadmap while she pitches you the Slowlane? Is she worth *millions* because she followed her own advice? Or because she sold *millions* of books? *Is her wealth equation different from the one she teaches?* Things that make you go hmmm…

In a 2007 article Suze was quoted as admitting to having the bulk of her wealth (an estimated $25 million) in bonds, primarily municipals. Additionally, she admits that only 4% of her wealth is tied-up in the stock market because "if I lose a million dollars, personally I don't care."

Wow, and yet, this is the vehicle you should entrust to build *your* wealth?

How exactly did Ms. Suze acquire that $25 million nest egg? Because of her advice which champions the stock market, mutual funds, IRAs, bonds, and treasuries? Or, did she use the Fastlane roadmap, amass wealth fast via explosive net income, and then pour her wealth into these instruments? Yet, her advice for people at the precipice of poverty is that they should invest in the stock market to *create* wealth when it appears like she hasn't. Folks, *the rich use the markets for income and wealth preservation—not to create it!*

Then there's David. As I thumbed through David's many books, I was inundated with an alarming quantity of Slowlane ilk: compound interest tables, save 10% of your paycheck, stop drinking expensive coffee, and other chronic Slowlane diatribes. Again, the Paradox of Practice rears its ugly mug.

Is David rich from his advice or from money management fees? Or from selling 11 books, over and over several million times, often regurgitating the same Slowlane sludge until you can't take it anymore?

And finally, we have Robert, who hails from Hawaii and has two dads—one rich, one poor. Robert bellicosely explains the real definition of assets and that sophisticated investors are deep into real estate. On national television, Robert once bragged about his Lamborghini and I found this extravagant boast ironic, yet disingenuous. Why? Isn't Robert showcasing the fruit of his teachings? Perhaps.

Robert is a Fastlane success story. He created and built a brand worth millions. But the curious question is this: Which came first? The best-selling book or the Lamborghini? Is there a Paradox of Practice underneath? Did Robert have this status icon "pre-book" by leveraging his real estate teachings? Or did the Lamborghini arrive after selling millions of books? Robert has undoubtedly amassed a great deal of wealth selling books, games, and seminars. Is it possible you're being sold *one wealth equation* while the player of the game *uses another*?

Gurus fill a market need and I don't deny it. However consider this: Are they being truthful about their paradox and their magic potion?

Are they rich because of what they preach, or what they sell?

Once you're familiar with Fastlane mathematics, it should become clear to you which gurus are likely guilty of the paradox. Is the underlying mathematical equation which governs their teachings the same one that made them rich? If the "do as I say" doesn't match the "do as I do", you should be suspicious.

What makes me different is this: The Fastlane concepts in this book gave me financial independence. I already have financial freedom—the nice house, the sports cars, and the flashy rapper credit card. I don't need this book to get me these things. I also confess this Fastlane disclaimer: This book has the power to make me wealthier because it leverages the same wealth equation I teach you. In other words, the "do as I say" either as an author or an entrepreneur, matches the "do as I do."

SLOWLANE GURUS ADMIT FAILURE

On a Slowlane financial radio show, a caller sought advice: In a few months the recession destroyed more than 50% of her savings, which had taken her nearly 10 years to accumulate.

The Slowlane guru's advice?

A palliative "Stick to the plan." Recommit. Rebuild.

In other words, my crappy plan has failed you, has taken 11 years to fail you, yet stand by it.

Hope the economy rebounds.

Hope the economy never sees another recession.

Hope, hope, and hope.

And yes, please buy my newest book, *Rebuild Your Nest Egg . . .*

Economic recessions expose the Slowlane as a risky fraud with lifetime ramifications. Since these gurus make their rich livelihood selling the Slowlane roadmap, they need you to believe it works.

Their wealth comes from your belief.

Despite the recession's masterful exposé in 2008, the Slowlane illuminati will never admit that their strategy is woefully inept, and instead they have deviously recalibrated their message to conceal the truth: They continue to spew the same failed rhetoric by writing new books, with new titles and new platitudes. Titles like:

Rebuild Your Wealth . . .

Start Over . . .

Recommit . . .

Notice the shift in language, exposing the truth: If the plan is so good, why do you need to "rebuild" or "start over?"

If the strategy worked, such words wouldn't be necessary.

For the charade to continue, the gurus need to lipstick the pig by reinforcing the old strategy with new books, selling the same old crap. Inside these books you'll find words like "patience" and "rebound" and "discipline."

And the bigger question . . .

Do you think the gurus need to "start over" or "rebuild"?

Of course not. They don't use the plan they sell!

They operate in an entirely different wealth universe not predicated on uncontrollable limited leverage.

CHAPTER SUMMARY: FASTLANE DISTINCTIONS

- Take advice from people with a proven, successful track record of their espoused discipline.
- Many money gurus often suffer from a Paradox of Practice; they teach one wealth equation while getting rich in another. They're not rich from their own teachings.

Slowlane Victory... A Gamble of Hope

I'd rather live in regret of failure than in regret of never trying.

~ MJ DEMARCO

EXODUS: LIFE IN THE SLOWLANE

Wealth by the Slowlane roadmap is analogous to Exodus, the biblical story of Moses. God leads Moses out of Egyptian bondage into a harrowing 40-year journey through the desert, with the promise of a triumphant future in the land of "milk and honey." After a lifetime of toil and struggle, Moses arrives at the doorstep to his destination and—wham! He dies. He never sees the promise of the journey because life has no guarantees.

Sadly, Slowlane wealth is akin to this hardship through the desert. It's a trip that takes decades to finish, starves your life, and makes no promises. Yes, graduate from college, get a good job, entrust your money to Wall Street, serve the boss well, and you might be rewarded. In today's harrowing financial climate of printing money and government recklessness, I'm surprised people still believe it.

But people do, and in legions.

When I see sales figures for Slowlane books, I'm dumbfounded. Millions sold. How sad. Millions being led astray down a path littered with dangerous potholes and detours, a road that takes years to travel for a far-fetched promise of a freer tomorrow.

To assume that you will live a long, healthy life is arrogant. To assume that life won't throw you any curves is naïve. For the Slowlane to prevail, it assumes life is predictable and forgiving.

It isn't. You lose your job. You get sick. The car needs a new transmission. You get married. You get divorced. You have kids. You have a child with special needs. You have aging parents who need care. The economy dips into recession or depression. Life is a menagerie of crisis points making the Slowlane roadmap a risky bet that consumes your most precious asset: time.

SEVEN SLOWLANE DANGERS

People drive the Slowlane because it's what they've been told to drive. They believe the risks are minimal and it's safe. After all, 90% of all new businesses fail after five years, so the "Fastlane" can't be any safer! If you lob a little logic into the Slowlane narratives you'll find that it's extremely hazardous and a plan based entirely on *hope*. Assumptions—decades of them—expose the Slowlane's true risks. Choose to travel the road and choose to gamble. Here are the risks:

1) The Danger of Your Health

The Slowlane HOPES you will live long enough to enjoy the fruits of your savings as you hit your late stage years. Remember, you will have millions when you retire at 65! Will you be healthy enough to enjoy it? Alive? If you can't work your job, you can't make money. If you can't work, what happens to this plan? Also, avoid other calamities; hope your job stress doesn't kill you and your family remains healthy.

2) The Danger of the Job

The Slowlane HOPES that you'll be gainfully employed at all times, safely climbing the corporate ladder year after year. You must avoid layoffs, corporate politics, firings, poor industry cycles, job skill degradation, and bad job markets.

3) The Danger of Your Home

Home equity is lauded as a middle-class wealth vehicle. Many gurus shout from the rooftops, "Retire on your home equity!" and "Your home is an asset!" Capital BS. The Slowlane HOPES that real estate values always rise, and it's patently false. In 2008, the value of my home equity plummeted $800,000. I disavow my home as an investment and, thankfully, I do not rely on it.

4) The Danger of the Company

Not many companies outlive the centuries. If your retirement faith is put into one company in the form of either 1) your job, 2) your pension, or 3) their stock, you HOPE the company survives. You make a bet. Many retirees discover too late that their retirement pensions are lost to mismanagement by company executives. Others who bet their wealth with one company stock accept great risk that the stock will be worth more in the future. If your retirement is assigned to others, you accept uncontrollable risks. When the torque of your financial plan rests with others, you're likely to lose control.

5) The Danger of Your Lifestyle

The Slowlane begs you to settle and become a miser. Want to own an exotic car? Forget it. Want to live on a beach? Wishful thinking. If you cannot control your temptations of lifestyle improvement (a nicer home, a nicer car, a nicer meal out), the Slowlane becomes slower and reverses course. The Slowlane HOPES your "delayed gratification" moves to "no gratification."

6) The Danger of the Economy

The Slowlane HOPES that your investments will yield a predictable 8% return year after year. You must believe the theory that "buy and hold" works. It doesn't, because economic busts, recessions, and depressions happen. For example, in 2008–2009, the equity markets lost nearly 60%. If you saved for 15 years and amassed $100,000, it would now be worth $40,000. It would take you 14 years at 8% yearly returns just to get back even! That equates to almost 30 YEARS GONE! And this doesn't account for inflation, which makes your $100,000 more like $50,000!

7) The Danger of the Sidewalk

Frustrated Slowlaners often revert to the Sidewalk. Why? Hope over control. When you can't control time, your job, or five days of your life each week, you feel powerless. Emotions of helplessness create an environment ripe for instant gratification and Lifestyle Servitude. A study published in 2008 by the *Journal of Consumer Research* found that when people feel powerless and out of control, they have a strong desire to buy things that convey a high status. Why do they feel powerless? Simple. In the Slowlane, you relinquish control because time is in control and the gates to the Sidewalk reopen. Hope is not a plan.

RESISTANCE IS FUTILE

When you perform an autopsy on the Slowlane you see its true colors: It's slow, it eats time, and it's risky. When a Slowlaner realizes the plan isn't working, he goes into overdrive. Overdrive in the Slowlane is like pushing a car's accelerator to the floor, hoping its upper speed limits somehow will mystically extend higher, when in fact, the racetrack itself is the problem—not the accelerator.

Yet, a Slowlaner will try to manipulate his weak mathematical universe by trying to make the variables malleable.

- Manipulate intrinsic value by increasing hours worked. (I need to make more money!)
- Manipulate intrinsic value by changing jobs or adding jobs. (I need to get paid more!)
- Manipulate intrinsic value by going back to school. (I need a better career!)

- Manipulate compound interest by seeking better investment yields. (I need better investments!)
- Manipulate compound interest by expanding investment time horizon. (I need more time!)
- Manipulate compound interest by increasing the investment. (I need to save more!)

Each of these six responses is a futile attempt to manipulate the impotence of the Slowlaner's wealth equation. Unfortunately, the limitations of the mathematics cannot be subverted, and doing so results in dangerous cause-effects cycles. When a Slowlaner wants to make more money, he increases his hours worked, switches to a better paying job, or adds jobs. When a Slowlaner wants to get paid more, he goes back to school, hoping to increase intrinsic value. When a Slowlaner realizes that a 3% investment return isn't building wealth fast enough, bigger risks are assumed for bigger returns. When a Slowlaner watches 40% of his nest egg disappear in an economic recession, he goes back to work arguing that five years is not enough to "get back to even."

You can't overcome mathematical limitations.

A car that has a top speed of 10 mph will always have a top speed of 10 mph, no matter HOW HARD YOU PUSH THE ACCELERATOR. If you travel across the country at 10 mph, you're going to need 40 years!

The Slowlane is predisposed to mediocrity because the numbers are always mediocre.

The Slowlane is risky because its variables are uncontrollable and leverage is absent. ULL really means "ULL" never get rich. Yet, lifestyle is the one variable Slowlaners can effectively manipulate. Unfortunately, this quickly turns Slowlane life into a stale exhibition of misery. Yes, settle for less.

WEALTH FAIL: WRONG EQUATION. WRONG VARIABLE

At some point, the Slowlaner realizes he can't force the stock market to yield bigger returns. He can't force a 200% pay raise. He can't afford an advanced education to raise intrinsic value. Job-hopping offers little incremental pay upgrades. The Slowlaner is enslaved to his equation and resorts to manipulating the only controllable variable, personal net income, which is increased by reducing expenses.

Personal Net Income = Intrinsic Value – Personal Expenses

Slowlane gurus praise this strategy. The edicts are clear: Pay down your debt. Dump the new car for an old one. Raise your insurance deductibles. Cancel your credit cards and pay cash for everything. Quit buying $10 coffee at Starbucks.

Bag your lunch. Shop in bulk. Spend four hours clipping coupons. C'mon buddy, slash those expenses—some day you're going to be rich! Hilarious!

These tiresome strategies are a classic response to being stuck in the Slowlane. *Lifestyle degradation.* When you're married to a bad wealth equation, this is resistance. This is like getting a divorce by sleeping on the couch.

Since wealth is tied to time and can't be controlled, you're left with kitchen scraps . . . lifestyle degradation in the form of expense reduction. Yup, become a cheapskate.

Wrong.

Hoodwinking expenses does not create wealth. *Exploding income and controlling expenses creates wealth.*

For example, when I routinely earned over $100,000 per month, I accumulated wealth fast because I controlled and restricted my expenses. As my income exponentiated, expenses grew linearly and weren't neglected. If my income increased by 100%, expenses only grew by 10%. I didn't accumulate wealth because of expense dickery. *Income explosion and relative expense containment created wealth.*

So what happens when a Slowlaner commits to the expense variable?

Life becomes about what you can't do.

You can't take that trip. You can't buy your kids a decent pair of shoes. You can't own a dream car. You can't subscribe to the movie channels. Yes, the good old "sacrifice your today for the promise of tomorrow."

You settle.

SLOWLANE VICTORY: FAME OR A GERIATRIC WARD

Why invest in a plan that consumes 40 years of your life and fails most of the time? I wouldn't. The dreary reality is that Slowlane failure doesn't happen overnight; failure transpires over the years like a termite-infested woodshed, and when its denizens come to judgment, it's too late. Yes, Slowlane victory is as tough as a truck-stop sirloin.

In a 2002 AARP (formerly the American Association of Retired Persons) survey, 69% of the respondents said they would need to work past retirement age. A year earlier, 45% said they would need to work into their 70s and 80s. Fifteen years later, a 2017 GALLUP POLL revealed this number to be now 74%. We can deduce something disturbing from this data: *The Slowlane's failure rate is nearly* 75%.

Despite the risks, despite the mathematical limitations, despite the typical five-day trade for a weekend, despite all of it, you might stand firm and try your luck. While victory isn't impossible, I need mention a few things: Slowlane winners are usually extremely talented, elderly, or overworked.

HOW TO WIN THE SLOWLANE: THE "SECRET EXIT"

The Slowlane can be defied if you find its "secret exit," its "get out of jail free" card that neutralizes the limitations of Uncontrollable Limited Leverage. That secret Slowlane escape?

Fame.

Fame breaks the mathematical limitations of intrinsic value. Those who defy the Slowlane are the most pervasive in our culture because of fame—the pro athletes, rappers, musicians, actors, and entertainers. If you want to bludgeon the Slowlane's weakness you need to get famous. Why? Fame and notoriety carries a high intrinsic value. People pay extraordinary rates for you or your services. (Even if, like a reality-show star, you have no skills.)

When a 20-year old basketball player leaves college and scores a $30 million contract, you've just witnessed Slowlane defiance. When an actress lands a $15 million lead role in a major motion picture, you've just witnessed Slowlane defiance. When a homely Irish guy ascends from waiter to top finalist on *American Idol*, the limitations of the Slowlane roadmap are shattered because intrinsic value explodes. Suddenly, *intrinsic value has leverage because of demand.*

Unfortunately, most people who seek wealth do so through Slowlane defiance, not via the Fastlane. Fortune-leading fames are the obvious attack. Why do stadiums breach to capacity for singing competition auditions? Fame explodes intrinsic value!

You can defy the Slowlane's limitations by becoming so indispensable that your value to society skyrockets. If millions seek you, you will be paid millions. Pro basketball player LeBron James is paid millions because his skills are in short supply. Famous actors and entertainers are paid millions because millions demand their brand in entertainment form. Extreme talent is paid extremely well.

OVERWORKED INTO CORPORATE MANAGEMENT

The other highly sought-after Slowlane "secret exit" is good ol' corporate management. No doubt you've heard the Slowlane missive "climb the corporate ladder."

When a corporate CEO cashes $20 million in stock options, you've witnessed another Slowlane defiance. Surely you've heard about all those overpaid CEOs of large companies raking in the big dough.

Have you ever looked at their age?

Exclusive of the founders and owners, most of them are in their 50s and 60s. Obviously, the roads through corporate management don't happen overnight; from mailroom to CEO can take 40 years. And if it does, you certainly don't get there by taking it easy. Nope, you arrive early and leave late.

Sorry, but waiting for a golden parachute after 40 years of patience and prayer isn't a gamble I'd like to bet.

SUCCESSFUL SLOWLANERS GET STUCK IN THE "MIDDLE"

I have no desire for fame or corporate droneship—heck, I don't even own a suit or tie, so how would I climb the corporate ladder? If you're allergic to fame and corporate ascension as a road to riches, what's left? Society enforces the Slowlane as your only option. Unfortunately, that strategy leads straight into the "middles"—middle class or middle age.

Every lottery has a winner. Yes, bad odds have winners!

"Oldlaners" (Slowlaners who succeed using a Slowlane strategy) who survive the Slowlane road-map eventually become millionaires, but please, don't pop the cheap champagne quite yet.

The distinction between a Slowlane millionaire and a Fastlane millionaire is like the difference between a Buick and a Ferrari. When you recognize the difference, you can critique advice properly and assign it to its correct Fastlane or Slowlane box.

MILLIONAIRES ARE RICH . . . OR ARE THEY?

I recently read an article about a young woman named Callie from the U.K. who, several years ago, won millions in a lottery, only to lose most of it shortly thereafter. Of course, "lose" implies that the entire bag of cash flew out of her brand new convertible while cruising down the boulevard.

She didn't "lose" it—*she spent it.*

She was just 16 years old when she won the $3 million, and it took only six years for her to blow it: drugs, partying, exotic cars, breast implants, and a jaw-dropping $730,000 in designer clothes. The problem? *Callie thought she was rich* and spent like she was rich. Surely she bought into her title: "I'm a millionaire." While $3 million is a decent chunk of change, she needed $30 million for her lifestyle.

Which brings us to our famous word, "millionaire."

When you hear that word, what do you think? Like wealth, you probably have visions of an extravagant lifestyle: boats, helicopters, mansions, and expensive jewelry. For decades, the term "millionaire" has been ubiquitously used to describe someone "rich."

Except these visions of opulence describe a lifestyle of a millionaire elevated by the Fastlane, not the Slowlane.

Slowlane millionaires who don't escape by fame or corporate prostitution *live differently.* They own homes in innocuous middle-class neighborhoods. They drive unassuming cars like Hondas or Toyotas, they vacation infrequently, they limit their dining expenses, they cut coupons, and they max out their retirement accounts. They work five days a week at jobs they most likely hate and diligently save 10% of their paychecks. Others own small businesses, franchises, and retail stores. Several international best-selling books have enlightened us: Yes, these are the "millionaires next door."

Sadly, in today's terms, a "millionaire" (net worth of $1,000,000) is simply upper middle class. *A millionaire is not rich.* Ten million is the old one million.

Depressing, I know.

This hidden truth is why many lottery winners go broke after a few years. Winners envision a lavish lifestyle and live it not realizing that several million dollars won't support it! If you win a million bucks (which after taxes is only $500,000), your lifestyle shouldn't change. If you try to live the "millionaire lifestyle" as shown on Instagram, a fool and his money are soon parted.

Playing the lottery is a symptom of the Sidewalk.

It shouldn't shock you that a newly crowned lottery winner goes broke just years later. Lottery winners assign "rich" to the word "millionaire," so their fortune is fast spent on the illusion, and soon thereafter, they're bankrupt. The word "millionaire" fooled them. Millionaire is middle class.

To live a lifestyle normally reserved for "millionaires," you need much more than $1 million. Having $1 million doesn't entitle you to a lifestyle of the rich and famous. You need at least $10 million to even think about it. So, when the media spoon-feeds you the word "millionaire," determine its perspective: Is it Slowlane and middle class? Or Fastlane and rich?

12 DISTINCTIONS BETWEEN SLOWLANE AND FASTLANE MILLIONAIRES

1) Slowlane millionaires make millions in 30 years or more. Fastlane millionaires make millions in 10 years or less.
2) Slowlane millionaires need to live in middle-class homes. Fastlane millionaires can live in luxury estates.
3) Slowlane millionaires have MBAS. Fastlane millionaires hire people with MBAS.
4) Slowlane millionaires let their assets drift by market forces. Fastlane millionaires control their assets and possess the power to manipulate their value.
5) Slowlane millionaires can't afford exotic cars. Fastlane millionaires can afford whatever they want.
6) Slowlane millionaires work for their time. Fastlane millionaires have time working for them.
7) Slowlane millionaires are employees. Fastlane millionaires hire employees.
8) Slowlane millionaires have 401(K)s. Fastlane millionaires offer 401(K)s.
9) Slowlane millionaires use index-funds and Wall Street instruments to get rich. Fastlane millionaires use them for income, liquidity, and capital deployment.
10) Slowlane millionaires let other people control their income streams. Fastlane millionaires control their income streams.
11) Slowlane millionaires are cheap with money. Fastlane millionaires are cheap with time.
12) Slowlane millionaires use their house for net worth. Fastlane millionaires use their house for residency.

The Fastlane isn't about becoming the next middle-class millionaire with tiresome mandates about what you cannot do; it's about what you can do.

CHAPTER SUMMARY: FASTLANE DISTINCTIONS

- The Slowlane has seven dangers, five of which cannot be controlled.
- The risk of "lifestyle" is the one risk Slowlaners will try to control.
- The Slowlane is predisposed to mediocrity because its mathematical universe is mediocre.
- Slowlaners manipulate the "expense" variable because it is the one thing they can control.
- Exponential income growth and expense management creates wealth—not just by curtailing expenses.
- You can break the Slowlane equation by exploding your intrinsic value via fame or insider corporate management.
- Successful Slowlaners not famous or in corporate management end in the middle . . . middle class and middle age.
- Slowlane millionaires are stuck in the middle class.
- $10 million is the new $1 million.
- A millionaire cannot live a millionaire lifestyle without financial discipline.
- Lottery winners fall into the millionaire trap and go broke because they attempt to live a "millionaire" lifestyle, not understanding that a few million doesn't go very far.

Part 5

Wealth: The Fastlane Roadmap

Wealth's Shortcut: The Fastline

People would do better, if they knew better.

~ JIM ROHN

WHAT ABOUT DOOR #3?

Sidewalk or Slowlane? Sacrifice today or tomorrow? You can walk the Sidewalk with no financial plan and convince yourself that today's indulgences don't have tomorrow's consequences. Or, you can drive the Slowlane and gamble your today for the risky bet of a secure tomorrow.

But wait! There is another choice . . . an alternative, a hybrid financial roadmap that can create wealth fast and slash 40 years from wealth accumulation. "Fast" however is relative; if you're 18 you can be filthy rich by 25. If you're 30, you can be retired by 36. Broke at 48 and you can retire by 54. But is it likely? Risky? If you could play one of three raffles, which would you play?

Raffle Sidewalk: First prize: $50,000,000 awarded immediately.
Your odds of winning: 1 in 6 million (.0000016%)

Raffle Slowlane: First prize: $500,000 awarded in 40 years.
Your odds of winning: 1 in 6 (17%)

Raffle Fastlane: First prize: $10,000,000 awarded in 6 years.
Your odds of winning: 1 in 7 (14%)

Which did you pick? Hopefully Raffle Fastlane because its rewards far exceed the incremental risk of Raffle Slowlane. Raffle Sidewalk is a wasted long shot. Your choice of financial roadmaps—Sidewalk, Slowlane, or Fastlane—is like this hypothetical raffle. Once you understand the roadmaps and their respective wealth equations, you can choose the one that will serve as your compass.

WHAT IS THE FASTLANE?

The Fastlane is a business and lifestyle strategy characterized by Controllable Unlimited Leverage (CUL), hence creating an optimal environment for rapid wealth creation and extraordinary lifestyles. Definitively, pay attention to these four segments:

1) **Controllable Unlimited Leverage (CUL)**
   Whereas the Slowlane is defined by uncontrollable variables with no leverage, the Fastlane exploits the opposite conditions: maximum control and leverage.

2) **Business**
   Your own business, self-employment, and entrepreneurship are centrist to the Fastlane, much like a job is to the Slowlane.

3) **Lifestyle**
   The Fastlane is a lifestyle choice: a commitment of blended beliefs, processes, and actions.

4) **Rapid Wealth Creation**
   The Fastlane is about creating large sums of wealth rapidly and beyond the confines of "middle class."

Here is a story that best describes the Fastlane, and yes, this story is inspired from a real story posted on the Internet.

> *After four long years, I sold my company for $32 million [RAPID WEALTH CREATION] and I wouldn't change a thing. I'm happy I sold because I wanted to make money fast and transform paper money into real money. This decision changed my life permanently.*
>
> *Now, I do whatever I want and I'm not the least bit bored. The world is my playground; I travel, I learned two new languages and how to play piano. I play water sports, hike, and snowboard at least a month a year. I own three homes, I watch pro sports and my favorite teams whenever I choose, watch 3–4 movies a week, and read 1–2 books a week. Most of my time is spent with my family, and I literally watch my two daughters grow before my eyes.*

> *My family has lived on all four corners of the planet, including Australia and the Caribbean.*
>
> *Looking back, it wasn't easy. I worked 12–16 hour days for four years, almost always six days a week, and always a few hours on Sunday. We created an awesome service and sold the crap out of it.* [THE BUSINESS WITH C.U.L.] *I remember tough times, and I had to put every dime of my money into the company . . . we had less than 50 bucks in our account at least five times. Except for my family during those startup years, I sacrificed plenty; I canceled cable TV and I temporarily stopped doing a lot of things I enjoyed because I was committed to a goal and a dream of something far greater than a lifetime job.* [THE LIFESTYLE]
>
> *Now, I am an investor in multiple startup companies and am making an impact I could have never imagined. I have no apologies or regrets. My life rocks and I wouldn't change a thing. If I didn't make a choice to get into business and start a company, I don't know where I'd be.*

This story epitomizes the Fastlane. A business was created; a lifestyle grew the business, which opened up the expressway, and the expressway led to extraordinary wealth, which led to freedom. And yes, it isn't easy and it isn't for everyone. Question is: *Is it for you?*

THE FASTLANE MINDPOSTS

Like the other roadmaps, the Fastlane Roadmap contains the same mindposts or behavioral characteristics that drive the Fastlaner's actions along the journey. They are:

Debt Perception: *Debt is useful if it allows me to build and grow my system.*

Time Perception: *Time is the most important asset I have, far exceeding money.*

Education Perception: *The moment you stop learning is the moment you stop growing. Constant expansion of knowledge and awareness is critical to my journey.*

Money Perception: *Money is everywhere, and it's extremely abundant. Money is a reflection of how many lives I've touched. Money reflects the value I've created.*

Primary Income Source: *I earn income via my business systems and investments.*

Primary Wealth Accelerator: *I make something from nothing. I give birth to assets and make them valuable to the marketplace. Other times, I take existing assets and add value to them.*

Wealth Perception: *Build business systems for cash flow and asset valuation.*

Wealth Equation: *Wealth = Net Profit + Asset Value*

Strategy: *The more I help, the richer I become in time, money, and personal fulfillment.*

Destination: *Lifetime passive income, either through business or investments.*

Responsibility & Control: *Life is what I make it. My financial plan is entirely my responsibility and I choose how I react to my circumstances.*

Life Perception: *My dreams are worth pursuing no matter how outlandish, and I understand it will take time and money to make those dreams real.*

These mindposts are what formulate the Fastlaner's lifestyle. *It drives action.*

THE FASTLANE ROADMAP: PREDISPOSED TO WEALTH

The Fastlane Roadmap is predisposed to wealth because it operates under a wealth equation with controllable, unlimited variables, and the mathematical cage of time is removed. ULL is replaced with CUL. Correctly exploited, the roadmap reveals a rapid road to wealth via unlimited mathematics evolving via "profit" or "asset value" or both. This rapid wealth accumulation extricates years from the wealth journey because time is removed or exploited during the process. The Fastlane produces wealth in short periods—millions, sometimes billions of dollars.

Yes, it's true: "Get Rich Quick" exists.

THE SHADOW BEHIND "GET RICH QUICK"

Successful Fastlaners "Get Rich Quick." Don't let those three words scare you; I know when you hear them you're inundated with a flurry of negative associations starting with "scam:" things like "one tiny classified ad" and seminars that cost $5,000, memories of infomercial gurus, foreign lotteries, the Interior Finance Minister from Nigeria who needs help unloading $9 million dollars (USD), and the phony "Bill Gates," who needs you to "forward this email beta test to everyone" and be rewarded $50,000 in quick cash because, gosh golly, the attorney listed on the letter says so.

"Get Rich Quick" is such an abused phrase that it has no credibility. Beaten and battered, we're numbed to believe it doesn't exist. Like Santa or a unicorn, we're advised, "Get rich quick is a scam!"

I don't blame you, but is it true?

Can't fast millions be made as advertised on infomercials and websites?

The distinction is that "get rich schemes" aren't endemic of "Get Rich Quick" but its evil twin, "Get Rich Easy." "Get Rich Easy" shadows its innocent sibling, leaving a trail of victims to be blamed by its brother. "Get Rich Easy" parades in the limelight and on Instagram feeds with pictures of beaches, palm trees, and used Ferraris. It lies, deceives, and casts a mirage of vanity that all desire. Just watch buy this $197 PDF or buy this stock software program, and wham, you will be rich in 10 days! No! That's not "Get Rich Quick" but "Get Rich Easy"—and that only leads to a lighter wallet.

Fastlane success stories embody "Get Rich Quick." For people to proclaim "It doesn't exist" is another untruth advanced by ignorance. Don't allow Slowlane losers to corrupt truth. Don't concede. Don't make "That only happens to other people" your truth. Many people have lived "Get Rich Quick" because it was preceded by process.

TALES FROM THE FASTLANE

Unless you live in a vacuum, you're already familiar with the Fastlane. When anyone experiences a get-rich-quick event via business, you're witnessing the Fastlane. Here are some Fastlane stories pulled from the headlines:

- The inventor who creates a gadget and sells millions of them to 15 wholesale distributors.
- The YouTuber with thousands of subscribers who monetizes it into a subscription service or a product offering.
- The guy who builds a cell phone application and sells it 50,000 times.
- The guy who formulates an energy bar to help him stave off hunger and later is offered $192 million for his company.
- The guy who builds a blog and three years later sells it for $4 million to a big pharmaceutical company.
- The woman who invents a mop and sells 500,000 of them on QVC.
- The teenager who builds a website that profits $70,000 month and later sells it for millions.
- The guy who patents a product process and then licenses it to a *Fortune 500* company and goes on to make $14 million.
- The guy who creates a website to help him listen to his favorite basketball team and later sells the company for $5.5 billion.
- The guy who builds a software company and later becomes the richest man on the planet.
- The doctor who researches anti-aging treatments and sells them to a drug company for $700 million.

- The author who writes a book about a teenage wizard and goes on to become a billionaire.
- The gal who manufactures and sells 20 million undergarments that help women fight body gravity and later becomes a billionaire.
- The entrepreneur who refines and improves a product process and goes on to sell $150,000/month through a variety of channels, including Amazon.
- The guy who creates a $20K/month supplement business allowing him to travel the world and later sells it for $560K.

Don't let some of the big stories fool you. Most "Fastlanes" aren't publicized and fly under the radar: fortune but no fame. The larger "Get Rich Quick" Fastlanes make news, the smaller ones set their owners free.

THE FASTLANE: WEALTH'S INDUSTRIAL REVOLUTION

The Industrial Revolution was a historic period when humans learned how to leverage the speed and efficiency of machine-based manufacturing. Manual labor was replaced by systems, a union of distinct parts that coalesced into a specific production outcome. Long and arduous tasks manually handled by humans transformed into mechanization, expelling most human labor out of the production equation. For that era, it was their version of "Get Rich Quick." Products that formerly took months to manufacture now took days.

Likewise, financial freedom via the Fastlane Roadmap is like an industrial revolution for wealth. The default road to wealth is manual labor, a fight against *time* and *intrinsic value*. The rapid road to wealth is to industrialize the wealth process, to systematize it like our ancestors systematized production. The differences between the default road (the Slowlane) and the shortcut (the Fastlane) are best demonstrated in an Egyptian parable.

THE PARABLE OF FASTLANE WEALTH

A great Egyptian pharaoh summons his twin nephews, Chuma and Azur, and commissions them to a majestic task: Build two monumental pyramids as a tribute to Egypt.

Upon completion of each nephew's pyramid, Pharaoh promises each an immediate reward of kingship, retirement amidst riches and lavish luxury for the rest of their natural lives.

Additionally, each nephew must construct his pyramid *alone*.

Chuma and Azur, both 18, know their daunting task will take years to complete. Nonetheless, each is primed for the challenge and honored by the Pharaoh's directive. They exit Pharaoh's chambers ready to begin the long pyramid-building process.

Azur begins immediately. He slowly drags large heavy stones into a square formation. After a few months, the base of Azur's pyramid takes shape. Townsfolk gather around Azur's constructive efforts and praise his handiwork. The stones are heavy and difficult to move, and after one year of heavy labor, Azur's perfect square foundation to the pyramid is nearly finished.

But Azur is perplexed. The plot of land that should bear Chuma's pyramid is empty. Not one stone has been laid. No foundation. No dirt engravings. Nothing. It's as barren as it was a year ago when Pharaoh commissioned the job.

Confused, Azur visits Chuma's home and finds him in his barn diligently working on a twisted apparatus that resembles some kind of human torture device.

Azur interrupts, "Chuma! What the hell are you doing!? You're supposed to be building Pharaoh a pyramid and you spend your days locked in this barn fiddling with that crazy machine?"

Chuma cracks a smile and says, "I am building a pyramid, leave me alone."

Azur scoffs, "Yeah, sure you are. You haven't laid one stone in over a year!"

Chuma, engrossed but unfazed by his brother's accusation retorts, "Azur, you're short-sightedness and thirst for wealth have clouded your vision. You build your pyramid and I will build mine."

As Azur walks away, he chides, "You fool! Pharaoh will hang you in the gallows when he discovers your treason."

Another year passes and Azur solidifies the base of his pyramid and begins the second level. Except a problem arises. Azur struggles in his progress. The stones are heavy and he cannot raise them to the pyramid's second level.

Challenged by his physical limitations, Azur recognizes his weakness: he needs more strength to move heavier stones, and to do so, seeks the counsel of Bennu, Egypt's strongest man. For a fee, Bennu trains Azur to build bigger and stronger muscles. With great strength, Azur anticipates the heavier stones will be easier to lift onto the higher levels.

Meanwhile, Chuma's pyramid plot is still vacant. Azur assumes his brother has a deathwish since, by all appearances, Chuma is violating Pharaoh's mandate. Azur forgets about his brother and his nonexistent pyramid.

Another year passes and Azur's pyramid construction slows to a disheartening crawl. One stone placement takes one month. Moving stones to the upper levels require great strength and Azur spends much of his time working with Bennu to build greater strength. Additionally, Azur is spending most of his money on counseling fees and the exotic diet required for the training. Azur estimates at his current construction pace, his pyramid will be completed in another 30 years. Unfazed, Azur lauds, "After three years, I've far surpassed my brother. He hasn't placed one stone yet! That fool!"

Then, suddenly, one day while hauling a heavy stone, Azur hears a loud commotion erupting from the town square. The townsfolk, regular observers to his work, abruptly abandon his plot to examine the celebratory fuss. Curious himself, Azur leaves to investigate.

Surrounded by a cheering crowd, Chuma trolls up the town square commandeering a 25-foot contraption, a towering machine built from a twisted maze of gantries, wheels, levers, and ropes. As Chuma slowly moves up the village street amidst the jubilant crowd, Azur fears the explanation. After a short trawl to Chuma's barren pyramid plot, Azur's suspicions are confirmed.

Within minutes, Chuma's strange machine starts moving heavy stones and begins to lay the foundation to his pyramid. One after another, the machine effortlessly lifts the stones and softly places them side-by-side into place. Miraculously, the machine requires little effort for Chuma's operation. Crank a wheel attached to a rope and cantilever entwined by a gear system, and bingo! Heavy stones are moved quickly and magically.

While Azur's pyramid foundation took over a year to build, Chuma lines up the foundation to his pyramid within one week. The second level that Azur struggled with is more shocking: Chuma's machine does the work 30 times quicker. What took Azur two months takes Chuma's machine two days. After 40 days, Chuma and his machine accomplish as much as Azur's three years of toilsome work.

The revelation destroys Azur. He spent years doing the heavy lifting *while Chuma built a machine to do it for him.*

Instead of honoring the machine, Azur stubbornly vows, "I must get stronger! I must lift heavier stones!" Azur continues the hard labor of pyramid building while Chuma continues to work the crank of his machine.

After eight years, Chuma finishes his pyramid at age 26: *three years to build the system and five years to reap the benefits of the system.* The great pharaoh is pleased and does as promised. He rewards Chuma with kingship and endows him with great riches. Chuma never has to work another day in his life.

Meanwhile, Azur continues to dredge away at the same old routine. Lift rocks, waste time and money to get stronger, lift rocks, and get stronger. Sadly, Azur refuses to acknowledge his flawed strategy and endures the same old process: Carry heavy stones until you can lift no more . . . then get stronger so you can lift heavier stones.

This mindless prescription leads Azur to a lifetime of sweat and drudgery.

He never finishes his pyramid promised to Pharaoh simply because he decides to do the heavy lifting himself when he should have focused on a system to do it for him.

Azur has a heart attack and dies while on the 12th level of his pyramid, just two levels from finishing. He never experiences the great riches promised by Pharaoh.

Meanwhile, Chuma retires 40 years early in a crown of luxury. Sloshing in free time, Chuma goes on to become Egypt's greatest scholar and an accomplished inventor. He is entombed alongside Pharaoh in the same pyramid he built.

THE FASTLANE IS A BUSINESS SYSTEM: THE SLOWLANE IS A JOB

The Slowlane is a job: your hard work traded for your employer's cash. Azur's struggles resemble that of a Slowlaner; to get rich, you're told to get stronger (spend money, return to school, and earn more in the job market) so you can lift heavier stones.

The Fastlane is about building a better system, a better contraption, a better product, or a better "something" that will *leverage* your work. In the Slowlane, you are the source of heavy lifting, while in the Fastlane, you construct a system that does it for you.

On your wealth road trip, the Slowlane roadmap asks that you endure a long, tiresome walk to wealth. The toil of wealth is the process itself. In the Fastlane, wealth is driven in a business system you create—the toil is the creation and management of the system itself.

CHAPTER SUMMARY: FASTLANE DISTINCTIONS

- The risk profile of a Fastlane strategy isn't much different from the Slowlane, but the rewards are far greater.
- The Fastlane Roadmap is an alternative financial strategy predicated on Controllable Unlimited Leverage.
- The Fastlane roadmap is predisposed to wealth.
- The Fastlane Roadmap is capable of generating "Get Rich Quick" results, not to be confused with "Get Rich Easy."

Switch Teams and Playbooks

A man wrapped up in himself makes a very small bundle.

~ BENJAMIN FRANKLIN

THE FASTLANE ROADMAP: THE PLAYBOOK FOR WEALTH

Losing teams use losing playbooks. Play for a losing team and you're stuck using their losing playbook. To win, switch teams and use the winner's playbook. The Fastlane roadmap creates financial winners because it uses a winning formula rooted in unlimited and controllable mathematics.

Where is this playbook and how do you get it?

You have to forsake the majority ideology and *become a Slowlane traitor.*

SWITCHING TEAMS AND THE PLAYBOOK

From the day you were born, you were baptized to play for *Team Consumer*, from the Barbie Doll and the Tonka Truck to the *Star Wars* action figures. You've been conditioned to demand: to want products, to need products, to buy products, and of course, to seek out the cheapest of those products.

The correlation between the Slowlane and the Sidewalk is this: Jobs exist to facilitate the consumer process. You become a brand manager for a consumer products company, you become an insurance agent, you become an accountant for some corporation—it's consumer driven and focused to move goods and services into the hands of consumers.

This "consumer" focus acts like a gravitational pull to anti-Fastlane thinking and immediately puts you on the wrong team.

CRACKING THE CODE

Decoding the Fastlane roadmap is as simple as joining the team that is custodian to the decryption key.

The winning team is *Team Producer.*

Reshape life's focus on producing, not consuming.

When you reframe your thinking from majority thinking (consumer) to minority thinking (producer), you effectively switch teams and allegiances.

Yes, *become a producer first and a consumer second.*

Applied, this means instead of buying products on TV, sell products. Instead of digging for gold, sell shovels. Instead of taking a class, offer a class. Instead of borrowing money, lend it. Instead of taking a job, hire for jobs. Instead of taking a mortgage, hold a mortgage. Break free from consumption, switch sides, and reorient to the world as producer.

I know; it's not easy.

However, once you see the world from a producer perspective, your perception sharpens like a fine-tuned radio frequency, from static to clear stereo sound. Suddenly, opportunities have clarity, ideas surface, and scams are exposed. This new minority status is critical to strengthening your wealth-creation temperament. Remember, the rich are a minority, and you want to be in that minority. It starts with a producer mindset.

PRODUCER REORIENTATION

When you encounter an advertising message that coaxes you to buy something, examine it from the producer perspective. How does this company make money? What psychological tactics are used in its marketing messages? What kind of operational processes are involved in offering this product or service? Is this company making a profit? What is the revenue model? Is this product manufactured overseas or locally?

I've never bought a product on late night television, because I'm on the same team. As a producer, I see the infomercials for what they are: producers (the minority) serving the consumer (the majority). The "act nows," the "but wait, there's more!" the "free bonuses"—these are marketing weapons in a producer's arsenal. I watch infomercials not to buy, but to see what the pros are doing.

As producers, our job is to entice consumers to buy. As a producer locked into a producer mindset, I attract wealth because *consumers seek producers.* Consumers are the majority who demand their fill!

TO CONSUME RICHLY, PRODUCE EFFECTIVELY

And the irony of this producer/consumer dichotomy? Once you succeed as a producer, you can consume anything you want with little consequence because you'll be rich.

To consume richly, *produce richly first.*

Unfortunately, most people have it backward: consumption and no production.

Producers get rich.

Consumers get poor.

Switch teams and reorient as a producer first, a consumer second. Make wealth attracted to you!

BE A PRODUCER: LEVERAGE THE BUSINESS OF A SYSTEM

To switch teams and become a producer, you need to be an entrepreneur and an innovator. You need to be a visionary and a creator. You need to give birth to a business and *offer the world value.*

While the centrist theme to the Slowlane is a job, *in the Fastlane, it's a business.* Yes, good old self-employment. I know, not breaking news for "get rich" books, however, it's important to note that most small business owners are light years away from a Fastlane and dickering with Slowlane metrics. *Some businesses masquerade as jobs!*

A Fastlane business is the key to the Fastlane wealth equation *(Wealth = Profit + Asset Value)* because it unlocks LEVERAGE, a new set of wealth variables that are unlimited and controllable, whereas in the Slowlane, they are limited and uncontrollable. Yes, ULL is swapped for CUL.

For example, the sale of this book extricates me from the Slowlane wealth equation and its universe. This book puts me into the Fastlane universe, which is governed by its wealth equation of NET PROFIT and ASSET VALUE. This book is a business system that has unlimited leverage in both time and money!

First, it *survives time* and it is capable of earning income long after my original time investment. This book effectively transfers the act of income generation from me (the human asset) to the book (the business asset).

From start to finish, this book cost roughly 1,000 hours of my time. If I sell 100,000 books at $5 profit each, I earn $500,000, or roughly $500 per hour invested. If I sell 500,000 books, I will earn $2,500 per hour invested. The more I sell, the greater the return on my original time investment, as I already paid the time. I finished this book in 2010 and specifically wrote it to be transcendent and relevant no matter what the year (the rules of mathematics don't change!) and years later, it still sells consistently. I earn $5 from a time investment I made years ago!

But it gets better!

If I guest-speak on a radio show for 10 minutes and that appearance yields 1,000 book sales, this 10-minute investment yields $5,000 in income (1,000 books × $5 profit) and yields a return on my time at $30,000 per hour.

Can you get rich trading your time for $30,000 per hour?

Yes you can, and awfully fast.

You see, when you unlock yourself from the handcuffs of time imposed by the Slowlane roadmap, you assign income to a system that leverages unlimited mathematics, and fast wealth becomes possible.

The variables in my wealth universe can be controlled and leveraged.

In the next chapter you will discover why the Fastlane can deliver financial freedom and wealth faster than any indexed-fund can.

CHAPTER SUMMARY: FASTLANE DISTINCTIONS

- Producers are indigenous to the Fastlane roadmap.
- Producers are the minority as are the rich, while consumers are the majority as are the poor.
- When you succeed as a producer, you can consume anything you want.
- Fastlaners are producers, entrepreneurs, innovators, visionaries, and creators.
- A business does not make a Fastlane—some businesses are jobs in disguise.
- The Fastlane wealth equation is not bound by time and its variables are unlimited and controllable.

How the Rich Really Get Rich

Only those who will risk going too far
can possibly find out how far one can go.

~ TS ELIOT

THE BURNING QUESTION: "HOW DID YOU GET RICH?"

Drive any car that costs more than most people's homes and strangers will accost you with the question, "What do you do for a living?" This seemingly innocuous question "fronts" for the real question burning inside . . . "How did you get rich?"

People want to know the road I've taken so they can assess their likelihood to travel that same road. When I prompt for a guess, the answers are typical: Athlete. Actor. Plastic surgeon. A spoiled brat indulged by rich parents. A lottery winner.

These speculative "answers" unmask the reality behind people's perceptions: To get rich you have to get famous, inherit or win money, or be a high-paid professional. That's what I thought, until I met that stranger in his Lamborghini so many years ago.

THE FASTLANE WEALTH EQUATION

Living wealthy in youthful exuberance has to shatter the myth of "Get Rich Quick." If you're 30 years old and worth millions, and you aren't rich or famous via inheritance, you dirty all fabrics of normality. We can't have that, now can we?

Once again, the secret is unmasked in the universal language of mathematics. The secret is to divorce yourself from the communist dictatorship of the Slowlane equation (ULL) and trade up to the free-wheeling libertarian—the Fastlane equation (CUL).

Wealth = Net Profit + Asset Value

Underneath this equation lies the true power of the Fastlane and how to build wealth fast. Its variables are controllable and unlimited. If you can manipulate the variables inherent to your wealth equation, you can get wealthy. Those variables are:

Net Profit = Units Sold × Unit Profit

~ and ~

Asset Value = Net Profit × Industry Multiple

All business owners leverage this equation, in which [UNITS SOLD] × [UNIT PROFIT] determines net profit.

Using my Internet company as an example, my unit profit was approximately $4 for every website conversion. (A conversion was a user who generated a lead). On any given day, I had 12,000 people visiting my website. This means my "units sold" variable had an upper threshold of 12,000 per day. I had the opportunity to "sell" 12,000 people per day.

Let's compare this variable to the Slowlane's counterpart of hours worked. Under my wealth equation, my upper limit of wealth is "units sold" and currently stood at 12,000. Of course, 100% conversion is unreasonable, and "converting" all 12,000 is unlikely. Likewise, in the Slowlane, the unreasonable upper limit is 24 because there are only 24 hours in the day. Logically, the real upper limit is 8 to 12 hours per day.

What is going to make you rich? An upper limit of exposure to 12,000 people per day? Or maximizing your hours worked in the day? That's 12,000 vs. 24. No contest. I get rich and the Slowlaner gets old.

Controllable unlimited variables will make you rich. So how did I control this variable? How is it unlimited? Simple. My average conversion ratio was 12%. If I want to make more profit, I don't walk into the boss's office and ask for a raise. No, I have several weapons available for deployment.

1) Raise Units Sold by Increasing Conversion Ratio

A 1% increase from 12% to 13% would give me an instant raise of about $480 per day. That's $14,400 per month. If I redesign the website, hit a home run and get conversion to 15%, now I've expanded my income to over $43,000 PER MONTH.

2) Raise Units Sold by Increasing Web Traffic

To raise profit, I can increase traffic. If I increase web users to my website from 12,000 to 15,000 and conversion stays at 12%, my daily income rises by $1,440 per day, or $43,200 per month! Not likely? It happened! On some days I would have traffic spikes where over 20,000 users would visit.

3) Raise Unit Profit

If I detect a weakness in supply for my service or improve value, I can raise prices and increase my unit profit. If my unit profit moves from $4 to $4.50, I raise my income to $10,800 per day from $8,000. That translates to an additional $84,000 per month! Is your mouth on the floor yet?

Isn't it wonderful to have control? These were my options to create wealth. I had reasonable control over both variables, "unit profit" and "units sold," whereas in the Slowlane you're left pleading with the boss for a measly 3% salary raise.

Second, notice how my wealth variables are virtually unlimited. I controlled only a small part of my market, and conceivably my upper threshold of traffic wasn't the current 12,000 people but upward of 50,000–100,000 users PER DAY. Unit profit is also pliable. I could experiment with increased prices or new services.

I remember when I introduced a new service that cost me nothing and I sent an email to my advertisers outlining the program. Within minutes, I made a few thousand dollars in reoccurring yearly income. My invested time was negligible and the results were accumulative.

Limitless variables = high speed limit = high potential income.

The power of this example is to illustrate why I got rich and most others don't. I changed my universe because *my wealth equation was unlimited and controllable.*

When I make tiny, incremental changes in my strategy, I explode my income. A mere 1% increase in the variables could mean thousands and a new Lamborghini. When your wealth variables have high leverage, so does your income potential—or would you rather stick with the ceiling of 24 hours native to intrinsic value?

Unfortunately, many enthusiastic business owners engage in opportunities with low, punitive speeds. For example, if you sit outside the Home Depot and sell hot dogs from your hot dog cart, you've muzzled your speed with no accelerative leverage. The variables are limited because your reach is confined to a small area. How many hot dogs could you conceivably sell in the day? 40? 100? Is it possible you can go home and rave to your wife "Honey! I sold 20,000 hot dogs today!" It would never happen! Again, this isn't much different from the 24-hour cage on intrinsic value.

Small numbers have a strong gravity toward mediocrity.

Another example is this book itself. How many people are interested in financial independence or early retirement? My market, *my upper speed limit*, is virtually hundreds of millions of people all over the world. To weaponize the Fastlane wealth equation, you must deploy a Fastlane business that has the potential for leverage or high speed limits. Retarded numbers retard wealth!

MILLIONAIRES CREATE AND MANIPULATE ASSETS (ASSET VALUE)

In a survey of 3,000 penta-millionaires ($5 million net worth) the Harrison Group (HarrisonGroupInc.com) reported that almost all penta-millionaires made their fortunes in a big lump sum after a period of years. Worth repeating: a big lump sum, not "by saving 10% of his paycheck for 40 years." "A big lump sum" is just another phrase for "asset value." Furthermore, 80% either started their own business or worked for a small company that saw explosive growth. Explosive growth is another phrase representing asset value. And yet, none of these multimillionaires had a cushy union job down at the DMV. Surprised? Don't be.

The primary wealth accelerant of the rich boils down to one concept: *Appreciable and controllable assets.* Within our Fastlane wealth equation, this second component is called "Asset Value." Asset value is simply the worth of any property you own that has marketplace value.

Slowlaners and Fastlaners have two antagonistic views of "assets." Slowlaners and Sidewalkers buy and sell depreciating assets that decline in value over time. Cars, boats, electronics, designer clothes, gizmodos, and sparkly bling to impress that newly divorced woman in the adjacent cubicle—these are all assets that lose value the moment your credit card is charged.

Contrary to this, Fastlaners buy and sell appreciating assets: businesses, brands, cash flows, notes, intellectual property, licenses, inventions, patents, and real estate. As it relates to the Fastlane wealth equation, the power of "Asset Value" lies in your ability to control the variable in a virtually limitless fashion.

WEALTH ACCELERATION BY ASSET VALUE

The rich accelerate wealth by accelerating asset value and selling those upgraded assets in the marketplace.

> *Twenty-four-year-old Sheila Hinton quits her job to start a business as a roving computer technician. At first, her business operates in the local city, but growth forces her to hire additional technicians, expanding into nearby cities. In a few years, Sheila owns a company that operates in 6 Midwestern states. She moves from a technician to a facilitator of the system, and her company enjoys an impressive $3 million profit. After enjoying the profits (and saving $6M of it), she sells her company for $21 million to a large computer manufacturer. She built an asset from nothing to something. While she never enjoyed "passive income," the asset was her system, and now with a $27 million nest egg, she has passive income for life, never needing to work again.*

The preceding story best represents the two variables that comprise "asset value":

$$\textit{Asset Value} = (\textit{Net Profit}) \times (\textit{Industry Multiplier})$$

Any time an asset has sustainable profits, an industry multiplier governed by prevailing market conditions determines the asset's value. Other people or companies will buy that asset based on the asset's net profit multiplied by the assessed multiple. For example, if you own a manufacturing company that nets $100,000 and the average multiple for your industry is 6, your asset value is worth $600,000. Industry multipliers are subject to intense negotiating as they rise and fall with the economy and within industry sectors.

You already might be familiar with "multipliers." Stocks trading on the public markets define the multiplier for each respective company by the price-to-earnings ratio, or PE. If a company's stock trades at 10 times PE, investors are purchasing that company at a multiple of 10 times. Price-to-earnings is relevant regardless of whether your company is a small private company or a large publicly traded company: *The valuation of your company is predicated on the subjective* PE *for your particular industry.*

For example, in my particular web space, industry multipliers ranged from 2 to 6. For this analysis, let's use the middle: 4. This means that any time I increased my net profit, *the value of my business increased by a minimum factor of* 4, *or* 400%. 400%! Where can you get a return of 400% in today's financial market? Are there any mutual funds paying 400%? Forget about today, how about ever?

In effect, this puts a phenomenal wealth-building tool at your disposal. Since net income, profit, or earnings can determine asset value, I experienced asset growth of 400% every time I increased net profit. For every dollar I profited, the value of my company would increase by a factor of 4, or $4. If my net profit increased $500,000 for the year, my company's valuation increased by $2 million.

Below is a list of average multiples per respective industry.

Industry	Multiple
Advertising	2.85
Beauty Shops	4.10
Bars/Drinking Places	2.70
Carpet Cleaning	5.22
Computer-Related Services	8.19
Employment Agencies	5.40
Engineering Services	6.32
Gasoline Stations	3.70
Grocery Stores	11.34
Medical Labs	2.62
Misc. Retail Stores	3.62
Patent Owners and Lessors	14.56
Physical Fitness Facilities	3.56
Plumbing/HVAC Services	4.52
Surgical and Medical Equipment	17.32
Used Merchandise Stores	4.92

Source: *Inc.* Magazine, June 2009

THE WEALTH ACCELERATION FACTOR (WAF)

Suppose you're a disgusted engineer employed by a multinational corporation. You've been employed for three years and diligently save 10% of your paycheck and invest it into a indexed-fund earning an average of 8% a year.

Your Wealth Acceleration Factor (WAF) is 8%.

Now suppose you quit your job and take your experience and set off to create a company manufacturing medical devices. You estimate that your total market (potential buyers) for your medical product(s) is 16 million. According to our chart above, the average multiple for the "medical devices" industry is over 17. This means within your scope of wealth acceleration, you can accelerate wealth at a FACTOR of 17, or 1,700%.

Your Wealth Acceleration Factor (WAF) is 1,700%.

Let's extend this example further. For the next six years, you grow this company to the point that its net income is $1.2 million per year. This means you now earn $100,000 per month (your net profit) AND your company (the asset) is now worth in the neighborhood of $18.4 million based on the average multiple ($1.2MM × 17.32 multiple). You could continue to grow the business (grow wealth via asset value) and cash flow (grow income) or seek to liquidate (sell asset value) to realize wealth acceleration.

Contrast the two wealth acceleration options for the Slowlaner and the Fastlaner. Your wealth acceleration options if you stay as an employed engineer:

1) Raise your intrinsic value and HOPE the boss gives you a pay raise.
2) HOPE the company doesn't lay you off, so you can continue receiving your income.
3) Save 10% of your paycheck in an indexed-fund and HOPE for an 8% return for the next 40 years.

Your wealth acceleration options if you owned your own medical device company:

1) Grow net income with an income potential only limited by the number of devices you can sell, that is, 16 million.
2) Grow asset value at a factor of 1,700%.
3) Liquidate asset value and turn paper money into real money.

Can you see now why some 30-year-olds are worth $50 million and some are worth $19,000? The Fastlane universe operates on gains of 1,700% and millions, while the Slowlane universe 8% and 40. One plan is about *HOPE* while the other is about *CONTROL*. Breaking news: 8% and 40 makes millionaires in 40 years: 1,700% and 16 million makes *billionaires* in four years.

WEALTH'S DUAL-FLANKED ATTACK

Zealous pursuit of net profit is a double-flanked attack at creating wealth. Since asset value is tied to net profit, raising net profit simultaneously elevates asset value by the average industry multiple. Of course, this works in the opposite as well; if your company stalls and net income falls, so will the corresponding asset value. When I repurchased my company, I paid $250,000. Then for the next several years I manipulated the asset and increased its value.

1) I expanded my customer base by 30%.
2) I reduced expenses, improving profitability.
3) I streamlined operations, which created passivity.
4) I elevated "net income."

Over this process, my net income exploded and, with it, asset value. Then, subsequently, and after profiting millions passively, I put the company up for sale and entertained multimillion dollar offers. I bought an asset for $250,000, appreciated and manipulated the variables, and then sold it for millions.

I controlled my financial plan; the plan didn't control me.

In the Fastlane, your Wealth Accelerator is based on creating or buying appreciative assets, adding value and manipulating the variables, and then selling. Or you can opt for the Slowlane alternative—give $200 a month to Wall Street and pray for 8% per year and 40 years of employment.

Excuse me while I laugh.

SUPER-FAST WEALTH ACCELERATION: LIQUIDATION EVENTS

Liquidation events create millionaires overnight, but only if liquidation occurs. Liquidation events are the process of selling your appreciable asset to the market. It's a Fastlane exit strategy.

> *John Hammerstein creates a social networking website that goes viral. Soon millions of people are using his service and John finds himself entertaining buyout offers and venture capital investments.*
>
> *Despite having no revenue and no profit, John has built an asset that has value to the marketplace. He receives a $640 million offer for his service from the web's leading search engine.*
>
> *John declines, arguing that his business will be worth more money once he starts generating revenue. While this is true, it is a gamble.*
>
> *After 18 months, John's social networking service falls out of vogue, proving that the service was nothing more than a fad. The company becomes a bad party joke.*

In search of rich valuations on a declining property, John no longer receives investor or buyer interest. He realizes too late that he should have taken the $640 million and experienced a liquidation event. He eventually sells the company at a "fire-sale" price of $2.5 million to a private equity firm. His poor timing cost him more than $600 million.

Asset valuations of businesses, real estate, and other appreciable assets are nothing, but just that—valuations based on subjective analysis and market data. If the company you build from scratch has a paper valuation of $60 million and your bank account only has $10,000, are you really a millionaire?

Not really.

Illiquid, paper-millionaires can't buy Ferraris and palatial estates; money does. And to get the money, you have to increase profit and save it, or go for the big exit: liquidation.

Fastlaners accelerate wealth by building cash-flowing assets that can be sold in the marketplace to realize gains. Their wealth equation has controllable, unlimited leverage.

CHAPTER SUMMARY: FASTLANE DISTINCTIONS

- The key to the Fastlane wealth equation is to have a high speed limit, or an unlimited range of values for units sold. This creates leverage. The market for your product or service determines your upper limit.
- The higher your speed limit, the higher your income potential.
- The primary wealth accelerant for the rich is asset value, defined as appreciable assets created, founded, or bought.
- Wealth creation via asset value is accelerated by each industry's average multiplier. For every dollar in net income realized, the asset value multiplies by a factor of the multiple.
- Your industry of specialization will determine the average multiple that determines your wealth accelerant factor. If the multiple is 3, your WAF is 300%.
- Liquidation events transform appreciated assets ("paper" net worth) into money ("real" net worth) that can be transformed into another passive income stream: a money system.

Divorce Wealth from Time

Time is the coin of your life. It is the only coin you have,
and only you can determine how it will be spent.
Be careful, lest you let other people spend it for you.

~ CARL SANDBURG

INDUSTRIALIZING WEALTH: DIVORCE FROM TIME

My first Fastlane taste was in my late 20s, when I had the worst month of my life: A brutal mix of a relationship gone south and some troubling health news served as a lethal cocktail to my business productivity. I spent most of the month in bed with the shades drawn, watching Judge Judy unleash a firestorm of common-sense whoop-ass. During this troubling time I had to cash in my Fastlane winning ticket—and let me tell you, it paid.

Despite being "checked out" on life, my income actually grew. Yes, grew. My income didn't stop because I stopped.

How did I get so lucky?

I was divorced from time.

Years earlier, I broke the chains of "my time for money." This allowed me to escape the stranglehold of the Slowlane equation and operate on the Fastlane playing field.

When your wealth is predicated on factors that you cannot control and that are implicitly limited, you aren't going to make fast progress. You aren't in control, because time is in control. You aren't in control, because the boss is in control. You aren't in control, because the stock market is in control.

How did I escape these controls that society finds perfectly acceptable? Instead of trading my time for money (manual labor), I traded it into a business system—industrialized wealth production.

In my situation, time was working for me, not against me. My business system earned money with the passage of time, and *yet was exclusive of my time.* It was a virtual money tree and it didn't care what I was doing. Whether I was watching *Jerry Springer* or jet skiing in Jamaica, the system was built to be its own machine—a living, breathing entity that did my dirty work. My system surrogated for my time. I owned my time instead of time owning me.

PASSIVE INCOME: THE HOLY GRAIL TO RETIREMENT

The buzzword in moneymaking circles is "passive income"—earning income while not working. While retired, I receive checks every month like clockwork and I don't lift a finger. Passive income is a successful divorce from the "work-for-money" equation indigenous to the Slowlane. The beauty of passive income is it doesn't care if you're 20 years old or 80. If your monthly income exceeds your lifestyle expenses including taxes, guess what? YOU'RE RETIRED!

The Fastlane Roadmap is engineered for two purposes. It's engineered to create a passive income stream to the excess of your expenses and lifestyle desires, and to make financial freedom a reality, exclusive of age.

TO BREAK TIME IS TO GROW A MONEY TREE

Mom convinced me it was true. "We can't afford that, do you think money grows on trees?" She was wrong. Money grows on trees if you own a money tree. And, you can own one if you know how and where to get the seeds.

Money trees are business systems that survive on their own. They require periodic support and nurturing but survive on their own, creating a surrogate for your time-for-money trade.

A few years ago, I was in Vegas and I lost nearly $2,000 gambling. After retreating to my hotel room with my tail between my legs, I realized, why fret? I lost $2,000. On that day, my money tree, my Internet company I created, earned $6,000. While I gambled (or slept, swam, or ate) my blooming money tree bore fruit.

A money tree is a business system, and it's the Fastlane roadmap's Main Street. Money trees create passive income streams BEFORE you "officially" retire. Yes, you can experience the destination of retirement and financial freedom without actually being retired. This is akin to taking a vacation to the South Pacific and magically bypassing the nine-hour plane ride.

MONEY TREE SEEDLINGS: A FASTLANE BUSINESS

Not all businesses are Fastlane, and many of them can't be transformed into money trees. Misled by gurus and life coaches, wannabe entrepreneurs are steered astray under the lure of "Be your own boss" and "Do what you love!" and head down a path of business servitude that is identical to wage slavery.

It is Jillian's dream to be her own boss. After a 13-year career on Wall Street, Jillian quits her financial adviser job and buys a well-known deli franchise. She liquidates half of her 401(k) to pay for franchise fees and startup costs. Three months later she is in business and expects to realize her dream. But Jillian discovers that her dream is only a nightmare. Between seven-day workweeks, long hours, and constant bickering between her and the corporate franchiser, she burns out in two years.

Her profit margins, slim and softened by franchise royalties, don't allow her to hire an operator to run the restaurant in her place. She feels trapped as she trades her time for dollars.

Although she earns a $90,000-a-year profit in her business, Jillian has no free time to enjoy the fruits of her labor. She could pay $60,000 to a general manager, which would give her free time. Knowing she can't survive on $30,000 per year, she feels trapped to her business while her profit is cornered into submission. Four years later, she puts the business up for sale and seeks the comfort of a 9-5 job.

Too many people plant businesses in barren, infertile soil that is incapable of spawning money trees. Instead they end up with a scrawny Slowlane twig that sucks time and money, no different than a bad job.

THE FIVE FASTLANE BUSINESS SEEDLINGS

There are five business seedlings to money trees. Mind you, these aren't absolute and can intersect with one another. Each system inherently has a grade that rates its level of passivity. A higher grade means a greater potential for passivity, but not necessarily a greater income.

1) **Rental Systems**
2) **Computer/Software Systems**
3) **Content Systems**
4) **Distribution Systems**
5) **Human Resource Systems**

Seedling 1: Rental Systems (Passivity Grade: A)

Real estate is one "rental system." I consider real estate money trees as Fastlane 1.0 or Wealth 1.0. It is the old way and still very much a road to wealth. For example, I own a single-family rental home with a great tenant. I could be living on the moon and each month I get a check in the mail because my time is detached from its income. Real estate is a perfect example of Wealth 1.0 because real estate is its own system. It is 95% passive. As time passes, tenants pay landlords to use their property. From single families to apartment buildings to massive commercial office buildings, real estate has always been the default choice for seedling money trees. Furthermore, real estate is an asset that can be manipulated and its value appreciated. Appreciative assets (asset value) are cornerstones in the Fastlane wealth equation.

Don't want to get involved in real estate? No problem. Rental systems aren't just reserved for real estate.

Rental systems can come from a variety of other sources: leases, royalty payments, and licensing are other forms of "rental systems" that can produce recurring income. For example, when you own the rights to a music collection, corporations have to pay you a royalty to use the music. The work might have been recorded decades earlier, but it still generates royalties.

Likewise, if you invent and patent a product process and license it to other companies, you again earn income from the licensing fee. The patent was invented and registered, yet its income survives time exclusive of your time. Photographers can earn licensing revenues by allowing others to use their photos. Cartoonists license their artistry to book authors and newspaper producers. The cartoon might have been created years ago, yet, it survives time and generates rental income for the owner.

And finally, this book has been translated and published into over 20 languages worldwide. These foreign book sales earn me yearly royalties from countries spanning the planet, yet, I've never visited them. Rental systems are powerful money trees because they are high on the passivity scale and survive time.

Seedling 2: Computer/Software Systems (Passivity Grade: A-)

My preferred system is computer and software systems, including the Internet. It's no shock that the Internet has paved the road to millions more than any other road out there. In fact, I heard a statistic that the Internet created more millionaires in the last five years than the previous five decades combined. What makes the Internet and computer systems so potent?

Computers are miraculous inventions and fertile seeds to money trees. They work 24 hours a day, 7 days a week, and they don't bitch about working conditions or that you don't pay them enough. They don't whine about co-workers like Lazy Joan or Same-Shirt Bob. Computers aren't late, they don't ask for pay raises, and they don't care you just bought a new Mercedes. Nope, they just do what they're programmed to do and it's done.

What sets the Internet apart from real estate is it implicitly contains leverage. When you own a website, you're accessible to millions. When you own a three-bedroom home on Elm Street, it's accessible to a few. This duality makes Internet systems one of the best business seedlings in existence.

Additionally, computer systems aren't limited to the Internet. It could be software or applications. Some of the richest people on the planet like Larry Ellison of

Oracle or Paul Allen of Microsoft are software billionaires. Software enjoys plump margins because it is easily replicated. Once the code is written, it's done. You can easily sell one or 10,000. Can you replicate an office building with ease? You can't.

Software millionaires can be "average Joes." Facebook and iPhone application developers are making money fast. One iPhone developer, Nicholas, raked in $600,000 in a single month with a single iPhone game. In a phone interview, Nicholas said that he wouldn't be shocked if he became a millionaire by year's end. Wow. One day Nicholas is treading the Slowlane at his nice cushy job and popping a few Benjamins into his 401(k), when suddenly he finds himself smack in the middle of a Fastlane. Of course, the road to the Fastlane wasn't easy for Nicholas. An engineer at Sun Micro Systems, he worked on his application after working eight-hour days, cradling his one-year-old son in one hand and coding with the other. How did he learn how to code an iPhone app? Nicholas couldn't afford books so he taught himself by scouring websites. Hmmm . . . do you smell process behind the event?

Software, when tapped into potent distribution, can be replicated to millions. It scales without significant degradation to passivity.

Seedling 3: Content Systems (Passivity Grade: B+)

Content systems are systems of information. That information can be fused to a variety of other systems, like the Internet and physical distribution systems. This book is a content system that I can effectively move through other channels, like Amazon, book distributors, or other mediums of reach.

In the old days of wealth, striking it rich via content meant you had to be a newspaper mogul, magazine publisher, or successful author. Control the press. Distribute content. Information, like software, often has ease of replication. I can print 10 million of these books. I will never own 10 million pieces of real estate, nor do I have any desire. Like their software counterparts, some of the richest people on the planet are successful authors.

In a few short years, JK Rowling, author of the *Harry Potter* brand, went from being a 32-year-old divorced English teacher to a media mogul worth over $400 million. The single mom has sold over 30 million copies of her books in 35 different languages. I guess she didn't hear the excuse, "I'm a single mom and I don't have time." Ms. Rowling recalls the happiest point of her life—not the acquisition of millions, but the point at which she could write full-time.

Similarly, Dan Brown has sold over 80 million copies of the *DaVinci Code* in 51 languages. Let me be perfectly clear: If you sell 80 million of ANYTHING, you will be a very rich human being.

The latest trend of content distribution has merged with computer systems. Video blogging (YouTube), social networks (Facebook pages/Instagram channels), e-books, and online magazines all serve the newest hybrid of computers systems and content distribution. In fact, this new combination is so powerful that it is driving many of the old, hard-line models out of business. Paper newspapers and magazines are officially endangered to be extinct in the coming decade.

Change creates millionaires. Those who see the changes and take advantage of it will become the new millionaires and billionaires. And because change is constant, millionaire opportunities also remain constant.

Content also survives time. This book might have taken me years to write, but it also survives years. If someone buys this book five years from now, I will earn a small profit on a time investment I made years earlier. The content is an asset that is salable, over and over again, and with each sale, the effective time cost declines while the hourly rate of return expands.

Seedling 4: Distribution Systems (Passivity Grade: B)

A distribution system is any structure or organization designed to move products to the masses. Distribution systems can be hybrids with the other seedlings, such as content and computer systems.

If you invent and manufacture a new product and sell it on QVC, you are leveraging a distribution system. If you sell that product via infomercial at 2 a.m., you are leveraging a distribution system. If you sell your product to four wholesale distributors that, in turn, sell it to retailers like Wal-Mart and Target, you are leveraging a distribution system.

When inventing any product, the invention is always half the battle. Distribution is the other. The greatest product in the world goes unused if it isn't leveraged into the proper distribution system—either one that exists, or one that you create.

Amazon.com is one example of a distribution system that I use. This book sells on Amazon and is available to millions. However, a book sitting on Amazon represents unrealized potential, like a 1,000 horsepower car sitting in the garage. It is my job to push the engine and drive the distribution system's power. The tool exists, ready to be exploited by successful (or failed) execution.

Our iPhone developer leveraged the iPhone "App Store" to move his software. This was his distribution point. Without the distribution, he couldn't sell software.

Distribution is a means to move product to the masses. Some systems are better than others and when it comes to distribution, it all depends on the control structure. If you *create* a network marketing company to sell your new vitamin product, you are creating a powerful distribution network capable of earning millions. If you *join* a network marketing company, you are electing to be a gear in the distribution process.

Another potent form of distribution is franchising and/or chaining. When a successful store concept is branded and systemized, it can be replicated and sold to other individuals. Savvy Fastlane entrepreneurs recognize that a successful local business with weak leverage can be made highly leveraged by franchises or chains. Does this path sound familiar? It should; this is what Starbucks did to become the biggest coffee chain in the world.

Other restaurants deploy a combination of chains and franchises. Dairy Queen and McDonalds have both chains and franchises. If your business operates in limited scale, it can be conquered with chains and franchises. If you own one hot-dog cart and sell at one location, there is no leverage. If you own 500 hot-dog carts and sell at 500 locations through 500 owner-operators, suddenly leverage appears. The Fastlane wealth equation has power.

Seedling 5: Human Resource Systems (Passivity Grade: C)

Amazon.com is a distribution system backboned by a computer system and operated by a human resource system. Human resource systems are the most expensive and complicated to run. Humans are unpredictable, expensive, and difficult to control. Ask anyone with a company that relies on employees how challenging it is to keep employees happy.

I came to the employee crossroads with my own company. I had to either suffer technology obsolescence or hire two more people to scale my company to the next level. Since my business was already 80% passive, I knew adding employees would erode business passivity because employees need management. At a certain level, even managers need managers.

The other alternatives were to keep my company on autopilot and watch it slowly degrade over the years (web companies need to be constantly reinvented), dig in and return to "startup" mode (long hours in "Chuma" mode), or sell it. After evaluating the options, I chose to sell. In my case, human resource additions would have subtracted to passivity, not added. While I would have made more money hiring more people, I wasn't willing to forgo my free time for it.

A year after I sold my company, I examined the possibility of a parking business near the airport. Local travelers to the Phoenix airport could valet-park their car in a neighboring parking lot and get chauffeured to the airport. In general, this was a rental system. People would pay to park their car and I would earn a daily fee for each parked car. It had Internet-like qualities; it ran 24/7 and generated income with the simple passage of time. It was great idea with high potential for passivity. I found land for sale near the airport and it was perfect. I started to run numbers, projections, and scenarios to see how I could make this business a reality.

The numbers uncovered something important. The business model had the DNA of a "rental system," but the operation was a "human resource system." To succeed at this idea, it would have required a payroll of at least two dozen people. That stopped me cold and I didn't pursue it further. Human resource systems can be unpredictable with management difficulties making "passivity" an unlikely and/or distant possibility.

A member of the Fastlane community owns a few self-storage facilities. Her business is a rental system. People pay money to store their junk and she receives monthly income. You'd assume that her facility is run by a human resource system—managers, property assistants—but it isn't. Her properties have automated kiosks that run each property—a computer system. This makes her business 85% passive. Remove the kiosk, add human resource systems, and passivity drops.

Does this suggest that human resource systems are a drain to passivity?

It depends.

First, what is the existing level of passivity to the business as it is now? If you own a coffee shop and work 80 hours a week, you have ZERO passivity. A general manger—a human resource system—would raise passivity by an estimated 40%. In my business, I was operating at 80% passivity. Adding any human resource system would have lowered passivity.

Good employees nurture money trees. Bad employees pluck the fruit of money trees and require pruning. However don't let that stop you. If you want to make millions or billions, human resource systems (employees) will be needed. While solopreneurs can make a lot of money, you can't do everything yourself. At some point, managing your time and growth has to take precedence.

CHAPTER SUMMARY: FASTLANE DISTINCTIONS

- To divorce yourself from the Slowlane's transactional relationship of "time for money," you need to become a producer, specifically, a business owner.
- Business systems break the bond between "your time for money" because they act like surrogate operatives for your time trade.
- If you have a passive income that exceeds all your needs and lifestyle expenses including taxes, you're retired.
- Retirement can happen at any age.
- The fruit from a money tree is passive income.
- A Fastlane objective is to create a business system that survives time, exclusive of your time.
- The 5 money-tree seedlings are rental systems, computer systems, content systems, distribution systems, and human-resource systems.
- Real estate, licenses, and patents are examples of rental systems.
- Internet and software businesses are examples of computer systems.
- Authoring books, blogging, and magazines are forms of content systems.
- Franchising, chaining, network marketing, and television marketing are examples of distribution systems.
- Human resource systems can add or subtract to passivity.
- Human resource systems are the most expensive to manage and implement.

Recruit Your Army of Freedom Fighters

The rich rule over the poor, and the borrower is slave to the lender.

~ PROVERBS 22:7 (NIV)

HOW THE RICH EXPLODE WEALTH

I spent a few years chauffeuring clients in limousines, so I heard a lot. I remember Gary, a young 20-something client who hired our limousine several times a month to serve as his personal escort to parties and drunken excursions. Oddly, this guy wouldn't just hire us on Friday or Saturday; he'd hire the limousine during the week. Every day of his life was his weekend. When he hired us, I knew it was going to be a long and profitable night, since he tipped fabulously.

Being broke and a student of wealth, I couldn't bottle my curiosity. I asked the limo company owner, "What's Gary's story?" He told me that Gary was semi-retired and just sold his administrative office company for millions. Wow. This guy couldn't have been much older than I and he was already retired and living large!

The next few times I chauffeured the man, I eavesdropped on his conversations hoping to catch a tasty tidbit of the rich.

And I did.

To his club wingman, I heard Gary drunkenly declare: "Thanks to municipals and treasuries, I never have to work another day of my life."

Another piece of the wealth puzzle solved.

THE BEST PASSIVE INCOME VENUE IN EXISTENCE

In the prior chapter, I neglected to mention the best money-tree seedlings in existence. I omitted it because it isn't really a business seedling but a seed you already possess. Whether you're broke, in a dead-end job, or without a business, you already have the raw materials for the best money-tree seed in existence.

What is it? Guess. Real estate? An Internet business? A network marketing company? Licensing an invention? No. No. Hell no. And no. The best money tree in existence sits right in your pocketbook: The good old-fashioned buck.

Yes, money. *Money is the king of money trees.*

How is money passive? If you have a lot of money, you're given the gate key to switch teams from consumer to producer. Specifically, you move from borrower to lender. You move from employee to employer. You move from customer to owner. In other words, people pay you to use YOUR MONEY in the form of interest or ownership.

For example, let's examine interest, which is a fee earned to lend money. Right now you're probably someone who doesn't earn interest, but pays it. Someone lent money for your home mortgage, and in return you pay the note-holder interest. That interest is profit or income to someone else.

While the act of becoming a lender sounds complicated, it isn't. Anytime you buy a certificate of deposit from a bank, you become a lender. Anytime you buy a municipal bond, either directly from the source or indirectly via mutual fund, you become a lender. When you deposit money in the bank, you become a lender.

As a lender, you don't administer the loans; you just sit back and collect checks. It's super easy and super passive. Gary, my rich limousine passenger, was a lender who never had to work another day in his life.

SAVERS BECOME LENDERS, OWNERS, AND PRODUCERS

I once heard a radio commercial from a "Two-Dad" guru who was pushing a seminar. He declared: "Savers are losers!" I couldn't believe my ears. Savers are losers? And who are the winners? The people you advised to borrow millions on risky real estate investments? Savers aren't losers. Savers are winners because they eventually become lenders. Savers are winners because they become owners in companies. Savers are winners because they become producers and build assets.

Open your wallet and look at a dollar. One buck. It doesn't buy much but it is the embryonic start to a passive income stream. One dollar has the power to give you a nickel of passive income for life. Yes, for life. While one nickel buys squat, it unlocks the DNA implicit in money—it's fully passive.

I retired in my thirties because of this simple reality. I'm a lender, and when you have a lot of money to lend, you live free because passive income arrives every month.

If you had $10 million and lent it at a mere 5% interest, you'd enjoy a passive income of $41,666 *every single month.* At 8% your monthly income would be $66,666 per month—fully passive. Over $60,000 every month! This is WITHOUT touching the principal. You can do this for years and still have 10 million dollars left over!

Imagine opening your mailbox every month to a $40,000 check—and you didn't have to do anything for it. What kind of trouble can you get into earning $40,000 per month? I bet a lot. Unrealistic? It isn't. This is how I live. Even in this low-interest-rate environment I can find safe investment yields in the 4%–6% range, some tax-free. While most people shudder at the thought of an interest rate increase, I love it. I get a pay raise. A 1% interest rate hike translates into thousands per month for me. And since inflation rises in unison with interest rates, my income has an element of inflation protection. If inflation rises, so do interest rates.

So how does all of this become a reality? I created a passive income stream via my Internet businesses (a business money tree seedling), which funded my passive income system from lending. While my Internet business was 80% passive (yes, I had to work several hours per week), my lending passivity is 99.5%. I do virtually nothing and the checks arrive.

Instead of trading my time for dollars, *I invested my time into an autonomous system simultaneously capable of passivity and capable of funding my money system.* It was a dual-flanked attack where passive income was both the short and long term goal.

AMASS YOUR ARMY OF FREEDOM FIGHTERS

Every dollar saved is another freedom fighter in your army. If your money is fighting for you, your time is freed and you break the equation of "time for money."

Money is your army. The more you have, the more they will fight for freedom. Slowlaners focus on the EXPENSE variable in the wealth equation when they should be focused on the INCOME variable. Income is the key to growing your army of freedom fighters. You aren't going to recruit a massive army detailing cars down at the Jimmy's Auto Salon.

And I'm not referring to just the U.S. dollar, but all international dollar-denominated assets. As I write this, much of my income is derived from non-U.S.-dollar assets in other countries with stronger currencies and better yields. Fastlaners think globally, not locally.

What does a dollar represent to you? A mechanism that gets you bottle service at the club every Friday? Or is it the seed of your money tree? Is it your freedom fighter? Make money fight for you instead of you fighting for money.

HOW FASTLANERS (THE RICH) USE COMPOUND INTEREST

While examining the Slowlane, I impugned "compound interest" as an impotent wealth accelerator because of its attachment to time. When the Slowlane media bootlickers read that assertion I'll be crucified. Lambasting compound interest is the pinnacle of financial blasphemy. But I also exclaimed it to be a powerful passive income generator when leveraged against large sums of money. Contradictory?

Just like education, Fastlaners and Slowlaners leverage compound interest differently. Slowlaners (the middle-class) use compound interest to get wealthy while

Fastlaners (the rich) use it to create income and liquidity. Slowlaners start with $5; Fastlaners start with $5 million.

Compound interest pays me a lot of money. It's a tool I use. It's a great passive income source. *Yet, compound interest is not responsible for my wealth.* This is critical. Fastlaners aren't using compound interest to build wealth, because it's not in their wealth equation. The heavy lifting of wealth creation is left to their Fastlane business.

When a rich politician or public figure discloses his finances, notice the common themes. Their wealth comes from business interests, while liquid cash reserves are tied into fixed-income securities like municipal bonds, treasuries, and other highly liquid investments. The rich aren't using the markets to create wealth; *they're increasing their existing wealth with leveraged business assets.* Remember, that 25-year-old multimillionaire who got rich investing in indexed-funds is a fairy tale. The millionaires are the guys running the funds! They're the producers!

HOW TO REALLY USE COMPOUND INTEREST

Would you rather have $5 million right now, or a penny doubled every day for forty days? No-brainer, right? You'd take the $5 million bucks. But that would be a serious mistake. Accept $5 million now and you forsake nearly $5,500,000,000. That's $5.5 BILLION dollars. The chart below demonstrates the force of doubling.

One Penny Doubled

Days	Amount	Days	Amount
1	.01	21	10,485.76
2	.02	22	20,971.52
3	.04	23	41,943.04
4	.08	24	83,886.08
5	.16	25	167,772.16
6	.32	26	335,544.32
7	.64	27	671,088.64
8	1.28	28	1,342,177.28
9	2.56	29	2,684,354.56
10	5.12	30	5,368,709.12
11	10.24	31	10,737,418.24
12	20.48	32	21,474,836.48
13	40.96	33	42,949,672.96
14	81.92	34	85,899,345.92
15	163.84	35	171,798,691.84
16	327.68	36	343,597,383.68
17	655.36	37	687,194,767.36
18	1,310.72	38	1,374,389,534.72
19	2,621.44	39	2,748,779,069.44
20	5,242.88	40	5,497,558,138.88

Now transform the previous chart and replace the days with YEARS. Make day-one a person—you—at 21 years old.

One Penny Doubled

Years	Amount	Years	Amount
Age 21	.01	Age 41	10,485.76
Age 22	.02	Age 42	20,971.52
Age 23	.04	Age 43	41,943.04
Age 24	.08	Age 44	83,886.08
Age 25	.16	Age 45	167,772.16
Age 26	.32	Age 46	335,544.32
Age 27	.64	Age 47	671,088.64
Age 28	1.28	Age 48	1,342,177.28
Age 29	2.56	Age 49	2,684,354.56
Age 30	5.12	Age 50	5,368,709.12
Age 31	10.24	Age 51	10,737,418.24
Age 32	20.48	Age 52	21,474,836.48
Age 33	40.96	Age 53	42,949,672.96
Age 34	81.92	Age 54	85,899,345.92
Age 35	163.84	Age 55	171,798,691.84
Age 36	327.68	Age 56	343,597,383.68
Age 37	655.36	Age 57	687,194,767.36
Age 38	1,310.72	Age 58	1,374,389,534.72
Age 39	2,621.44	Age 59	2,748,779,069.44
Age 40	5,242.88	Age 60	5,497,558,138.88

The transformed chart is indicative of a Slowlaner's journey where compound interest doesn't enforce power until most of life has evaporated. Big money doesn't hit until your fifties and sixties, and this is with 100% returns year after year. Average market returns would be 7%. Yet at a doubling, at age 40 you have barely six grand. Again, this is the Slowlaner's predicament: Imprisoned in time and uncontrollable yield.

Fastlaners understand this weakness and realize that the compound interest weapon is most effective with large sums of money. For compound interest to be effective, you must bypass 30 years of mathematical ineptitude by riding the crest where it is effective.

THE TIDAL WAVE OF COMPOUND INTEREST

Like a tidal wave far out to sea, compound interest's strength isn't visible until it moves near land. As the wave approaches land, its force becomes incredibly powerful.

Most Slowlaners ride the compound interest tidal wave a million miles out at sea. And guess what—nothing happens. They float aimlessly, going nowhere. Ten percent interest on $5,000 doesn't make millionaires. Saving $200 a month from your paycheck in a 3% savings account isn't going to make you rich fast. You simply can't ride a wave miles out at sea.

One Penny Doubled

Can You Bypass 30 Years and Start Here?

Years	Amount	Years	Amount
Age 21	.01	Age 41	10,485.76
Age 22	.02	Age 42	20,971.52
Age 23	.04	Age 43	41,943.04
Age 24	.08	Age 44	83,886.08
Age 25	.16	Age 45	167,772.16
Age 26	.32	Age 46	335,544.32
Age 27	.64	Age 47	671,088.64
Age 28	1.28	Age 48	1,342,177.28
Age 29	2.56	Age 49	2,684,354.56
Age 30	5.12	Age 50	5,368,709.12
Age 31	10.24	Age 51	10,737,418.24
Age 32	20.48	Age 52	21,474,836.48
Age 33	40.96	Age 53	42,949,672.96
Age 34	81.92	Age 54	85,899,345.92
Age 35	163.84	Age 55	171,798,691.84
Age 36	327.68	Age 56	343,597,383.68
Age 37	655.36	Age 57	687,194,767.36
Age 38	1,310.72	Age 58	1,374,389,534.72
Age 39	2,621.44	Age 59	2,748,779,069.44
Age 40	5,242.88	Age 60	5,497,558,138.88

The Fastlaner observes the tidal forces near land and seeks to meet it at the shore. At the shore, the tidal wave can be ridden with impact.

To activate compound interest's power, start at the shore, with a large number that can be leveraged. Ten percent interest on $10 million is $1 million a year—$83,333 every single month.

The point of this illustration is to show that the rich aren't using compound interest to get wealthy; they're using it for income, liquidity, and capital deployment.

A 5% tax-free yield on $10 million suddenly creates a $500,000 per year passive income.

Like a tidal wave at the seashore, compound interest rears excruciating force when pitted against large sums of money. This is where money transforms into a fully passive income stream.

As for earning your $10 million (or more), that solution lies in exponential leveraged growth stemming from a Fastlane business—net income plus asset value—NOT in expenses, NOT in the stock market, and NOT in a job.

CHAPTER SUMMARY: FASTLANE DISTINCTIONS

- One saved dollar is the seed to a money tree.
- A mere 5% interest on $10 million dollars is $40,000 a month in passive income.
- A saved dollar is the best passive income instrument.
- Fastlaners (the rich) don't use compound interest or the markets to get wealthy but to create income, preserve liquidity, and deploy capital.
- A saved dollar is a freedom fighter added to your army.
- The rich leverage compound interest at its crest, applied against large sums of money.
- Fastlaners eventually become net lenders.

The Real Law of Wealth

Try not to become a man of success, but a man of value.

~ ALBERT EINSTEIN

EFFECTION, NOT ATTRACTION

The Law of Effection. Nope, not a misprint. Mathematics is the transcendent language of the universe. It cannot be controverted or debated. Two plus two equals four. The number 10 million will always be greater than 24. These statements are facts and not subject to interpretation by some mystical theory of philosophy.

Math is law.

"Secrets" and mystical philosophies are not.

If you want to get rich, start observing the true law of the universe—MATH—and not some hocus-pocus law that can neither be proved nor documented. Singing positive platitudes around the campfire isn't going to make you rich. Oh, don't get your panties in a wad; I know the Law of Attraction sounds great and has practical applications.

For those not familiar with The Law of Attraction ("LOA"), it's a mystical philosophy that states you become what you think and that your conscious and unconscious thoughts make your reality. The LOA contends that if you know exactly what you want, ask the universe for it, see it coming, then you will eventually receive it. Think riches and you will have riches! Sounds easy, huh?

I won't hide my candid sacrilege to the LOA crowd; I think it's a bunch of baloney orchestrated to sell books to those who think "thinking" will make you rich. In fact, the LOA is nothing but old principles of belief and visualization repackaged and remarketed for mass consumption. Who are the true Fastlaners? The LOA marketers!

BAKE A CAKE WITHOUT SUGAR?

Why did this book take me so long to write? I spent two years wishing and thinking positively about it. I let the Law of Attraction do the work. I asked the universe for this book. I was open to it. I saw it before my eyes. I even snapped a picture of a bookstore shelf and Photoshopped my book on the shelf. What happened?

Absolutely nothing. Nada. Zilch.

The universe never gave me my finished book. The fact is, despite all my positive thinking and meditations to the universe for my book, it never materialized until I sat my butt down in a chair and started to write it. I made a coordinated commitment to ACTION, a conscious choice, and then a commitment to that choice in the form of massive action.

If you're a Law of Attraction fan and find this critique offensive, that's OK; I didn't write *The Millionaire Fastlane* to make friends or to book speaking engagements about being a positive thinker. I wrote it to tell you exactly what you need to do to set yourself free. Thinking never made anyone free (or rich), unless that thinking manifests itself into consistent action toward application of laws that work.

In fact, I find it insulting that someone might assume my success is due to positive thinking. I'm a realist who understands human nature, and that nature is to take the path of least resistance. It doesn't surprise me that these "attraction" books sell millions. The books that promise the easiest roads to wealth do well because, like sex, easiness sells.

Events of wealth sell. Process does not.

Yes, positivity is favored over cynicism. Belief is the starting point to change. Visualization is crucial. Yes, if you don't believe you can do it, I've got news for you—you can't. This stuff isn't new, it's OLD. While The Law of Attraction is a nice hammer in the toolbox, its flaw is that it ignores the real secret that transcends all wealth, all people, all cultures, and all roads—and that is the Law of Effection.

The "Flaw of Attraction" is that it ignores mathematics.

THE LAW OF EFFECTION: THE FASTLANE PRIMER

The Law of Effection states that *the more lives you affect in an entity you control, in scale and/or magnitude, the richer you will become*. The shortened, sanitized version is simply: Affect millions and make millions. (Grammarians, I can hear you screaming. Relax. I know the difference between "affect" and "effect." I'm using "effection" as it appears in *Webster's Revised Unabridged Dictionary*, published in 1913 by C. & G. Merriam Co., as a noun meaning "creation; a doing.")

A while ago, I wrote an article titled *The Shortest "Make Millions" Article Ever Written*. Guess how long the article was? A paragraph? Maybe a sentence or two? Nope. Just two words. And those words?

Impact millions.

Impact millions and make millions. It doesn't get any simpler than that!

In other words, how many lives have you touched? Who has benefited from your work, your assets, and your handiwork? What problems have you solved? What value are you to society? If you're working the front desk at a hotel, you simply aren't making much of an impact, and your bank account will represent that same fact. The amount of money you have (or don't have) is a direct reflection on the amount of value you have provided (or not provided).

EFFECTION IS SCALE, MAGNITUDE, OR BOTH

To exploit the Law of Effection, your business needs to make an impact of either scale or magnitude, or both. Within our Fastlane wealth equation, "scale" and "magnitude" are implicit to our "net profit" variable.

NET PROFIT = Units Sold (Scale) × Unit Profit (Magnitude)

An example of SCALE is reflected on our Fastlane roadmap via the profit variable in our wealth equation: units sold. If you sell 20 million pens and make 75 cents profit on each, you just earned $15 million. This is having an impact on SCALE with tiny MAGNITUDE. Obviously, selling a writing pen doesn't have a major impact on anyone's life. The wealth is transmuted via SCALE, not magnitude.

Conversely, magnitude is having a great impact on a few and within our Fastlane wealth equation is reflected in UNIT PROFIT. Price always reflects magnitude. If you sell a product that's worth $50 million, you have access to magnitude. For example, if you owned an apartment complex with 400 units and profit $100 from each unit, you'd generate $40,000 in monthly income. Because you are providing housing for 400 families, you are making an impact of magnitude, not scale. Shelter has magnitude. Activities of magnitude have higher profit potential with smaller scales. Magnitude is always reflected by an item's price. High value = high price = high magnitude.

If you can combine both scale and magnitude, we won't be discussing millions but billions. Steve Jobs made an impact on both magnitude and scale and therefore died worth billions.

Scale creates millionaires. Magnitude creates millionaires. Scale and magnitude creates billionaires.

FOLLOW THE MONEY!

Unfortunately, the word "law" is loosely tossed around to represent concepts that aren't really laws. The Law of Attraction isn't a law but a theory. The word "law" is absolute. It works 100% of the time. When you drop a watermelon from your tenth-floor dorm window, the Law of Gravity takes over—the watermelon falls to the ground every single time. The outcome is a 100% certainty.

Unfortunately, positive thinking and visualization don't work with 100% certainty. Belief and manifestation aren't absolute so they can't be classified as laws. However, the Law of Effection is absolute.

Show me any self-made billionaire and I will show you a person who has touched the lives of many in scale or magnitude, directly or indirectly. To Woodward and Bernstein, Deep Throat said, "Follow the money," and when you do, you find the only one true law of wealth, and that is Effection. Why? Because Effection is rooted in mathematics, and because of this it operates exclusive of any roadmap.

A Slowlaner can use the Law of Effection to escape Slowlane confinement. Pro athletes, actors, and entertainers—intrinsic value explosions happen because of the effection: Society suddenly perceives your value to be meteoric. Yes, these people are still trading their time for money, but in an unprecedented stratum of value.

For example, if you're a comedian and make millions laugh, you undoubtedly will make millions. While you might still be trading your time for money, you're trading it at a profound level of compensation. *If you entertain millions, you will be paid millions.*

A rapper sells millions of songs and is paid millions. A housewife sells a million kitchen gadgets and earns millions. A lottery winner wins millions because millions entered the drawing. Daddy Warbuck's son inherits millions because Warbucks Company served millions. A plastic surgeon earns millions because he serves many in magnitude. A star athlete's agent earns millions because his clients serve millions. *Retrace the source of millionaire money and you will find millions of something.*

Effection of scale or magnitude always precedes money, either directly or indirectly. The more lives you impact, directly or indirectly, the more wealth you will attract.

BIG WEALTH FOLLOWS BIG NUMBERS

Athletes are a perfect example of Effection. If you play professional baseball, you're paid a meteoric intrinsic value. In 2014 Giancarlo Stanton signed a $325 million contract. How exactly is that justified? Simple. The Law of Effection justifies all wealth. Giancarlo Stanton, via baseball, entertains millions. He leverages SCALE. This is the same for any professional athlete. They get paid millions because they entertain millions. The corporate executive who facilitates a corporation that services millions gets paid millions.

Again, these are glorified power intrinsic-value positions that leverage the Law of Effection. If you want to get rich via intrinsic value, you must do it via the Law of Effection. Get into a position to impact millions. Become indispensable and irreplaceable like an athlete, entertainer, or a top-brass executive.

Can't get access to millions like an athlete?

Then go directly to the source and serve the source.

For example, agents of high-profile athletes are as rich as the athletes themselves because they have indirect contact to the Law of Effection. Real estate brokers who specialize in the homes of the rich become rich themselves because they indirectly connect themselves to arbiters of the Law.

The Law of Effection doesn't care about roadmaps or time trades or anything but the mathematical power of large numbers. Make a giant impact a few times or make a small impact millions of times.

Joe Magnitude owns a company that develops commercial real estate. He develops 14 office complexes and partitions the offices into condos. Each fully sold complex profits him $400,000 (magnitude) × 14 (scale) equals $5,600,000.

Joe Scale writes a book detailing a diet of the stars. He sells 800,000 copies (scale) and earns $7 per copy (magnitude). He earns the same amount: $5,600,000.

The closer you get to the source of large numbers, the closer you will get to wealth. To serve millions is to make millions.

Think big to earn big.

CHAPTER SUMMARY: FASTLANE DISTINCTIONS

- The Law of Effection states that the more lives you affect or breach, both in scale or magnitude, the richer you will be.
- Scale translates to "units sold" of our profit variable within our Fastlane wealth equation. Magnitude translates to "unit profit" of our profit variable within our Fastlane wealth equation.
- The Law of Attraction is not a law, but a theory. The Law of Effection is absolute and operates exclusive of a roadmap.
- All lineages of self-made wealth trace back to the Law of Effection.
- The Law of Effection's absoluteness comes from direct access and control (you are the athlete) versus indirect access (you are the athlete's agent).
- To make millions you must serve millions in scale or a few in magnitude.

Part 6

Your Vehicle to Wealth: YOU

Own Yourself First

Events and circumstances have their origin in ourselves.
They spring from seeds which we have sown.

~ HENRY DAVID THOREAU

THE PARALYSIS OF "PAY YOURSELF FIRST"

Fastlane success demands a well-tuned vehicle primed and prepared for the journey that awaits.

You are the vehicle to wealth.

You are impetus for action and progress.

You are responsible for the journey and the first step in taking charge of you, is to own you.

Surely you've heard "Pay yourself first," a common Slowlane declaration born from the classic 1926 book, *The Richest Man in Babylon* by George Clason. A good read, but fundamentally flawed.

If you aren't familiar with "pay yourself first," it's a Slowlane doctrine that urges you to save your money (pay yourself) before all else—food, gas, car payments, and other bills. This supposedly forces the Slowlaner's savings rate to accelerate their putrid wealth acceleration vehicle: compound interest via market investments.

The fact is, advising a Slowlaner to "pay yourself first" is like advising a quadriplegic to climb a flight of stairs. It's futile.

If you have a job, examine your last paycheck.

Is your gross pay that same as your net pay? It isn't and for some, it might be 35% less or more. Additionally, pre-tax saving weapons such as 401(k)s and IRAS severely limit your contributions to infantile amounts where creating wealth on a pre-tax basis in a job becomes organizationally penal.

If your primary income source comes from a job, your ability to pay yourself first is paralyzed because the governments are paid first! For "pay yourself first" to be legitimate, you truly need to pay yourself first in infinite amounts and the government last. *You must own your vehicle.*

TO PAY YOURSELF FIRST, YOU MUST OWN YOURSELF

You can't pay yourself first if you don't own yourself. Your vehicle (you) must be free and clear. *When you have a job, someone owns you.* And when someone owns you, you aren't paid first, but last.

The first step to controlling your vehicle—you—is to own yourself so you're paid first and the government last. That is accomplished by forming your business into a corporation that you control.

The corporation serves as the Fastlane frame because it offers the immediate tax benefit of "pay yourself first" versus "pay yourself last."

When you own a corporation, net profits are reduced by expenses. The remaining profit is taxed, and those taxes are paid to the government. Additionally, corporations exist separate from their owners and survive time. *It's the surrogate structure that serves as your business system.*

When you own a corporation, the government (assuming USA) is paid four times a year, once every quarter through estimated taxes. If you have a payroll, taxes are paid each time you pay your employees. I pay myself first 365 times a year while the government is paid four times a year. Doesn't that sound like a structure that is conducive to not only "pay yourself first" but also wealth?

HOW TO OWN YOURSELF

Like many entrepreneurs, I made the horrific mistake of getting into business as a sole proprietor. Any "adviser" who recommends a business structure as a sole proprietorship or general partnership should be avoided like an airport toilet. These entities are risky because they don't protect you and catapult unlimited liability onto you and your personal assets.

If you're a plumber organized as a sole proprietor and you accidentally leave a pipe cutter at a client's house and the client's three-year-old kills himself with it, guess what? They're coming after you because you chose an ill-protected business entity. Instead of suing a corporation, they sue you and everything you own is up for grabs. Assuming a US-based business, the best business structures for your Fastlane business are:

1) C corporation
2) S corporation
3) Limited liability corporation

Each has its advantages and disadvantages, but all share two common benefits: limitation of liability and tax efficiency.

The C Corporation

The C corporation is a business structure that survives time and can be easily transferred. Corporate profits are taxed at corporate income tax rates, with net income distributed to shareholders.

Some C-corp owners use this structure to deploy a strategy known as "income splitting." The strategy is to partition the business's income to both the owner and the business, effectively lowering the tax bracket of the two, versus a large income for just one. While it's not within the scope of this book to dive into tax strategy and corporate formation, it does offer up a Fastlane component, which is control.

While C corporations and their owners are subject to double taxation (tax on corporate profits and dividends to shareholders), they are advantageous for larger corporations and corporations with an "asset growth" strategy. In other words, if you don't plan on distributing profits and are focused on building "asset value" over "net profit," C corporations do the job. The majority of publicly traded companies are C corps that do not distribute dividends to their shareholders. They grow revenue and asset value.

The S Corporation

An S corporation is like a C corporation except that it isn't taxed as a separate entity. Considered a "pass-through" entity, taxes aren't paid at the corporate level, but at the individual level and reflected on the owner's personal tax return. S corporations also have some tax advantages because profits are not subject to the hefty self-employment tax that comes with sole proprietorships. However, unlike C corporations, which can have limitless owners, S corporations are limited to 100 owners and will have additional filing requirements.

The Limited Liability Corp (LLC)

An LLC operates just like a corporation with the benefits of a partnership or a sole proprietorship. LLC profit passes through to its owners, called members, and is reflected on their personal income tax. LLCs are also considered "pass-through" entities because profit passes directly to the owners. For partnerships, the LLC or the S corp is the recommended structure in lieu of a general partnership, which, again, does not offer liability protection.

For small startups, I recommend looking into either an LLC or an S corp. Personally, I steer clear from partnerships and sole-proprietorships, as they might not limit liability.

Creating a corporation is not as daunting as it seems. Depending on your state, it shouldn't cost more than $1,000. In Arizona, one can be created for less than a few hundred dollars.

SELECTING AN ENTITY

Selecting an entity depends on your goals and your vision for your business. Here are some general questions to help you decide.

- What is your exit strategy? Go public? Sell to private investors?
- What is your growth strategy?
- What is your liability exposure in the worst case?
- Do you plan on raising capital now, or in the future?
- Do you plan to hire employees?
- Do you plan to take on new partners?
- Do you plan on earning profits fast? Or not for a while?

Your answers determine the best entity. In my businesses, I use a variety of structures from S corps to LLCs to trusts.

And finally, I'm not an accountant or an attorney so please don't construe this as legal or professional advice. Always consult someone who has the appropriate up-to-date credentials to determine what is best for you. Laws, economies, taxes, and regulations are always changing, year to year, country to country.

CHAPTER SUMMARY: FASTLANE DISTINCTIONS

- "Pay yourself first" is fundamentally impossible in a job.
- To own your vehicle (you), start a corporation that formally divorces you from the act of business. Your corporation is the body of your surrogate.
- The recommended Fastlane business entity is a C corp, an S corp, or an LLC.

Life's Steering Wheel

Your life is the sum result of all the choices you make,
both consciously and unconsciously.
If you can control the process of choosing,
you can take control of all aspects of your life.
You can find the freedom that comes from being in charge of yourself.

~ ROBERT F. BENNETT

THE LEADING CAUSE OF POORNESS

If poorness were an illness, take a guess as to its cause. Of course, lack of money. But is that a cause or a symptom of the underlying problem?

Lack of education?

Lack of opportunity, positive role models, or determination?

Nope. Those are all symptoms.

If you retrace poverty's footprints you will find that poorness starts at the exact same place: *choice.*

The leading cause of poorness is poor choices.

THE HEART OF THE PROBLEM

As my income elevated, so did my cholesterol. The road of good living runs parallel to a cliff of gluttony. My doctor's preferred method of attack was prescription drugs. I refused because I wanted to fix problems, not mask symptoms.

If you approach wealth like a big pharmaceutical company and attack symptoms while neglecting problems, you will not succeed. Feeling tired? Take this pill. Want to lose weight? Another pill. The problems are ignored while the symptoms are addressed in catatonic cycles. I refused cholesterol medication because it addressed the symptom, not the problem. *The problem is poor diet; cholesterol is the symptom.*

If your car's fuel tank had a small leak, how would you fix it? The symptomatic solver would increase his trips to the gas station to ensure a steady inflow of fuel. The problematic solver plugs up the hole. One addresses the symptom (the gas tank leaks), while the other addresses the problem (there's a hole in the gas tank). While adding fuel addresses the symptom, it doesn't solve the problem. When the behavior stops the problem remains.

How does this relate to success and choices?

Simple: *If you aren't where you want to be, the problem is your choices.*

Your circumstances are the symptoms of those choices. For example, everyone loves success quotes. Here are two:

- *The will to persevere is often the difference between failure and success.*
- *Success means having the courage, the determination, and the will to become the person you believe you were meant to be.*

The problem with these quotes is they're asymptomatic. They're ambiguous to the real issue, and that is choice.

The first quote deals with perseverance. How do you persevere? You react from conscious choice. Not just one choice but hundreds, perhaps thousands. You cannot choose to persevere with one choice. You cannot wake up one day and say, "Oh, today I will choose to persevere." It must happen everyday, not just once! Perseverance is woven by many choices that fabricate lifestyle. If you quit after two tries, have you persevered? Can you claim perseverance after one failure?

Likewise, the second quote suffers from the same conundrum. Determination is not a solitary choice but thousands of them. You cannot decide to be determined; it must occur repeatedly, concertedly, and with commitment. The point of this rant is that Fastlane isn't something you *try,* it's something you *live.*

It isn't one choice but hundreds. And when you line a string of choices together, they create your process, and your process will create your lifestyle. Lifestyle choices will make you a millionaire.

YOUR LIFE'S STEERING WHEEL

Your choices spark the fires of future circumstances. The fabric of your life is sewn by the cumulative consequences of your choices—millions of them—that you set into motion. You act, react, believe, disbelieve, perceive, misperceive, and all of it engineers your existence. If you're dissatisfied with life, your choices take full responsibility. Blame yourself and the choices you've made.

Yes, you are as you have chosen.

It took me 26 years of life and a blizzard to grasp the horsepower of my choices. The blizzard impeded my limousine, but I was there because I chose it.

I chose to get the job.

I chose to pursue low-rent businesses.

I chose to continue life in Chicago.

I chose to avoid corporate after college.

I chose my friends.

I chose my business pursuits.

I chose all of it, and it engineered my life to that exact moment. I awoke to the epiphany that *I was the driver of my life* and my problems were the consequences of my choices. I steered myself there!

Wherever you are: reading on the train, on a plane, on the toilet in a run-down apartment, or on a beach in the Caribbean, you've chosen. I didn't force you to pick up this book and read it. You chose to. Yes, *you are exactly where you decide to be.* And if that's unhappiness, you need to start making better choices.

CHOOSE TO BE WEALTHY OR CHOOSE TO BE POOR

There's a big chasm between thinking wealth and choosing wealth. You can choose the Sidewalk, the Slowlane, or the Fastlane. You can choose to align your life with greater purpose, or choose to let life live you. You can choose to believe these theories or choose not to. The common denominator is CHOICE and YOU.

Your steering wheel (choice) is the most powerful control you have in your life. Why do I hate the Slowlane? Because it denies choice and gives it to someone else—the company, the boss, Wall Street, the economy, and a bunch of others.

People don't choose to be poor. They make poor decisions that slowly assemble into a poorness puzzle. Retrace the footprints to poverty and it happens slowly, systematically, and methodically, under a steady diet of poor choices.

- The choice to cheat on your exams or study.
- The choice to squander college because your parents paid for it.
- The choice to lie or to be honest.
- The choice to drive without insurance.
- The choice to befriend bad people over good people.
- The choice to watch TV or read a book.
- The choice to drive 105 mph in a 55 mph zone.
- The choice to rob the corner convenience store.
- The choice to overindulge in food or liquor.
- The choice to believe in people with no track record.
- The choice to cheat on your significant other.
- The choice to buy on credit.
- The choice to "try" crystal meth one weekend.
- The choice to hire a contractor without a background check.
- The choice to play video games 30 hours a week.
- The choice to get married after four weeks of dating.
- The choice to go into business with incompetent partners.

THE ROAD TO TREASON IS ALWAYS OPEN

I always loved a good street race. Having owned a variety of juiced-up Vipers, confrontation was standard. One summer evening after a few drinks, I let my ego take over and I street raced. I over-throttled, spun out of control, crossed into oncoming traffic, and crashed into a palm tree. By the time it was over the new occupant of the Viper's passenger seat was the trunk of a 30-foot date palm. I was arrested, taken to jail, and charged with DUI and reckless endangerment.

Luckily, I didn't kill anyone or myself. In fact, the arresting officer (who witnessed the entire race—brilliant, eh?) stated that had the impact been driver-side versus passenger-side, I would have been killed. I survived a life-or-death coin flip.

In reflection, my choice to race was a *treasonous choice.*

Treasonous choices are actions that do irreparable harm to your life, your dreams, and your goals. The consequences of treasonous choices throw life onto unintended detours and hazardous roads that are difficult to escape and often times, permanent.

Had I killed someone, I would have spent years in jail, spent half my fortune on lawyers, and had to live with the painful reality that I stole someone's life. Life would have instantly transformed, with new circumstances unveiled. No amount of money can keep you from prison or purge your soul from the foolish horror of taking someone's life. Treasonous choices change your life forever.

> *Jack finances his dream home and takes an $800K mortgage although he only makes $65K/year. Due to loose credit and an exploding housing market, he accepts the loan. He doesn't read the documents and assumes his mortgage lender has his best interests. Eighteen months later, his interest rate adjusts higher and he can't afford the mortgage, forcing him into foreclosure. His poor credit haunts him for 12 years. He can't qualify for a new mortgage and potential business opportunities go untapped.*

> *A Fastlane millionaire by age 28, Andre has everything: money, a beautiful wife, a healthy baby, and seven restaurants scattered across the Five Boroughs. Andre is on top of the world and feels invincible. One Friday night after a few drinks to celebrate his night manager's birthday, Andre drives home sloppy drunk. He chooses to think, "I'm OK." On his way home he gets into an accident and kills a family of four. Andre is arrested for drunk driving and charged with manslaughter. After his conviction he spends the next 11 years of his life in prison. He loses his businesses and his family.*

Andre's life forever changed because of multiple treasonous choices. The choice to drink. The choice to drive. The choice to think, "I'm OK." The series of choices is plentiful, his exit strategy is clear. He doesn't choose wisely.

Events from the sports pages always seem to illustrate the gravity of treason. Football player Michael Vick partook in criminal activity and it reshaped his life. His legacy (if you call it that) will never be the same. He lost respectability and two years of his life. He made multiple choices that started with the choice to commiserate with criminal derelicts.

Another NFL football player made a choice and it cost him his life. You'd never think that cheating on your wife could end so tragically. It did for Steve McNair when his mistress allegedly shot him to death in a Nashville, Tennessee, condo. While he didn't choose to be murdered, he chose to pursue the woman. He chose the relationship. He chose to cheat. He chose to act. You see, we aren't just talking about ONE choice here but many that make him complicit to the treason. His choices loaded the gun but someone else pulled the trigger.

More recently, a number of high profile men (Cosby, Weinstein, Lauer) decided that inappropriate (and perhaps criminal) actions toward women in a presumptive exchange for career favors would be "OK" choices. These choices were not acute, but chronic. And their treason caught up with them.

Your life's steering wheel is a dangerous weapon. Three inches is all it takes. Jerk your life's wheel three tiny inches while speeding and you can steer your life onto a path of no return, or worse, smack into a concrete wall. Like an automobile's steering wheel, your choices are super-sensitive. Unfortunately, treasonous roads always have a green light. People drown in the misery of their own choices while neglecting to acknowledge they are the cause.

WHAT'S CHOSEN TODAY, IMPACTS FOREVER

You'll see.

"You'll see" is my mother's code for "I'm right, you're wrong, and time will uncover that truth."

As a rebellious teen, Mother lobbed a "you'll see" at me after she surrendered to my pleadings for an off-road motorcycle. Mother didn't like the idea and levied her missive "you'll see." It didn't take long for that "you'll see" to come true. Full of testosterone, cocky, and invincible, a 15-year-old kid with no motorcycle experience gambled with his life. I crashed on a dirt road going 50 miles per hour and broke my wrist and two fingers, lost nerves in my knee, and screwed up my neck.

While the bones healed, the full array of consequences from that day has not dissipated.

Decades later I live with chronic neck pain and have to sleep in unorthodox positions to avoid discomfort. I've spent countless hours and money on physical therapy and chiropractic treatments. Many times I fantasize about going back in time to that day and bitch-slapping that arrogant kid—I wish I could tell him how things are; I wish I could have him read this chapter; I wish he would understand the trajectory, the *horsepower*, of his choices.

Our choices have consequences that transcend decades. This transcendence is HORSEPOWER. Every day my discomfort reminds me of that fateful day when I chose poorly. And today, I'm still paying the mortgage of that choice, a mortgage that never amortizes.

THE BUTTERFLY EFFECT

Can you make a choice this instant that can forever alter the trajectory of your future? You can, and it can be the difference between poverty and wealth.

When you make minor permutations (choices) that deviate from your initial conditions, profound effects transpire over time.

Think of it like a golf club striking a golf ball.

When the clubface hits the ball square, the ball goes straight and heads toward the hole. But when the clubface is rotated a fraction of one degree, the ball's trajectory lands far off course. At impact, the divergence is minor, but as the ball travels further it widens and widens until the gap is so large that getting back on track is nearly impossible. A bad choice can set your trajectory off by only one degree today, but over years the error is magnified.

Choices have this type of divergence over time and it's called "impact differential." When your choices are extrapolated throughout the years, the divergence widens. The divergence can be either positive or negative. For example, when I moved to Phoenix from Chicago, the "impact differential" exploded as time passed. Had I not made this choice my life would be significantly different. I also chose to get a dead-end job as a limo driver, which opened my eyes to a business need. That too was a choice that had extraordinary horsepower and created positive "impact differential."

The 2003 movie *The Butterfly Effect* starring Ashton Kutcher is great film that excellently illustrates choice horsepower. In the movie, the main characters engage in treasonous choices as youngsters, and you witness how each life unfolds as those treasonous choices permeate through time. You see the impact differential!

Recognize that every day you make decisions that will ripple through the years. Question is, will your choice ripple to happiness and wealth? Or depression and poverty?

THE EROSION OF HORSEPOWER

Your choices have significant trajectory into the future, and the younger you are, the more horsepower they exude. Unfortunately, horsepower fades with age.

If this is confusing, think about it in terms of an asteroid that is on a collision course with Earth. When an asteroid is millions of miles out in space (representing your youthful choices) a simple one-degree change in trajectory will save the Earth from destruction. This is the power of horsepower. For us older folks, the asteroid is closer to Earth (and closer to our death), which weakens the potency of our choices. A one-degree change isn't as effective, and for the same potency, it needs to be 10 degrees.

When you are under 25 you have maximum horsepower and your choices discharge an incredible amount of firepower. A simple choice I made more than 20 years ago is still felt today. That's a lot of torque!

If you reflect on your choices, you make them in an instant, yet their consequences transcend a lifetime, especially ones made early in life.

Your life's choices are like a mature oak tree with millions of branches. The branches symbolize the consequences of your choices. Near the trunk of the tree, the branches are thick, reflecting the decisions you've made early in life, while the top branches are thin, symbolizing decisions near the end of your life.

Youthful choices radiate the most strength and fabricate the trunk of your tree. As the branches ascend topside through time, they get thinner and weaker. They don't have enough power to bend the tree in new directions because the trunk is thick with age, experience, and reinforced habits.

My motorcycle crash had significant horsepower because I feel it today. If you are unmarried with five kids by age 23, where do you think the branches of your choice tree will lead? How thick and unbendable is your choice tree? If you skip classes and are drunk for four years in college, how will that ripple through your choice tree? If your best friend is dealing heroin, where will that branch lead?

At age 16, for a school prank, David ignites a smoke bomb in the school bus, and 14 children suffer smoke inhalation. Fortunately, those children recovered quickly, but David's 10-day stay in juvenile detention forever thrusts David's life down a different path. David meets Rudy, who teaches David the "rules" of the perfect burglary. This relationship forges David's new career choice—thievery. After avoiding the law for seven years, David is caught, convicted, and sentenced to nine years in prison.

Had David not met Rudy, where would he be? A fireman? Banker? Choice and its horsepower transcend.

At age 17 and against her parents' wishes, Alyssa, an honor student, leaves home to live with a 31-year-old man she met at the local bar four months earlier. Her boyfriend introduces her to crystal meth, and what initially started as a funny experiment becomes a life-consuming addiction. Alyssa resorts to illegal activities to support her habit, including stealing from her parents. Her reckoning occurs when she is caught at the local mall stealing and sentenced to three years in jail and state-mandated rehabilitation.

Had Alyssa listened to her parents, where would she be today?

Choice and its horsepower transcend.

The smallest choices made in your daily life create habits and lifestyle that forms process—they are the ones that can make the biggest impact.

You can't decide to "go Fastlane" because that itself is just an event.

A Fastlane process is hundreds of choices.

Regardless of age, reflect on your life and analyze the forks in the road and where those forks have taken you. The forks are choices, both large and small, and each shares the common thread of having the magnificent power to take you somewhere different. Whatever you decide today impacts tomorrow, weeks, months, years, decades, and yes, generations.

If you're younger than 30, your choices are at peak horsepower because they are growing the thick branches of your choice tree.

Time to put the pedal to the metal!

CHAPTER SUMMARY: FASTLANE DISTINCTIONS

- The leading cause of poorness is poor choices.
- The steering wheel of your life is your choices.
- You are exactly where you chose to be.
- Success is hundreds of choices that form process. Process forms lifestyle.
- Choice is the most powerful control you have in your life.
- Treasonous choices forever impact your life negatively.
- Your choices have significant horsepower, or trajectory into the future.
- The younger you are, the more potent your choices are and the more horsepower you possess.
- Over time, horsepower erodes as the consequences of old choices are thick and hard to bend.

Wipe Your Windshield Clean

Until we see what we are,
we cannot take steps to become what we should be.

~ CHARLOTTE P. GILMAN

WIPE YOUR WINDSHIELD CLEAN

While pumping gas into my Lamborghini, a teenager once asked me if he could snap some pictures. "Sure, go ahead!" I replied. After a few rants and raves about the car, he exclaimed, "I gotta get as many pictures as possible cuz I'll never be able to afford one of these."

See a problem in that conclusion? This young man made a choice to believe he would *never* own a Lamborghini. He couldn't see beyond his own windshield. Is this a small choice? A treasonous choice? A choice of significant horsepower?

This seemingly innocent choice of perception has the excruciating horsepower of treason. It is a crippler of dreams.

The teen's choice of perception was poor, and because of it, it would forever lead him to mediocre results. His jury had already deliberated, and the verdict was in: An extravagant car would be always "out of his league," and therefore, his choices would reflect that mindset. Unfortunately, he didn't understand the debilitating effect of being clouded to our own self-constructed windshield into the world.

THE CHOICE OF PERCEPTION

In the last chapter, we discussed choices and their impact on your life. Thus far it's been all about choices of action—physical actions that produce consequences. However, if you look deeper, what causes those actions? What motivates you to act and choose? We have two types of choices:

1) Choices of perception (thought patterns)
2) Choices of action (choosing to read)

Choices of perception precede choices of action. If you believe and perceive a certain idea, you are likely to act on that belief. The difference between the teen at the gas station and me was this: When I witnessed my first Lamborghini as a kid, I thought, "Some day, I'm gonna own one of those!" My choice of perception was strong and manifested into choices of action that reflected that perception.

You see, you choose to interpret events in your particular frame of reference. Your mind labels and categorizes events that surround you. For example, when someone says "dog," you might see a black Labrador, while other people see a poodle. When you see a mansion on the beach, do you think "lucky?" or "I'll never own something like that?" The first step in making better choices starts with your choice of perception, because your actions evolve from those perceptions.

If you lose your job, you can frame it as a negative or a positive. When you're caught speeding, you can be angry or thankful. The choice of perception and its choices start right between your ears and drive themselves into choices of action.

YOUR PERCEPTION IS NOT THE REALITY

A few years ago, my girlfriend and I were at friend's home for a party. We sat at a small table and noticed an overly exuberant gentleman talking from table to table. It was as if he was canvassing the room selling something.

He was.

He eventually got to our table and unleashed the uncouth, "Hey, how would you like to earn $10,000 per month?" The question was inappropriate for the party so I decided to respond with equal inappropriateness.

I asked, "$10,000 a month? Really?" Thinking I was hooked, he tried to sell me a network marketing opportunity for some herbal supplement. I interrupted him and laughed "Listen, I make $10,000 every two days, so for me your opportunity would be a 90% pay cut. Do you think I'm interested?" His eyes popped out of their sockets, and after he picked them off the table, he scampered away like a rat without his cheese.

In this brief exchange, this man made an assumption: $10,000 a month is a lot of money! It isn't. Money is infinite. Fastlane opportunists can drive opportunities that yield six and seven figures monthly. *The difference is perception.*

I remember the day when I thought $10,000 was a lot of money. It was perception and not reality. Earning $1 million in one month is possible if you make the right choices and drive the right Fastlane roads. This perception leads to better choices of action. That guy at the party? He chose a crowded road. Instead of creating a multilevel marketing company, he joined one.

Instead of serving the masses through Effection, he joined the masses.

WIPING THE WINDSHIELD CLEAN STARTS WITH LANGUAGE

You can expose your mindset by examining the words in your language and your thoughts. Take for example this comment made on the Fastlane Forum:

> *"I got engaged last Friday! I had been struggling with this for some time but decided to give marriage one more try. She's a great girl and deserves the best, and I think I can give it to her."*

When you read this statement do you see assured success? Or pending failure? While I wish the man the best marriage, I see flaccid words that lack confidence: "Try," "I think." This language spells trouble. What would have convinced me otherwise?

> *"I got engaged last Friday! I had been struggling with this for some time but I decided to get married for the last time. She's a great girl and deserves the best, and I will give it to her."*

Notice the difference. One is flimsy and the other is firm. Both might seem to say the same thing, but one implies possible failure while the other implies committed success. Your internal language carries weight. If a brain surgeon told you before surgery, "I'm think I can operate on you and I will try to succeed," you should freak out and trade in your hospital gown for some eternal nighties.

Altering your words and thought perceptions are akin to wiping your windshield clean and seeing beyond your bubble. How do you manage your choice of perception? What language do you use in your mind? "I never ... I can't . . . If only . . ." Or do you choose better words? "It's possible . . . I'll overcome . . . I will . . . I can."

If your world is canvassed with words like "never" and "can't," guess what? It's true—you can't and you never will!

Is it possible to earn $1 million in one month? Sure it is, just ask the guy who does it. What makes his windshield different from yours? Good choices of perception translate into good choices of action. To change your perception is to change your future actions.

The goal of this book is to change your perception about wealth and money. Believe that retirement at any age is possible. Believe that old age is not a prerequisite to wealth. Believe that a job is just as risky as a business. Believe that the stock market isn't a guaranteed path to riches. Believe that you can be retired just a few years from today.

So how do you upload new beliefs and overwrite the old ones?

Find the information, resources, and the people that align with the new beliefs. For myself, I pursued the stories of those who acquired wealth fast and soon learned that "Get Rich Quick" wasn't a myth. I never found that 19-year-old who got rich piling money into indexed-funds. However, I did find 24-year-old millionaire inventors, business founders, authors, and website owners.

If you want extraordinary results, you're going to need extraordinary thinking. Unfortunately, "extraordinary" is not found trapped in society's mediocracy and the beliefs that fuel them.

STEERING TIPS: BETTER CHOICES AND A BETTER LIFE

As your journey progresses, respect yourself and ask, is this a good choice of perception? A good choice of action? Is this going to be treasonous to my dreams and cloud my windshield to a better life? Have I chosen to be a victim or a victor? Have I accepted challenge or surrendered?

Changing your life starts with changing choices. The Fastlane vehicle to wealth is driven on choice, not asphalt. You start making better choices using two strategies dependent on the decision's gravity.

1) **Worse Case Consequence Analysis (WCCA)**
2) **Weighted Average Decision Matrix (WADM)**

WCCA is designed to steer you away from perilous detours and treasonous choices. Conversely, WADM is designed to help you make better big decisions with multiple contingencies. This dual-pronged attack works on the choice extremes: a prevention of disastrous choices and a facilitator of good choices.

WORSE CASE CONSEQUENCE ANALYSIS (WCCA)

The first decision tool is Worst Case Consequence Analysis (WCCA), which requires you to become forward-thinking and an analyzer of potential consequences. WCCA asks you to answer three questions about every decision of consequence:

1) What is the worst-case consequence of this choice?
2) What is the probability of this outcome?
3) Is this an acceptable risk?

While these three questions might seem lengthy, your analysis process shouldn't take longer than a few seconds. You don't need a pen or paper, just your head and a conscious choice of perception. When choices are analyzed using WCCA, potential disasters are exposed and alternatives chosen. Treasonous roads can be avoided.

I use WCCA extensively. For example, several years ago, after several drinks at a local bar, I went home with a woman who was making the moves and wanted to get busy. She pulled the old Harlequin whisper, "Make love to me." Of course, having known her for all of two hours, I knew this wasn't love but something else.

Behind my drunken passion, I ran through my WCCA analysis. What is the worse case outcome of this choice?

1) I could get a sexually transmitted disease.
2) I could get her pregnant and be handcuffed to this person for life.
3) I could be falsely accused of rape. (She voiced some head-scratching comments!)

What is the probability of these outcomes?

1) STD: 10% (based on her outward promiscuity!)
2) Pregnancy: 1%.
3) Falsely accused: 0.5%.

Is this an acceptable risk? I immediately reasoned HELL NO. The 10% or the 1%—I reasoned the risk was too great and that risk had outcomes that could change my life FOREVER. I denied the woman's advances and hid my lust in favor of a better choice. What if I hadn't? Sure, I would have enjoyed a quick romp of fun, but what about afterward? Would I be put in a position of an unplanned pregnancy with a woman I didn't know? Would I be condemned with a disease that would jeopardize my health and limit my search for a future partner? The potential consequences of this action had profound treasonous trajectories that I avoided.

WCCA comes into play when I drive. Viper, Lamborghini, doesn't matter—other idiot drivers looking for a street race constantly berate me. Sure, I might hit the accelerator hard for three seconds, but in those three seconds, WCCA takes over. What's the worst that could happen? I could kill myself or someone else. Odds? 3%? Knowing my racing competency, the risks are dangerously high. I release the accelerator and don't participate. The other driver? He speeds away with something to prove and in disregard to the potential outcomes. That's OK, maybe there's a reason he's driving a ten-year-old fart-can Honda and I'm in the Lamborghini.

Win the street race—I'll win life.

THE WEIGHTED AVERAGE DECISION MATRIX (WADM)

Ever wrestle with a tough decision? One day you favor option A and the next day you flounder back to option B. Wouldn't it be great if making a tough decision were as simple as picking the higher number?

The second decision tool I use compares and quantifies big decisions. You know them: Should you move or stay? Quit or continue? Go back to college or not? For WADM, you need paper and a pencil. Or, you can visit HelpMyDecision.com and let the web work the calculation for you. Keep in mind, WADM is for big decisions, so you might use this a few times a year whereas WCCA can be used daily.

With WADM, decision-making is easy as it isolates and prioritizes factors relevant to your decisions and then quantifies each decision with a value. The higher value reflects the better decision. For example, if you had a choice between moving to Detroit or Phoenix, WADM would yield a simple numerical valuation like Detroit 88 and Phoenix 93. Based on the number, Phoenix is the better choice. While WADM is subjective and requires your unfettered objectivity, it is a great tool for identifying which choice is more favorable to your preferences.

To use WADM, a minimum of two choices is needed, but it could be used for more. Let's say you do indeed live in Detroit and are considering moving to Phoenix. You struggle with the decision and can't get clarity. One day you want to move, the next you want to stay. Usually, this waffling occurs when there are too many decision factors within each choice.

Get a pencil and paper. Make three columns on your paper, one headed "Factors" and the other two for each choice, "Detroit" and "Phoenix."

Weighted Average Decision Matrix (WADM)

Factors	Detroit	Phoenix

Second, what decision factors are important in your decision? Weather? Schools? Cost of living? Being near family? Write down all factors relevant to the decision, no matter how small. Write these factors in the "Factor" column. Your WADM would now look like this:

Weighted Average Decision Matrix (WADM)

Factors	Detroit	Phoenix
Weather		
Schools		
Cost of Living		
Business Climate		
Taxes		
Safety		
Entertainment		
Near Family		

Thirdly, next to each decision factor, weigh its importance to the decision from 1 through 10, with 10 being the most important. For example, you are seasonally depressed, so weather is assigned a 10 in your matrix. Subsequently, your children are almost 18 so you decide that a good school system isn't a top priority and it receives a 3. Do this for all factors. Now your WADM looks like this:

Weighted Average Decision Matrix (WADM)

Factors	Detroit	Phoenix
Weather (10)		
Schools (3)		
Cost of Living (6)		
Business Climate (2)		
Taxes (7)		
Safety (4)		
Entertainment (8)		
Near Family (7)		

After each criterion is ranked 1 through 10, grade each choice 1 through 10 for each decision factor.

The school system in Detroit? You give it a 2. In Phoenix, you give the school system a 3, as you determine it is slightly better.

You assign entertainment in Detroit a 5 as they are home to your mighty Red Wings, while Phoenix gets a 2.

Continue for each decision factor within each choice. Your WADM should now look something like this:

Weighted Average Decision Matrix (WADM)

Factors	Detroit	Phoenix
Weather (10)	2	8
Schools (3)	2	3
Cost of Living (6)	5	7
Business Climate (2)	6	4
Taxes (7)	6	7
Safety (4)	3	6
Entertainment (8)	5	2
Near Family (7)	10	0

Next, for each row, multiply the weight times the grade and put that number next to the grade in parentheses. For example, in the entertainment row, Detroit receives a 40 (8 weight × 5 grade), while Phoenix receives a 16 (8 weight × 2 grade). Do this for all rows.

Your WADM should now look like this:

Weighted Average Decision Matrix (WADM)

Factors	Detroit	Phoenix
Weather (10)	2 [20]	8 [80]
Schools (3)	2 [6]	3 [9]
Cost of Living (6)	5 [30]	7 [42]
Business Climate (2)	6 [12]	4 [8]
Taxes (7)	6 [42]	7 [49]
Safety (4)	3 [12]	6 [24]
Entertainment (8)	5 [40]	2 [16]
Near Family (7)	10 [70]	0 [0]

The final step is simply to add up the graded weight columns to get a final number for each choice. The highest number will be the choice you favor. Your final WADM would look like this:

Weighted Average Decision Matrix (WADM)

Factors	Detroit	Phoenix
Weather (10)	2 [20]	8 [80]
Schools (3)	2 [6]	3 [9]
Cost of Living (6)	5 [30]	7 [42]
Business Climate (2)	6 [12]	4 [8]
Taxes (7)	6 [42]	7 [49]
Safety (4)	3 [12]	6 [24]
Entertainment (8)	5 [40]	2 [16]
Near Family (7)	10 [70]	0 [0]
	232	228

The better choice

In this hypothetical example, you should stay in Detroit because it received the highest score, 232 over 228.

The WADM is a great tool for making big decisions as long as you are perfectly honest with the factor weighting. I've used WADM many times in my life to bring clarity to tough decisions. It proved I needed to move to Phoenix, it offered insight into why it was time to sell my business, and it even steered me clear of some bad business investments.

In 2005, I had an opportunity to invest in a Las Vegas restaurant. After I conducted my diligence on the opportunity and the founders, it was time to make a decision. I couldn't decide. I solved my decision paralysis with a WADM analysis. It indicated that I should decline the investment, and I did. A year later, I heard through the grapevine that the investment went south. All of the investors lost their money. The WADM gave clarity to decision ambiguity and saved me from losing $125,000.

If you examine a map of the country, you'll find millions of roadways: freeways, streets, avenues, boulevards, all leading somewhere different. Your choices unearth those roads, and they are either impressive shortcuts or destructive detours. These two decision tools are navigational tools for your wealth journey.

GET YOUR EYES OFF THE REARVIEW MIRROR

Today is the starting line for the rest of your life. Yes, today is the tomorrow you worried about yesterday. The problem with the past is that we remember memories we shouldn't, and we don't forget what we should. If your eyes are stuck in the rearview mirror, you're stuck in the past. If you're stuck in the past, you're not looking ahead. If you're not looking ahead, you can't hit the mark of your future.

The universe doesn't care about your past. It is blind to it. The universe doesn't care that I wore pink pants in high school. (Hey, remember *Miami Vice*?) The universe doesn't care that I got in a fight with Francis Franken and lost. The universe doesn't care about your MBA from UCLA, your drug-dealing father, or that you wet your bed in junior high. The universe simply doesn't care. One person and one person only weaponizes past transgressions: you.

If the universe doesn't remember, why should you?

Being the youngest of three siblings, you can bet I was the subject of some vile comments. Fat, stupid, you name it. However, just because my brother called me an idiot for 12 years doesn't make it my reality.

Your past never equals your future unless you allow it.

Think about a coin flip.

No matter how many times it's flipped, the next flip is always random. Probability cannot be attached to a future flip based on the past.

Your past is the same.

Just because you failed at five relationships doesn't mean your next will fail, especially if you learn from them! Just because you flipped burgers three hours ago doesn't mean you can't be a millionaire next year. The universe forgets, just like the universe forgot I mopped floors and delivered pizza not long ago.

IS YOUR MEMORY TREASONOUS?

Your memories carry the same makeup as your choices. They're treasonous, muted, or accelerative. Unlike choice's consequences, you have a choice how your past is classified. The records of the past can be sealed.

For example, if you lost your life savings in a restaurant franchise that went bankrupt soon after you invested, your memory could be either accelerative or treasonous. Your memory and its perception could be:

"Business ownership is a big risk. I'll never do that again" or "Next time, I'm going to be selling franchises, not buying them." *The former is treasonous, while the latter is accelerative.*

You have a choice in framing failure and the past. It serves or hinders.

When I reflect on my own failures, they serve me to effect future change. It's a part of the responsibility/accountability process. What did I learn? What can I change in the future? What should I forget?

After I crashed my Viper and nearly killed myself, I remember the haze of almost losing everything. I didn't want to repeat those feelings, and their memories served future change: Street racing is for morons. Alternatively, I could allow ego to reign, keep street racing, and boast, "I'll never lose another race again!" While the consequences of our choices can't be manipulated, you can manipulate your memories to serve you. My life is not defined by being picked last in high school gym class. If you're defined by your past, it will be impossible for you to become who you need to be in the future.

CHAPTER SUMMARY: FASTLANE DISTINCTIONS

- Your choices of action manifest from your choices of perception.
- What you choose to perceive, or not perceive, will manifest itself to a choice of action, or inaction.
- You can change your choice of perception by aligning yourself with those who experience the perception as reality.
- Worst Case Consequence Analysis helps avoid treasonous choices.
- The Weighted Average Decision Matrix can help you make better big decisions by clarifying alternatives and their internal factors.
- The universe has no memory, only you do.
- Your past can be accelerative or treasonous. You choose the classification.
- If your eyes are transfixed to the past, you can't become the person you need to become in the future.

Deodorize Foul Headwinds

Ridicule is the tribute paid to the genius by the mediocrities.

~ OSCAR WILDE

THE FASTLANE'S NATURAL HEADWIND

The greatest invention of mankind was the airplane because it defied the natural force of gravity and seemingly violated the laws of physics. How could something so heavy float in the air? What made Orville and Wilbur Wright's breakthrough so spectacular wasn't just the act of flying, but the act of breaking free from society's gravitational pull.

"Flying is impossible."
"You guys are nuts."
"You are wasting your time."
"Foolish . . ."

Before they could even pursue flying, the Wright brothers had to break free of society's natural headwind—the natural social conditioning that poisons all young minds. A Fastlane Forum member posted this:

> *Go into a kindergarten class and ask the kids how many of them can sing. EVERY hand will go up. Fast-forward 13 years and ask the same class of seniors the same question. Only a few hands will go up. What changed? The kindergarten kids believed they could sing because no one had told them otherwise.*

Perfectly stated. We must not hear the naysayers, because they have been conditioned by society. Society will grind a constant headwind at your vehicle's grille. You can't worry about deviating from social norms, because the norm is to be two paychecks from broke. If you want to push beyond average results produced by average people, you'll need to adopt an uncommon approach that doesn't fall in the favor of "everyone."

The more uncanny and exceptional you strive to be, the more you need to fight through social indoctrination.

Extraordinary wealth will require you to have extraordinary beliefs.

TURN YOUR BACK TO STINKY HEADWINDS

If you turn your back to a headwind, it becomes an accelerant. I had to do this, otherwise I would have failed. After graduating from college, I was expected to find a good job. I didn't and instead dove into entrepreneurial ventures.

My family thought I was crazy and proclaimed, "You're wasting a five-year education!" Peers thought I was delusional. Oh dear, delivering pizza and chauffeuring limousines while two business degrees hung from the wall?! Women wouldn't date me because I broke the professional, "college-educated" mold the fairy tale and its white picket fence promised.

Going Fastlane and building momentum will require you to turn your back at the people who spew foul headwinds in your direction. You have to break free of society's gravitational force and their expectations. If you aren't mindful to this natural gravity, life can deteriorate into a viscous self-perpetuating cycle, which is society's prescription for normal: Get up, go to work, come home, eat, watch a few episodes of *Law and Order*, go to bed . . . then repeat, year after year.

Before you know it, 45 years have passed and you need another 25 just to make your financial plan work. Time passes, dreams die, and what remains? An old withered body forlorn for what could have been.

Who farts headwinds? They are:

1) Friends and family who just don't get it.
2) Media and educational institutions who preach Slowlane dogma.
3) Parents who are conditioned to believe wealth is for other people.
4) Slowlane gurus who claim your house is the best investment.
5) Slowlane gurus who say $100 invested today will be worth $10 million in 50 years.
6) Your environment.

ESCAPING HUMAN HEADWIND BLOVIATORS

People who don't empower your goals are human headwind bloviators. They add friction to the journey. When you spout excitement over actions or ideas, bloviators react with doubt and disbelief and use conditioned talking points such as, "Oh that won't work," "Someone is already doing it," and "Why bother?" In motivational circles, they're called "haters" or "dream stealers."

You must turn your back on them. Every entrepreneur has bloviators in their life. Network marketers consider *me* a bloviator. These people are normal obstacles to the Fastlane road trip. Remember, these people have been socially conditioned to believe in the preordained path. They don't know about The Fastlane, nor do they believe it. Anything outside of that box is foreign, and when you talk Fastlane, you may as well be speaking Klingon.

As a producer, you are the minority, while consumers are the rest. To be unlike "everyone" (who isn't rich), you (who will be rich) require a strong defense; otherwise, their toxicity infects your mindset. Commiserating with habitual, negative, limited thinkers is treasonous. Uncontrolled, these headwinds lead directly to the couch and the video game console. Yes, the old, "If you hang out with dogs, you get fleas."

This dichotomy makes you a blossoming flower that needs protection, water, and plenty of sun. Negative friends, family, or coworkers are dark clouds. Defend yourself or suffer the consequence of slow assimilation to mediocrity.

ESCAPING ENVIRONMENTAL HEADWINDS

While you might redirect human-originated headwinds, environmental factors aren't so easily controlled. What are environmental headwinds?

For me, it was Chicago. I was seasonally depressed and needed sun for motivation. Chicago was my hurricane force headwind, and if I wanted success, I needed to turn my back. I escaped and moved to one of the sunniest places on the planet. Had I not turned my back to my environmental headwind, this book would not exist. Where would I be today if I hadn't turned my back to the tornado? I know I wouldn't be here, happy, and retired 30 years early. Nope, I'd be on the Kennedy Expressway fighting traffic and strung-out on anti-depressants. I'll pass.

I made a choice to turn my environmental headwind into a tailwind. While I can't blame all my problems on my environment, they enforced this disconnect between "interest" in wealth and "commitment."

Another headwind could be your work environment. If your hated job drains the life out of you, it's a headwind. After a long workday and you have nothing left for your dreams and your Fastlane plan, you're done. The headwind keeps you trapped.

While growing up, one of the successful entrepreneurs I studied was Sylvester Stallone. While Sly is thought to be an actor, he's really an entrepreneur. His *Rocky* screenplay was his product that touched millions, and he sold it under a specific set of circumstances, which included the provision that he had to play the lead role.

Sly was no stranger to the Law of Effection. One of the telling elements of Sly's success story was his resistance to getting a "normal" job. He mentioned that if he'd taken a corporate job, his dream would have died because he knew the gravity of a job was inescapable for him. He recognized a corporate environment was a headwind.

If your environment puts a stiff headwind in your face, you must take proactive steps to remove the headwind. What headwinds are blocking your dreams? Take control and make choices that can shift the trajectory of your life.

CREATING ACCELERATIVE WINDS

My headwind was my environment. For you, it might be negative friends or other Slowlane influences. When you turn your back on these people, you break the headwind. When you associate with people who empower your goals, you create a wind at your back and build momentum. Positive people nurture your growth, sooth your failures, and invest in your dreams. Good people are conduits to your dreams, not just in motivational fuel, but in extending your opportunely reach.

People are like roads—they can either bring opportunity or distress into your life. The quality of these roads solely depends on the quality of the person.

Think of the relationships in your life like an army platoon readying for battle. Who are you going to war with? Your friend Mark who is always late, lies, and passes out drunk every Saturday night? Your friend Lucy who has a new job every three weeks, was caught forging checks, and is only looking for a super-rich guy to carry her off into the sunset? Are these people you can count on? Are these the people you want to go to battle with? If not, you need to pick better warriors to have on your team.

How? Join entrepreneur clubs, attend networking events, ally yourself with like-minders, get yourself around people who subscribe to a Fastlane, anything-is-possible mindset, and decide who you want on your team of warriors. Read books and autobiographies of those who have the kind of success you want. Find a mentor. Join entrepreneur forums with a Fastlane mindset, like the Fastlane Forum! Not a week goes by when someone doesn't email me, "This forum changed my life!" That's a tailwind!

Folks, this is war and your life is in the balance. You need warriors who are impervious to the Death Star and can deactivate the Slowlane tractor beam, not fearful pansies who drop their cargo at the first sign of Imperial Slowlaners. Reflect on your environment and your relationships, and recognize the headwinds. Then choose accelerative action: Can these headwinds be removed, ignored, or managed? Unlike natural wind, you are the arbiter of your headwinds. Success follows those who break the headwind and put it at their back.

SIGNIFICANT OTHER OR SIGNIFICANT DISTRACTION?

The worst headwind can be the person who sits in your vehicle's passenger seat. They sit and lecture you on your dumb ideas and remind you of your failures. Or they don't say anything and just distract you: They fiddle with the radio, adjust the climate control, mess with the windows, and hum old Duran Duran tunes. Or they play the role of a back seat driver: "Charles! Charles! Do this! Do that! Turn there! No, dummy!" What possibly can be so hazardous to your trip and who is this person? How did they get in your car?

This person is your significant other. By talking with other aspiring entrepreneurs, I've learned that significant others (spouses, fiancées, girlfriends, boyfriends) can be some of the biggest headwinds out there. Having a life partner who doesn't ascribe to your ideals and goals is like towing a trailer full of wet manure. If your partner doesn't subscribe to an entrepreneurial philosophy and toes the Slowlane road, can you expect to grow together? Someone fighting with you in your corner is accelerative; if they oppose, they become treasonous.

One of my first girlfriends was A+ marriage material. But she fully subscribed to the Slowlane philosophy. She couldn't understand why I was so fervent to be an entrepreneur. Our relationship soured as my failures grew, and the relationship eventually ended. This wasn't anyone's fault; we just were two different people on two different paths.

Bad relationships are roadblocks to Fastlane success. They drain energy and dim dreams. It's like rowing a boat upstream. Unwilling passengers add weight, distract, and sometimes are expensive to remove. Yes, divorce is treasonous and expensive, both emotionally and financially. Traveling down the road less traveled is already difficult. Why compound the journey by weighing down the car with someone who doesn't share your destination? Are you in the right relationship with a person who believes in you and your goals? Or is your relationship just like lukewarm water, not bad, not good, just comfortable enough to stand pat? If so, it might be time to evaluate your passenger.

CHAPTER SUMMARY: FASTLANE DISTINCTIONS

- The natural gravity of society is not to be exceptional, but average.
- Toxic relationships drain energy and detract from your goals to be extraordinary.
- The people in your life are like your comrades in a battle platoon. They can save you, help you, or destroy you.
- Good relationships are accelerative to your process, while bad relationships are treasonous.

Your Primordial Fuel: Time

Time isn't a commodity, something you pass around like a cake.
Time is the substance of life.
When anyone asks you to give your time,
they're really asking for a chunk of your life.

~ ANTOINETTE BOSCO

THE $6 BUCKET OF CHICKEN

Why will most people never get rich? Look no further than a $6 bucket of chicken. It made big news: A major fast-food restaurant offered a free bucket of chicken to anyone who had an Internet coupon. People flocked to restaurant locations and waited for hours, all for a free $6 bucket of chicken. Know anyone who would stand in line for hours just to get something free?

Are you one of them?

These stories are common, and yet my reaction is the same: What the hell is wrong with people? I'll tell you: *These people value their time at zero.* It's free. Like the air we breathe, they're convinced that time is abundant and in endless supply. They live as if they were immortal. They are certain that time, the fuel of their life, never runs empty.

I wonder if these people had three weeks left to live, would they be standing in line for a bucket of chicken? What if they had three months? Three years? At what mortal threshold would logic and reason smack sense into people? And affirm that waiting three hours for a free bucket of chicken is not time well spent? The greasy chicken truth: *Value your time poorly and you will be poor.* When time is wasted as a lifestyle choice you will be stranded in places you don't want to be.

Take a look around. How do your friends, family, and peers value their time? Are they standing in line to save four bucks? Are they driving 40 minutes to save 10 dollars? Are they parked on the sofa anxiously waiting to see who wins *Dancing With the Stars*?

The average American watches more than four hours of TV each day. In a 65-year life, that person will have spent *nine years* glued to the tube. Nine years Ms. Bueller. Nine.

Why?

Simple.

Life sucks. Life needs an escape. Life is no good. Show me someone who spends hours online playing *Clash of Clans* or *Candy Crush*, and I'll show you someone who probably isn't very successful. When life sucks, escapes are sought. I don't need television because I invested my time into a real life worth living, not a fictitious escape that airs every Tuesday night at 8 p.m.

Again, majority thinking yields mediocrity, and for that majority, time is an asset that is undervalued and mindlessly squandered. Instead of wasting nine years on *Game of Thrones* and *How I Met Your Mother*, why not invest those nine years into a business system that can pay dividends for the next thirty years?

THE TITANIC: HOW FAST IS YOUR SHIP SINKING?

People standing in line to save money ought to hold a picket sign announcing to the world, "I value money more than my life." That choice is a primal mistake.

A great example to time's reigning dominance over money comes from the 1997 movie, *Titanic*. As the ship sinks and few lifeboats remain, Caleden Hockley, a wealthy steel industrialist played by Billy Zane, bargains for his life with a ship's officer and offers cash in exchange for a lifeboat seat. The officer rebukes the tycoon's proposition with a stiff certainty: "Your money can't save you anymore than it can save me."

Reflect on that for a moment.

Your money can't save you anymore than it can save me.

Powerful.

In those eight seconds, the true value of time is exposed and we intersect with the certainty to our own ticking death-clock. You see, once your time is gone, you're dead. And when your clock ceases to tick, no amount of cash will save you from the end.

Fastlaners understand that *time is the gas tank of life*. When the gas tank runs dry, life ends. Time is the greatest asset you own, not money, not the 1969 restored Mustang, not grandpa's old coin collection. Time.

The fact is all of us are on a sinking ship. Is your time treated as such? Is it treated fairly or carelessly? Or is your primordial fuel squandered as if the tank will never run empty?

YOU WERE BORN RICH AND WILL DIE BROKE

Time is the great equalizer. You were born with a full tank of gas. There are no refilling stations, and your one fill-up occurred the moment you took your first breath.

Time can't be created outside of your mortal limits. Sure, we might be able to stretch a 76-year lifespan to 82 with good health and diet, but within mortality, time is transformed from infinite to finite. The greatest theft of all humanity is to act as if our time on this Earth is infinite when it isn't.

The reality is that time is deathly scarce, while money is richly abundant.

On any given day, $3 trillion is exchanged in the world currency markets. That's $3,000,000,000,000. To give that perspective, you can spend a million dollars a day for 8,000 years and you still wouldn't have spent $3 trillion. That's 109 lifetimes to quantify the total currency trading volume that exists for ONE DAY. Money is abundant and will be abundant as long as the world's governments print more.

Now, since you don't have 8,000 years of life, isn't it logical to conclude that money is an abundant resource while time is not? You can always acquire more money, but you cannot defy mortality. The irony of financial fortune is that no matter how much you have, you'll die flat broke. You cannot escape time's continual combustion as your tank bleeds away every second. You can live in blissful happiness or in a miserable depression—time is indifferent and it just drips away. Since time is scarce, wouldn't it make sense not to waste 3 hours of your life for a $6 bucket of chicken?

INDENTURED TIME IS THE RANSOM OF FREE TIME

There are two types of time that will make up your lifespan: Your *free time* and your *indentured time.*

Your Lifespan = Free Time + Indentured Time

"Free time" is yours to spend as you please: TV, a jog in the park, video games, sleeping, eating, vacation. If you're like most, your free time is lumped on evenings and weekends, where time is not exchanged for money.

"Indentured time" is the opposite: It's the total time spent earning money and the consequences of that spent time. When you awake in the morning, shower, dress, drive to the train station, wait, ride to work, and then work for eight hours—this is indentured time. When you spend your entire weekend "recharging" from the workweek, this is indentured time. Indentured time is actual work and the work you must do for the work. Morning rituals, traffic, compiling reports at home, solitary "recharges"—whatever time spent earning a buck is indentured time.

If you won the lottery, you'd quit your job because indentured time is no longer required and is suddenly replaced with free time.

Money buys free time and eliminates indentured time.

However, the irony of your free time is it isn't FREE; it's bought and paid for by your indentured time. You enjoy a two-week vacation because it was paid by a year of indentured time. You can relax with a cold beer on the couch because you paid eight hours of indentured time earlier in the day.

Indentured time becomes the ransom of your free time.

THE RIGHT TIME VERSUS THE WRONG TIME

There's the right time and the wrong time. The right time is free time; indentured time is the wrong time. The Slowlane ransoms time—time at the job and time invested in the markets. Remember, five indentured days for two free days is a bad trade! A financial plan with time as the linchpin is not a good plan.

If you were born into slavery, your life would be 100% indentured time with 0% free time. While total time can't be manipulated, you can manipulate your time ratio.

Wouldn't it be nice to have one day of indentured time and six days of free time? If you can steal free time from the hands of indentured time, life will have more of the "right time" versus the "wrong time."

DUMP THE JUNK IN THE TRUNK!

If you race cars at the drag strip, you know that every ounce of weight counts. Racers remove everything nonessential to make the car as light as possible. This increases efficiency, speed, and performance, resulting in faster finishes. Unnecessary weight forces the car to work harder.

Yet on our road trip to wealth, we're guilty of adding weight. Our vehicle is burdened with junk-in-the-trunk that coerces us to work harder. And when you work harder long enough, it wears you out and breaks you down.

This debilitating weight is *parasitic debt.*

Parasitic debt is everything you owe the world.

It is the excrement of Lifestyle Servitude.

Your shiny new Infiniti financed at 60 monthly payments, your home mortgage financed over 30 years, your fancy designer clothes four months removed from out-of-fashion, and yes, even that insidious furniture that seemed like such a good idea at the time.

All of this crap creates servitude and forces indentured time.

When you're forced to work, you limit choice, and limited choices close roads. Aside from my mother's creepy doll collection, nothing is more frightening than a parasite leeched to my neck, sucking my blood. Parasitic debt is a counterweight to your road trip; it's a bloodsucker that steals free time, energy, freedom, and health—all foes to true wealth.

PARASITIC DEBT CONSUMES FREE TIME

The leading cause of indentured time is parasitic debt. Surely you've heard the phrase "thief of hearts." When it comes to parasitic debt, it is the "thief of lives."

Parasitic debt is a gluttonous pig that gorges on free time and shits it out as indentured time. Any debt that forces you to work is expensed from free time and shifts it to indentured time.

Debt needs a constant drip of blood, and that blood comes from your gas tank of life: time. And since time is fixed, an increase in indentured time comes from only one source: your free time.

THE COST OF PARASITIC DEBT

The average American owes more than they are worth. Having a lifestyle built on credit creates Lifestyle Servitude in the form of indentured time. And because total time is finite, indentured time grows by pilfering from free time. Indentured time leads to the Sidewalk.

The next time you buy some fancy gadget on credit, know exactly what you are buying. You're buying parasitic debt that eats free time and transforms it into indentured time.

For example, if you buy an audio system that costs $4,000 and you make $10 per hour, what's the real price? What is the weight of the poop?

That price is 400 hours of your free time, since you must work 400 hours × $10 per hour to repay the debt. Add 10% interest and your final cost stacks up to 440 hours of your free time added to your weight burden.

So next time ya whip out the Visa, calculate the real cost. How much free time is this going to cost me? Everything we buy has not one cost, but two:

1) The actual dollar cost
2) The free time transformed into indentured time.

THE LAW OF CHOCOLATE CHIP COOKIES

When I first moved out on my own, I quickly learned the Law of Chocolate Chip Cookies: If the cookies don't get into the grocery cart, they don't get home. And if they don't get home, they don't get in my mouth. And if they don't get in my mouth, they don't transform into belly fat.

Parasitic debt follows the same law. Control parasitic debt by controlling its source: instant gratification, a trait of the Sidewalk. The next time you feel compelled to buy some trinket at Macy's, ask yourself: Will this be obsolete in six months and land in the garage with the rest of the junk? In four months, will these stupid sequin jeans be relegated to the dusty side of the closet reserved for painting smocks? Again, when you purchase the next hot fashion fad without being able to afford it, you open the floodgates to parasitic debt that flows downstream to the Sidewalk.

If the cost of that product doesn't make it to your credit card, it doesn't become parasitic. You protect free time!

Think!

Will this purchase TAKE FREEDOM?

Will I own this or will it own me?

While some choose servitude behind iron bars, others choose servitude behind velvet walls. Both are the same. The ultimate wealth is having the free time to live how you want to live. The Fastlane is about being both lifestyle rich as well as time rich.

A POOR VALUATION OF "FREE TIME" LEADS TO POORNESS

Rich or poor, time is equally possessed, shared, and consumed by all. Every day, you use it. I use it. Your neighbor uses it. No one gets more and no one gets less. Twenty-four hours for everybody. No one has an unfair advantage. You, me, we all have 24 hours to consume, expire, and spend.

Time is the planet's ultimate equalizer.

Then why do so few get rich while the rest wallow from paycheck to paycheck? The distinction lies in the valuation of free time, the chosen roadmap, and the acquisition of parasitic debt. Guess the behaviors—rich or poor?

- This person sleeps until noon.
- This person watches hours of reality TV.
- This person drives two hours to save $20.
- This person buys airline tickets with multiple layovers to save $100.
- This person spends hours surfing social networks and gossip blogs.
- This person is a Level 10 Druid in *World of Warcraft*.
- This person watches every Chicago Cubs game.

Behind poverty's tangled roots, you will find a poor valuation of free time, which breeds from bad choices.

"Time losers" are poor evaluators of time.

These are the people camped out at Wal-Mart at 4 a.m. waiting to grab the early-bird sales. They're sleeping outside Best Buy hoping to score a free 32" HDTV. They're waiting outside IKEA hoping to get a free breakfast.

Time losers are also inconvenient savers.

The inconvenient saver desperately clutches onto every dollar, fearful it may never return. Extreme inconvenience is never a match for saving money.

For example, an old friend of mine wanted an exercise bike and found it on sale at a store miles away her home. I told her just to buy the darn thing locally and pay the higher price, which was an extra $29. Nope, she was an inconvenient saver. Instead, she drove one hour to save $29.

Total time spent? Two and a half hours. Subtract gas and the total valuation of her time is about $5 per hour.

Last I checked, she doesn't work for $5 per hour, but has no problem wasting her free time at this rate.

The inconvenient saver gladly wastes time to save money. From plane tickets with multiple stops to shared-shuttle airport service, inconvenience is no match for saving a few bucks an hour.

If these people had three months to live, would they be outside Best Buy in a sleeping bag waiting? Six months? Six years? At what threshold will these people pack up their sleeping bag on the sidewalk and say, "Gee, what the hell am I doing lying on a sidewalk outside of an electronics store? Is this a smart use of my life?"

Sidewalkers sleep on sidewalks.

And yes, I've been always stingy with my time, even when I was broke.

Fastlaners exalt time as their primary consideration in decision-making because it's our most valued asset.

Fastlaners are frugal with time, while Slowlaners are frugal with money.

Sidewalkers and Slowlaners use money as the sole criterion in decision-making: Which job pays the most? Where is the cheapest item? How can I get some free chicken? Money is scarce and time brings up the rear and sweeps up the mess. If you want to be rich, you have to start thinking rich...

TIME IS KING.

CHAPTER SUMMARY: FASTLANE DISTINCTIONS

- Fastlaners regard time as the king of all assets.
- Time is deathly scarce, while money is richly abundant.
- Indentured time is time you spend to earn money. Free time is spent as you please.
- Your lifespan is made up of both free time and indentured time.
- Free time is bought and paid for by indentured time.
- Fastlaners seek to transform indentured time into free time.
- Parasitic debt eats free time and excretes it as indentured time.
- Lifestyle extravagances have two costs: the cost itself and the cost to free time.
- Parasitic debt has to be stopped at the source: instant gratification.

Change That Dirty, Stale Oil

Education is what remains after one has forgotten everything he learned in school.

~ ALBERT EINSTEIN

CHANGE THE OIL EVERY 3,000 MILES

The first lesson of car ownership: Change the oil every 3,000 miles. Neglect the lesson and your car dies well before its useful life. Frequent oil changes keep your car running efficiently; unchanged oil goes stale and turns the ride rough. Rough rides stall to the shoulder of the road.

The Fastlane road trip demands fresh oil changes. But what is oil? *Oil is education.* Knowledge. Street smarts. But be careful . . . it must be the right oil and for the right purpose.

Sidewalkers don't bother with oil. After 3,000 miles, they're done. Graduation is the last oil change. Slowlaners oil their vehicles for the explicit purpose of raising intrinsic value. Advanced education and certifications: What's going to command a bigger salary? Fastlaners oil their vehicles until they hit the junk yard.

GRADUATION IS NOT THE END; IT IS THE BEGINNING

Face it. *What you know today is not enough to get you where you need to be tomorrow.* You must constantly reinvent yourself, and reinvention is education.

Unfortunately, graduation traditionally signals the end of education. Regardless of your graduating age, adulthood begins. The party is over and real life begins. To cease learning at graduation is wealth suicide.

Your most effective earning years happen AFTER graduation, so wouldn't it be smart to continue the educational process long after formal schooling?

> *Jim Gallagher graduated 11 years ago and is unemployed. Jim is a stockbroker, but because of Internet technology his expertise has become endangered and flirts with extinction. Jim's education for that specific job-set has become dated and no longer applies to the current world. The world has moved on, yet Jim and his education have not. Jim contemptuously takes a menial sales job at a local furniture store. His financial plan stalls because he operates with the same stale oil last changed 11 years ago. Jim fails to change his oil so Jim's road trip to wealth also fails.*

Education, your oil, is a critical component to your wealth road trip. When you continually inject yourself with new education, new skills, and new competencies, new roads open and things run smoothly. The right education has incredible horsepower. New opportunities rarely follow an old education.

EDUCATION'S ROLE

Education is virtuous under both Slowlane and Fastlane roadmaps, but their roles are profoundly different. In the Slowlane, education is used to elevate intrinsic value, while in the Fastlane it is used to *facilitate and grow the business system.* Also, Fastlane education is secured by methods that do not produce parasitic debt or conformity. The purpose of education within the Fastlane is to amplify the power of the money tree and the business system. You're not a cog in the wheel; *you learn to build the wheel.*

For example, if I go to a training seminar that gives me skills to "hire top-gun sales people," I'm engaged in activities that specifically enhance the fertility of my business and my money tree. If I read a book on a new computer technology that illustrates how to create new interactive website features, I'd be learning to facilitate the system. Again, Fastlane education is to foster growth of the business system. Conversely, Slowlane education is designed to specifically enhance the intrinsic value of the person receiving the education. It is to become a gear in the system.

A Fastlane Forum user had an opportunity to pursue an MBA and he asked if it was worth it. My answer typically would be no, but this scenario was different. First, the MBA had no money cost, only time cost, as the government was paying for it. Second, this gentleman espoused the Fastlane ideology so his purpose was not intrinsic value elevation, but expansion of his knowledge to facilitate a Fastlane system. I voted yes.

"I DON'T KNOW HOW!"

If an oil change puts your car on a lift for months or years, what's the point? Your continued education must not come laden with conformity or parasitic debt, but must facilitate your Fastlane system. How? Make the real world your university. Yes, *you are your own university.*

Ask any successful entrepreneur and they will validate this truth: You learn from engagement, from doing, and from getting out and taking repeated action, more so than from any book or professor.

But "I don't know how!" you cry. Oh, stop. Public enemy No. 1 on the most-used excuses list is, "I don't know how!" Well, why don't you know how? I'll tell you why. You don't know because you haven't taught yourself how, nor have you wanted to "know how" badly enough. You see, it is easier to relent under the weight of "I don't know how" than it is to actively pursue the knowledge.

In today's information society, *there is absolutely no excuse not to find out how.*

I graduated from college with two business degrees, marketing and finance. Neither of them was related to computer science. I graduated with no computer programming experience. Yet I made my millions on the Internet. Funny, after 13 years of expensive institutional education, I NEVER took a formal class about the Internet or web technologies. Heck, my computer classes were limited to introductory business courses. If I didn't go to school to learn the Internet, how the heck did I learn these skills? I sought to change my oil frequently. I educated myself. I read books. I hit the library. I spent hours on the web and read articles, tutorials, wikis. I sought and consumed knowledge.

Years ago, when I started my career with Internet media, I could have easily quit and leaned on the obvious: I don't know how! I don't know how to program a website! I don't know how to design graphics! I don't know how to manage a server! I don't know how to write marketing copy! These excuses are like a plastic bag ready to smother your dreams, but only if you stick your head in the bag. Instead, my vision of a website didn't end with "I don't know how," but started there. So, get your head out of the bag!

Today I own a publishing company and a discussion portal for entrepreneurship. When planning those ventures, I started green with zero knowledge. To overcome the challenge, I had to learn. Study. Investigate. Solve problems.

Search engines were my teacher.

Had I not refreshed my skill set (my oil), all my journeys would have ended prematurely. My religious pursuit of knowledge kept me efficient in an ever-changing world and primed me for Fastlane opportunities.

Education didn't end with graduation, it started.

And best of all, my self-taught education was a twin-turbo acceleration into the Fastlane; my skills didn't come loaded with parasitic debt or conformity.

EDUCATION IS FREELY AVAILABLE

The greatest travesty of the free world is the underuse of knowledge. Walk into your local bookstore and inhale. Smell that? That's the smell of infinite knowledge.

Walk into your local library and look around. Amazing. Wall-to-wall books, free for the taking. Imagine if you could digest every book, every paragraph, and every sentence. Would "I don't know" be a detriment to your success?

I'm astonished that education is freely available, yet most choose to ignore it. Education is unplucked fruit from a tree, and all it needs is the ladder laying on the ground. Yet, most people cling to the limiting belief that "I can't afford education."

Sorry, but it's an excuse to be lazy.

Education is free for your consumption. Infinite knowledge is at your fingertips and the only thing preventing you from getting it is you. *Yes,* YOU.

Turn off the TV, pick up a book, and read it. Quit playing fantasy football and hit the library. Quit the XBOX grab-ass and hit the books. A committed Fastlaner has his nose in a book weekly. He attends seminars. He trolls business forums. He's on Google or YouTube searching different topics and strategies.

You have the innate power to become an expert at anything not requiring physical talent. Anything! No book in the world can make me a professional singer or a basketball player, but books can transfigure novices to experts in nonphysical disciplines. You can become a currency-trading expert. Real estate. Business. web programming. Sales. A public speaker. The expertise for any discipline not requiring physical coordination is out there. What does it take? Your commitment of pursuit, and then the biggy: applying it.

When I remodeled my house, my grand foyer walls needed to be faux painted. Faux finishing is a complicated painting technique that's used to create lavish surfaces with depth and luminance. I had two choices: Call a professional or learn to do it myself. Since I'm artsy and retired, I viewed this as a fun challenge. So I opted to do it myself.

I hit the Internet and watched a few hours of video tutorials. Then I hit the Home Depot and bought supplies. Over the next several days I practiced on cardboard boxes. Within a week I became proficient at faux painting. I built myself a skill in one week. Days earlier I was in the sphere of "I don't know how!" and days later, I possessed a new skill that I could aptly sell if I wanted. The best faux painters earn $12 per square foot. In one week, I built myself a skill that opened a tiny road into the Fastlane equation.

Skills and expertise are waiting just for you. No one drops a book on your lap and gifts knowledge. You have to seek it, process it, and then use it. *The acquisition and application of knowledge will make you rich.*

So where do you find infinite knowledge inexpensively? Like the air you breathe, it's all around you, like an apple tree waiting to be plucked.

Bookstores: Books possess the greatest return for your educational dollar. Buy them or borrow them. Just read them.

The library: The greatest free repository of knowledge and the disabler of the "I can't afford to buy books" excuse. I got my start at the library.

Internet forums/YouTube channels: Find like-minded congregations and learn from those who have succeeded. Find tailwinds!

Internet classes: Affordable and convenient, places like Udemy, Lynda, and Khan.

Internet blogs/podcasts/screencasts/Web casts: Another excuse destroyer.

Seminars: Good seminars bring good value, assuming they are sponsored by the right entities and not get-rich-quick gurus.

Television: Cable TV has turned television educational. Deviate from the mindless reality TV garbage and tune in to channels with educational value: History, Discovery, Science, HGTV, Military, and National Geographic.

Continuing education classes: Offered mostly by community colleges, these classes offer a wide array of formal training in specific disciplines.

Free magazines: Visit TradePub.com and FreeBizMag.com and sign up for free magazines subscriptions pertaining to your topic of interest.

Unfortunately, while infinite knowledge surrounds us, most people ignore it. Take for example this comment about education from successful real estate investor Lonnie Scruggs (LonnieScruggs.net):

> *I used to work two jobs.* EDUCATION *changed my life. Before I learned how to put my money to work, I was doing all the work. I was so uneducated back then that I thought the answer to financial freedom was working two jobs. And that's what I did for many years. Finally, I realized there weren't enough hours in a day and I couldn't work enough hours in a month to reach financial security. There had to be a better way. I started looking for it.*
>
> *When I realized that education and knowledge was the answer, I made up my mind to get an education. Before that, all I had was some "schooling." Now I realized I needed some education.*
>
> *Now I look back and see that I didn't do all the easy and fun things like others were doing, but I did all the right things. And today, we enjoy financial security and financial freedom. We can do what we want. Many of our friends are still working jobs, searching for financial security that they will never know. They had the same chance to make choices that I had; they just*

made the wrong choices. They all had schooling but they didn't have the necessary education that provides financial freedom. Now they tell me how lucky we are.

The best investment you can make is in yourself. So be willing to pay for your education now, or be prepared to pay a much bigger price for your lack of education later. The choices you make today will determine your financial future. Be sure you make the right choice, because you will have to live with the results of that choice.

The rich understand that education doesn't end with a graduation ceremony; it starts. The world is in constant flux, and as it evolves your education must move with it or you will drift to mediocrity.

"I DON'T HAVE TIME!"

Tailgating the crutch of "I don't know how!" is "I don't have time!" Where on earth will you find time to change your oil? I mean seriously, between the full-time job and the two kids, where is there time? It's in between everything else.

Changing your oil isn't difficult when you attach it to existing activities of repetition and consistency. While time might be linear, it can be manipulated by performing double-duty on one time block, as in the old cliché, "Killing two birds with one stone." Maximize time and you maximize wealth. Accomplish two objectives in one time frame. Make life your university. Here are some time-cheating, "life university" strategies that work for me, without killing efficiency .

Driving University: Listen to audio books or financial news radio while stuck in traffic. Traffic nuisances transformed to education.

Exercise University: Absorb books, podcasts, and magazines while exercising at the gym. In between sets, on the treadmill, or on the stationary bike, exercise is transformed to education.

Waiting University: Bring something to read with you when you anticipate a painful wait: Airports, doctor's offices, and your state's brutal motor vehicle department. Don't sit there and twiddle your thumbs—learn!

Toilet University: Never throne without reading something of educational value. Extend your "sit time" (even after you finish) with the intent of learning something new, every single day. Toilet University is the best place to change your oil, since it occurs daily and the time expenditure cannot be avoided. This means the return on your time investment is infinite! Toilet time transformed to education.

Jobbing University: If you can, read during work downtimes. During my dead-job employment (driving limos, pizza delivery) I enjoyed significant "wait times" between jobs. While I waited for passengers, pizzas, and flower orders, I read. I didn't sit around playing pocket-poker; no, I read. If you can exploit dead time during your job, you are getting paid to learn. Dead-end jobs transformed to education.

TV-Time University: Can't wean yourself off the TV? No problem; put a television near your workspace and simultaneously work your Fastlane plan while the TV does its thing. While watching countless reruns of *Star Trek*, boldly going where no man has gone before, I simultaneously learned how to program websites. In fact, as I write this, I am watching the New Orleans Saints pummel the New England Patriots on *Monday Night Football*. Gridiron gluttony transformed to work and education.

Think about the time you already use. How many hours are wasted in life's trivialities? The nine years on television? This time doesn't need to be lost, wasted time. This time is ripe for Fastlane oil changes. Just pick your multitasking sessions wisely—it has been proven that multitasking can hurt deep focus and concentration.

To start your oil recharge, choose a topic that interests you or an area in your life that needs improvement. Not good at sales or writing? Get to the library and start reading. Before I started writing *Fastlane*, I bought six books relating to publishing, writing, and authoring. I didn't blindly write and publish a book; I educated myself thoroughly during the process.

Set a goal to read at least 12 books per year, or one per month. If you are aggressive like me, you'll read a book every week. I can't stress enough that the more knowledge you consume, the more torque you create on the Fastlane road trip.

THE $50,000 OIL CHANGE

The last time I went to one of those while-you-wait oil change places, an advertised $21.99 oil change morphed into a $110 bill because of extra service suggestions. An oil change shouldn't cost more than 30 bucks, and anything heavier should arouse your suspicions. Twenty bucks is the average price of a book. Used books are less. Library books are free. Continuing education at a community college is $30 per credit hour. Oil changes are cheap. Yet, we continue to strap the chains of debt to our ankles and pay thousands of dollars for our oil changes.

I saw a picture the other day of a student publicly protesting one of the government financial bailouts. She hoisted a large placard that read: "I've got a 4.0 GPA, $90,000 in debt and no job—where's my bailout?"

Where's your bailout?

Let me tell ya, walk into the bathroom, flip on the light-switch and look in the freaking mirror. There's your bailout.

I'm tired of sob stories from well-intended college graduates with mountains of debt who can't get a job. Take responsibility. You bought into the myth that college ensures a job. The fact is, when you allow market forces to drive your vehicle you're likely to end on the street with a homemade poster proclaiming the value of your 4.0 GPA and the crushing burden of your six-figure debt.

No one cares. You're in debt because you borrowed. You're in debt because you bought into the scripted lie and relinquished control. You bought the Slowlane. Were you forced to take loans? You don't have a job because you voted for politicians who penalize producers and reward consumers. Face facts.

An expensive oil change that forces a lifetime of indentured time is stupid. Again, parasitic debt doesn't care about the source; it only wants to eat your free time, preferably seasoned with a little salt and pepper.

THE SEMINAR FAIL

What idiot would pay $50,000 to attend a seminar? Many do. This is a common question at the Fastlane Forum. So-and-so is offering a three-day seminar on real estate investment for $50,000. Should I buy it? What? Are you a smoking crack? Do you know what you're buying? Let me tell you. You're paying $50,000 for someone to explain a book that's found at the bookstore for 19 bucks.

A $50,000 seminar is exploitation of what we producers know: *People are lazy.* People want it handed to them. They don't want to read and connect the dots. They want to be steered and hand-held, or even better, have it done for them entirely. People want events, not process, and what better event than a $50,000 seminar!

Seminars can be great for education, but it has to be the right seminar, which is affordable and given by producers and experienced experts, not by professional, career public speakers. Most high-dollar seminars are well-orchestrated marketing machines tailored to extract every dollar from your wallet. Most cheap seminars are day long up-sells to a more expensive seminar. And those well-suited presenters? They suffer the typical Paradox of Practice: rich from public speaking to millions but not rich from what they teach.

A member of the Fastlane Forum reflected on her recent seminar experience with a popular book guru:

> *First, you won't be "allowed" to network. If you were allowed to network then people would find out quicker that the seminar is just one giant sales pitch for a larger, more expensive seminar to the tune of $50,000. Second, you won't learn a damn thing, except that you should have listened to your gut and not gone. There really is a sucker born every minute. Amazing how people have nothing in the bank but can come up with $50K just for the hope of something better. And finally, there is a segment in the seminar where they have you increase your credit card limits, because after all, the rich make*

money and the poor earn it. So then everyone goes and increases their credit limits, and then guess what—they hit you with the purchase price of anywhere from $16K to $50K, depending on how "serious" you are. Ridiculous? Apparently not, because people go rushing to the back of the room like cattle to slaughter, credit cards in hand. They leave with a nervous sense of self-satisfaction and a cute little sticker on their shirt that says "I invest in myself."

A $50,000 oil change is as shocking as a $50,000 seminar. Good seminars are under $1,000 and are given by respectable experts, practitioners, and seminar firms. Good seminars are educational and don't come at the price of a new Cadillac Escalade. Bad seminars are hyped, high-pressure, and exploitative. Bad seminars are about making money and not about helping you.

How can you tell a good seminar from bad? The first tipoff is price. Anything unreasonable is a warning sign that the provider is more interested in making money than education. The second is price again. Be wary of FREE. FREE usually means eight minutes of education and eight hours of up-sell to a higher-priced seminar. Thirdly, who is giving it? Is it a professional speaker? Or someone who actually practices what he or she teaches? Read the fine print. "Johnny Guru's strategies have made millions!" and then the fine print says, "Johnny Guru will not be in attendance." Huh? Would you allow an acting surrogate to perform surgery on you if the real surgeon wasn't available? Fail!

CHAPTER SUMMARY: FASTLANE DISTINCTIONS

- Fastlaners start their education at graduation, if not before.
- A Fastlaner's education serves to advance their business system and their money tree, not to raise intrinsic value.
- Fastlaner's aren't interested in being a cog in the wheel. They want to be the wheel.
- "I don't know how" is an excuse dismantled by discipline.
- Infinite knowledge is everywhere and it's free. What's missing is discipline to assimilate it.
- You can become an expert in any discipline not requiring physical skills.
- Educational recharges can occur within time blocks already allocated for other objectives.
- Organizers of expensive seminars take advantage of Sidewalkers and disenfranchised Slowlaners by marketing empty promises as "events."

Hit the Redline

If things seem under control,
you are just not going fast enough.

~ MARIO ANDRETTI

FASTLANE WINNERS ARE FORGED AT THE REDLINE

Winners are forged at the Redline. What's the Redline? The Redline is pure, unadulterated *commitment.*

Money trees, businesses, and systems aren't built overnight. It took Chuma years to construct his pyramid machine. Commitment is money-tree water, sun, fertilizer, and cultivation. I know commitment is a word likely to cause a riotous exodus. If you think Fastlane process is easy, stop now and go back to the Slowlane, which isn't easy either!

Remember, "Get Rich Easy" is a lure with a hook. The creation of a vibrant business is like raising a child from birth to adulthood. Like a parent has to commit to their children, you must commit to your system and your business. It is at the Redline where the limits of a car are tested, and that is where your limits will be tested.

ARE YOU INTERESTED OR COMMITTED?

Too many people saunter through life coasting in first gear and then wonder, how did I get here? Who doesn't want to worry about money? Unfortunately, it doesn't take any effort to be "interested" in wealth and financial security. Interest is kindergarten; it isn't enough, and those who have "interest" live in first gear.

To leave first gear, a string of good choices have to happen, to the point it becomes a lifestyle. No, this isn't an overnight thing. There's a profound difference between interest and commitment. It is defined by the quality and consistency of your actions.

Interest reads a book; commitment applies the book 50 times. Interest wants to start a business; commitment files LLC paperwork. Interest works on your business an hour a day Monday through Friday; commitment works on your business seven days a week whenever time permits. Interest leases an expensive car; commitment rides a bike and puts the money into your system. Interest is looking rich; commitment is planning to be rich.

Mark Zuckerberg, founder of Facebook, didn't build the most-used social networking site by being interested. He was committed. Elon Musk didn't improve rocketry by interest; he was committed. Interest is quitting after the third failure; commitment is continuing after the hundredth.

While I was building my company, my system, my surrogate, I was committed. I'd spend 12 hours a day for weeks perfecting and building my system. I'd forgo nights drinking with friends. I lived in a cramped studio apartment. I'd eat cheap pasta for lunch and dinner. I was ready to wash dishes to work my plan. While my friends were more concerned with bragging rights for having the fastest car on a racing video game, I wanted financial freedom. I wanted a fast car in reality, not on a video game. My friends were committed to being winners in a fantasy world, while I was committed to being a winner in the real world. *Fastlane winners are forged at the Redline.*

DISTANCE YOURSELF FROM "MOST PEOPLE"

How bad do you want it? How willing are you? Are you willing to sleep in your car for it? Are you willing to live in a tiny apartment while your friends own houses? Are you willing to forgo the new BMW in favor of a rust-bucket with 150,000 miles? Are you willing to wait tables at Maloney's Bar and Grill when your friends have cushy $50K/year jobs? How willing are you?

Most people aren't willing, and it separates the winners from the losers. The idea of living in the rat race for 50 years has to be more painful than the idea of working your ass off to escape it. You can have mediocre comfort now or meteoric comfort later. The Fastlaner trades short-term comforts with the foreknowledge that long-term extraordinary comfort is to be gained.

When it comes down to getting in the mud and getting dirty, most people will opt for the smooth sailing of first gear and avoid the discomfort of Redline. The Redline busts through roadblocks and hardens process.

When Carnegie Mellon University professor Randy Pausch was diagnosed with terminal cancer, he blessed us with his last lecture. In a video talk, he said:

> *The brick walls are there for a reason. The brick walls are not there to keep us out; the brick walls are there to give us a chance to show how badly we want something. The brick walls are there to stop the people who don't want it badly enough. They are there to stop the other people!*

The last two words of the quote are "other people." You want to be damn sure you aren't "other people," because "other people" is synonymous with "most people." Most people are consumers who are two paychecks from broke. Most people won't invest long hours into their business system while friends are living it up on credit. Most people will allow friends and family to deflate their dreams with "that won't work" directives. Most people start excited and gush with exuberance but give up at the first pothole or failure. Most people succumb to "I quit" and give up not knowing that they are one or two plays away from a touchdown—the Fastlane exponential growth curve.

"Are we there yet?" Wealth is a devious entity, and its elusiveness weeds out the weak. Your journey will follow a predictable path of excitement, questioning, commitment, and rebirth. Fastlane success requires an investment toll of time and effort. This is the toll that makes you special and keeps everyone else OUT.

This Redlined effort cannot be bypassed nor outsourced. Prime your expectations for work and sacrifice, know your destination and know that you are simply paying the toll because you don't want to trade 5-for-2 for life! If you don't do the hard work that Fastlane opportunity demands, someone else will. And if you aren't like everyone, you will discover something miraculous: *You can live unlike everyone.*

GET YOUR FOOT OFF THE BRAKES!

The sweat of success is failure, and I am soaking wet.

If you've taken a step, spin, or aerobics class, you know the objectives: sweat, cardiovascular endurance, and weight loss. If you went to a cardio class and the instructor forbade sweating, it would negate its purpose. Hard work naturally produces sweat, and sweat becomes evidence of your effort.

Unfortunately, this is the paradox you'll face if you fear failure and refuse to release the brakes. *The sweat of success is failure.* While you can't build cardiovascular endurance without sweating, you can't experience success without failure. Failure is simply a natural response to success. If you avoid failure you will also avoid success.

You can't drive the road to wealth with the brakes engaged. You have to take risks. Get uncomfortable and fail into progress.

What causes fear of failure? Answer: an overestimated worst-case consequence analysis. What is the worst that could happen and the probability of it happening? You have to go back to work? You or the wife needs a second job? Big deal. When you resist societal headwinds, you will sweat!

Take calculated risks. Do so and shit happens. You meet new people. New opportunities arise. Feedback pours in. "Lucky breaks" converge into your life. The act of doing does marvelous things.

Yes, the Fastlane is a risk. Failure is imminent. I learned how to code computers by trial-and-failure. I'd fail a code block hundreds of times before I found the right way. My other failures ranged from moronic network marketing gigs to jewelry retailing to direct marketing programs. Each time, I brushed it off, reanalyzed, learned, adjusted, and tried again. I acted, assessed, then adjusted. The brakes were disengaged, baby!

I once heard, "A smart man learns from his mistakes. A wise man learns from the mistakes of others." You can learn from my failures. I didn't learn the Fastlane overnight. I found it by the light of failure. Fear of failure is normal, yet failure creates experience and experience breeds wisdom.

FASTLANE RISKS CAN HAVE LIFELONG RETURNS

Bill Gates is a one-hit wonder. He built one company and made billions. One company was all it took. Despite two liquidation events and a current company worth millions, some might say I'm a one-hit wonder. Great. I'd rather be a one-hit wonder than a no-hit wonder. One hit is all it takes, and you could be set for life.

You have a challenge: If you want to hit home runs, you've got to get up to the plate and swing. Home runs or singles can't be hit sitting on the bench or on the couch inhaling *Cheetos* while killing grunts on Halo 3. Get up to the plate and start swinging! Start striking out! Foul balls and pop outs! After enough swings and acclimating yourself to the velocity of business, contact becomes easier.

TAKE INTELLIGENT RISKS AND SKIP THE MORONIC ONES

When it comes to risk analysis, there are two types of risk designated by best- and worst-case outcomes or consequences: *intelligent risks* and *moronic risks.*

Flying to Las Vegas and gambling a month's salary at the craps table is a moronic risk. Driving a car on the freeway with faulty brakes is a moronic risk. When you take intelligent risks and avoid the moronic ones, you amplify your wealth trajectory through time. *Intelligent risks* have a limited downside, while their upside is unlimited. *Moronic risks* have a bottomless downside and their upside is limited, or short term.

Most moronic risks fall into the asymptomatic category. They simply aren't clearly defined and it takes a little diligence to spot them. When I'm out racing on the streets of Phoenix in an 850-horsepower car, I'm taking an asymptomatic, moronic risk. My upside is a short-term burst of adrenaline and a temporary ego boost. The downside is crashing and killing myself or someone else. The upside is limited and short—the downside is unlimited and long. Yes, it seems so idiotic.

Here's another moronic risk, and it took me this chapter to uncover it. I'm writing this book on a cloud computing application. That means I'm writing to an external source, or an external server. I have not made copies of my work. If the cloud server fails, my work is gone.

Yes, moronic risks come in all sizes and flavors, and this makes me the idiot of the day. Excuse me while I go back up my work.

OK, I'm back.

Now let's talk about intelligent risks. When I invest $100,000 in an Internet company, I'm engaging in an intelligent risk. When I sold my Internet company, I reinvested part of the proceeds back into the company. Why did I invest $100,000 and expose myself to the risk? I assessed the acquiring company's probability of success to be decent. Their goal was to take my small company and transform it into a $100 million company. If they succeed, my small $100,000 investment would be worth millions. The downside? The company could fail and my investment's value would lose most of its value. My downside is limited while the upside is substantial. This is an intelligent risk.

If you quit your job to pursue a Fastlane business, it's an intelligent risk. Your upside could be millions. The downside? You might have to live below your standards: mop floors, flip burgers, eat rice and beans, and ride your bike to the grocery store. Or worse, deny your child the latest iPhone. Is that really that bad? Not if you know your destination and your commitment to the roadmap. Again, it all comes down to what you are willing to do and not do. Risk involves careful stewardship of choice. Minimize moronic risk and take advantage of intelligent risk. As for failure, trust me—*it is easier to live in regret of failure than in regret of never trying.*

SMACK "SOMEDAY . . ."

What prevents people from hitting the Redline?

Someday does. Someday I will . . . someday I'll do this, someday I'll do that, someday when the kids are grown, someday when the debts are paid . . . someday. And yet, someday never comes. Someday is a distant horizon in the theater of your mind.

Someday is dangerous and paralyzing. It traps you in land of Nowheresville. Someday is here, now, pristine and clean and begging no allegiance for tomorrow. The Fastlane petitions you for this simple transformation: *Make someday today.*

Ever drive somewhere and all the traffic lights are green? Unfortunately, when it comes to opportunity and risk minimization, people wait for perfect timing—they wait for all lights to go green, which summons the "somedays." Ask anyone seeking Slowlane escape . . . why haven't you made the leap? What are you waiting for? It's always some excuse . . .

"I'm waiting for a promotion."
"I'm waiting for my kids to be older."
"I'm waiting to be debt-free."
"I'm waiting until I inherit money."
"I'm waiting for the new year."
"I'm waiting to finish school."
"I'm waiting for my wife to get a job."

"I'm waiting for the economy turn around."
"I'm waiting until I fix the hot-water heater."
"I'm waiting for this . . ."
"I'm waiting for that . . ."

The common thread is always the same . . . "I'm waiting." But waiting for what? Someday! Someday for something, some event, or some precondition. Sadly, these mentally constructed provisions come and go, leaving the opportunity seeker stuck in the same rut for years. Waiting for all green lights is waiting for the skies to turn purple on the third Wednesday in November.

Let me be clear if I haven't been: There is never a perfect time. *Someday is today.* Today is now. A week is 7 todays strung together while a year is 365. Today is all you've got! And if you wait, opportunity passes. Your Fastlane journey never starts and year after year passes with new preconditions being added while the old ones are satisfied. While opportunity passes, guess what else passes? *Time.* Ring up the cheesy soap opera music. Yes, as time passes, so do the sands of your life . . . and these are the days of our lives.

OPPORTUNITY DOESN'T CARE ABOUT TIMING

Opportunity drives through your neighborhood frequently, and when it does, you have to grab it and don't let go. Evaluate the risk and take action. Unfortunately, opportunity doesn't care about your timing. Opportunity doesn't care about your circumstances, your broken-down car, or your life's turmoil. It comes and goes of its own will, has a mind of its own, and it's blind to predicaments. Opportunity comes dressed as changes and challenges. Remember, change makes millionaires.

The "Fastlane Forum" (TheFastlaneForum.com) is my example of seizing opportunity outside of my timing. My forum existed years before this book was written because opportunity drove through my neighborhood unannounced. My preconceived timing for the "Fastlane Forum" was after my book's completion. However, years before the first word was written, I revisited a business forum that I had once frequented. I recognized familiar forum contributors lamenting about "the old days" and how hucksters had invaded the forum: people pimping their spam, schemes, and scams. It was a garden that had become overrun by weeds. People demanded change or an alternative.

In my mind I had a forum coming at some point in the undefined future.

But this opportunity was not coming at my convenience.

Opportunity suddenly turned the corner and I heard its deafening exhaust. Even though I was in the shower, I got out, ran outside soaking wet, unprepared, premature, and met the opportunity. I greeted it, opened the door, and led it inside. Not in my time, but "opportunity's time," and someday became today. *That decision allowed me to pre-sell hundreds of books before the first word was written.*

Many of the world's successful entrepreneurs started businesses in college. You know their companies: Microsoft, Dell, FedEx, and Facebook. Their founders seized opportunity outside of their timing and chose to take an intelligent risk. These entrepreneurs captured opportunity and didn't wait for satisfaction of preconditions: "After I graduate" or "On summer break" or "After my Math 202 exam." Opportunities are dressed as unfilled needs, and when they ring your doorbell, answer it! Unanswered, opportunity leaves and rings another doorbell, knowing eventually, someone will answer.

Why not you? Timing is rarely perfect. Waiting empowers mediocrity. People sit around waiting their entire lives for the perfect this, the perfect that. The perfect scenarios and circumstances never arrive. What does arrive? Time, old age, and the specter of a dream lost.

And now you have the opportunity to get out of the garage and take the road. The road is where your Fastlane journey starts. Fastlane roads lead to wealth. You have the Fastlane roadmap, and you know how the Slowlane and the Sidewalk operate. You know how to tune your vehicle. You know which mindsets are assets and which are liabilities. You've exposed the gravitational forces that will conspire against your vehicle. You have all the necessary tools to get out of the garage and get on one of the many roads to wealth. Yes, it's time to hit the road.

CHAPTER SUMMARY: FASTLANE DISTINCTIONS

- Interest is first gear. Commitment is the Redline.
- Hard work and commitment separates the winners from the losers.
- Some choose short-term *mediocre* comfort over long-term *meteoric* comfort.
- To live unlike everyone else, you have to do what everyone else won't.
- Arm your expectations to hard work, sacrifice, and other bumps in the road. These are the land mines where the weak are removed from the road and sent back to the land of "most people."
- Failure is natural to success. Expect it and learn from it.
- One home run could set you financially secure for your life, perhaps generations.
- Home runs can't be hit in the dug out.
- Moronic risks have unlimited downside (long term) and limited upside (short term).
- Intelligent risks have unlimited upside (long term) and limited downside (short term.)
- There is never perfect timing and waiting for "someday" just wastes time.

Part 7

The Roads to Wealth

The Right Road Routes to Wealth

He who chooses the beginning of the road
chooses the place it leads to.
It is the means that determines the end.

~ HENRY EMERSON FOSDICK

IS YOUR ROAD-TO-WEALTH A DEAD-END?

What is the road as it relates to wealth journey? If you're a Slowlaner, your road is your job: doctor, lawyer, engineer, salesman, hairdresser, pilot. If you're a Fastlaner, your road is a business: Internet entrepreneur, real estate investor, author, or inventor.

Your road is your career or business path, and that road must route to wealth. Unfortunately, most jobs can't because of their mathematical limitations and, surprisingly, most businesses don't either! A road that starts in Chicago and leads east will never hit Las Vegas. It's a dead end! If you're on an errant business road you have to use your steering wheel and make a course correction: Exit, turn, or reverse course.

This impasse confronts millions of business owners. They fool themselves by driving the wrong road and then wonder why wealth has eluded them. Instead of fighting 8-hour workdays, they fight 12-hour store hours. Instead of leveraging the surrogacy of a system, they trade time for dollars. Instead of trading five days of work for two days off, they trade 6-for-1, or 7-for-0, in lifelong perpetuity.

If you heed the Fastlane philosophy and start a lemonade stand simply because the Fastlane said, "Start a business," I have failed. That road is unfit because it doesn't have probabilities for wealth. The right road must lead to wealth and carry real probabilities! How? Your road must go near or through the Law of Effection.

THE ROAD TO EFFECTION: THE FIVE FASTLANE COMMANDMENTS

The Law of Effection says to make millions you must impact millions. How can you impact millions? In the Slowlane you explode intrinsic value, become enormously indispensable, and earn millions. In the Fastlane, you engineer a business that touches millions of lives in scale, or many lives of magnitude. If your road doesn't lead through Effection's neighborhood or have an exit-ramp onto it, sorry, you're on the wrong road.

The power of the Fastlane wealth equation is ignited by a business that drives to the Law of Effection. Business opportunities are plentiful, and unfortunately most of them aren't Fastlane roads. If you're stuck in a retail store selling $15 haircuts, can you reasonably expect to serve millions? A kick-butt attitude is snuffed if your road is directionally challenged toward Effection, because Effection is the gatekeeper to wealth.

To light the Law of Effection and illuminate your Fastlane road, cross-examine it against the Five Fastlane Commandments, the CENTS FRAMEWORK.

1) **The Commandment of Control**
2) **The Commandment of Entry**
3) **The Commandment of Need**
4) **The Commandment of Time**
5) **The Commandment of Scale**

CENTS is a Fastlane litmus test and validates your road. Does your road (or potential road) route to wealth? Is it Fastlane? Can it be made Fastlane? Can it hit Effection? Can your road route to a multimillion-dollar enterprise, generate passive income, and end at a final liquidation event?

A road meeting all five commandments can make you filthy rich fast. As violations accrue, the road degrades in its wealth potential, and with it, your ability to get near Effection also degrades. While it's possible to violate one or more commandments and still create wealth quickly, you should aim for a road that satisfies all five commandments. Potent roads are potent wealth creators. Sadly, most business opportunities fail the commandments, and, if they fail, they don't deserve your respect or attention.

CHAPTER SUMMARY: FASTLANE DISTINCTIONS

- Not all businesses are the right road. Few roads move at, through, or near the Law of Effection.
- The best roads and the purest Fastlanes satisfy the CENTS FRAMEWORK; the Five Fastlane Commandments: Control, Entry, Need, Time, and Scale.

The Commandment of Control

There is no dependence that can be sure
but a dependence on one's self.

~ JOHN GAY

DEMAND THE DRIVER'S SEAT

Yes or no. You're either driving the Fastlane or you aren't. You're either in control over your financial plan or you aren't. There is no in between. And if you're not driving, you're sitting in the passenger seat and someone else is in control.

Envision your dream car, boat, or plane. Great, now here are the keys. You get it for one hour, unencumbered. Would you grab those keys and take it for a joyride, using every single minute? Or would you plop your butt into the passenger seat and resign, "Meh, you take control, I'll just sit here and hitchhike a ride." Senseless? Not exactly. This is how many people approach business: They hitchhike, give up the driver's seat, and violate the Commandment of Control. In doing so, they sacrifice control over their financial plan and ultimately, make someone else rich.

HITCHHIKING A FASTLANE

While life's hitchhikers tread the Sidewalk and are victims, the hitchhikers of business violate the Commandment of Control.

(CONTROL) - E - N - T - S

A business hitchhiker seeks refuge from risk and cowers within the confines of a matriarchal organization. This subservient relationship relinquishes control and leaves you vulnerable to the driver's actions. When you control your business, you control *everything* in your business—your organization, your products, your pricing, your revenue model, and your operational choices. If you can't control every aspect of your company, you're not driving! And if you can't drive, you set yourself up for sudden, unexpected crashes.

Fastlane drivers retain control. Those who violate the commandment do not. In general:

- Drivers create MLM companies; they don't join them.
- Drivers sell franchises; they don't buy them.
- Drivers offer affiliate programs; they don't join them.
- Drivers run hedge funds; they don't invest in them.
- Drivers sell stock; they don't buy stock.
- Drivers offer drop-shipping; they don't use drop-shipping.
- Drivers offer employment; they don't get employed.
- Drivers accept rents and royalties; they don't pay rents and royalties.
- Drivers sell licenses; they don't buy them.
- Drivers sell IPO shares; they don't buy them.
- Drivers don't JOIN the hottest trend, they SERVE the hottest trend.

So are you DRIVING a Fastlane? Or HITCHHIKING one?

If this hitchhiker description describes you, don't get discouraged or defensive. You can't be a driver in every instance. Heck, even I partake in hitchhiking activities. Fastlane hitchhikers can make good money, sometimes boatloads. However, understand this: The driver retains control and makes the *big money.* At best, the hitchhiker makes *good money.*

GOOD MONEY VERSUS BIG MONEY

There is a difference between good money, big money, and legendary money. Good money is $20,000/month.

The cattle call of every network marketing company is, "Hey, wanna make $10,000 a month?" Big deal. Remember your windshield. It's big money only in your head. That's decent money but nothing that's going to put you into a private jet and 40-foot yacht on Newport Beach.

Big money is $200,000/month. Now we're talking—$200,000 every month puts a dent into your lifestyle. At this income level, life changes.

And then there is legendary money, where you earn more than a million dollars every month. Outrageous? Not at all. When you leverage all five commandments and control your company, one million a month is not impossible.

To hit big money or legendary money, you need to control every aspect of your system. When you relinquish control and defer power to a higher authority, you cede big money to the driver and accept good money as the passenger.

For example, my company offered an affiliate program. My best affiliate consistently earned $20,000+/month. Yes, he was making good money. He was the hitchhiking passenger, and I, the driver, controlled the affiliate process. However, think about the danger he assumed. At any moment I could have instituted a "new policy" that would have reduced his earnings. I drove his income stream, and he absorbed the risk that I wouldn't disturb, alter, or modify the affiliate agreement. And most importantly, as a driver, I was the one making big money ($200,000/month), while he settled for good money ($20,000/month).

Similarly, you might have heard of a unique group of Internet entrepreneurs called "AdSense" millionaires. Google Adsense is an advertiser network that online content publishers leverage to earn income from their websites' traffic. There are affiliates, bloggers, and publishers who earn good money from using Google's AdSense program. Some content providers and bloggers earn six figures monthly. Arguably, this is big money, yet Google (the driver) makes the legendary money.

NO CONTROL = CRASHES

Think about the dangers of hitchhiking. You get into a stranger's car and you let them drive. Hitchhiking a Fastlane is an incredible risk, especially when your family is the cargo. My experience has repeated itself for countless entrepreneurs who learned the hard way.

Some background: My forum leverages the Google advertising network, which pays revenue for ad clicks that evolve from my forum. It is a hitchhiking relationship—Google is the driver and my forum is the passenger. A thread at my forum discussed an e-book marketing program. As the thread progressed, a joke was made about a former bankrupt NBA player, and (long story short) the folks at Google claimed the content violated their terms. My ads were terminated and the revenue stopped. Now imagine if my forum and its Google revenue were responsible for feeding my family. Imagine if I was earning $15,000/month from these ads and in one big swoop, poof! Gone.

No control. No say. No power. It took me eight days to fix the problem, but it exposed the hitchhiking dangers as a passenger versus driving it. For those eight days, my income from that activity was zero. In any driver/hitchhiker relationship, the driver always makes more money than the hitchhiker and retains a critical component to Fastlane strategy: *control.*

I can't imagine running a company in which another entity has the power to instantaneously kill your revenue stream. If someone can "flip a switch" and destroy your business, you're playing roulette with your financial plan. The congenital danger of hitchhiking is that you give up the keys to the driver. If the driver crashes into a wall, guess who goes with them.

You.

The problem with hitchhiking is you really never know the driver. The driver could be ethical, moral, and just, or the driver could be corrupt and evil. Either way, you waive power to your driver. *He who owns the keys owns the power.*

Yet millions of people submit to this type of organizational control without pause. They sign franchise agreements, giving control over crucial business decisions, including marketing, ads, and royalties. They join distributorships in which others dictate their compensation structure. Their product funnel is directed by a centralized source. They're told like automatons what they can and can't do. They're held hostage to a corporate matriarch, not realizing that they aren't really their own boss. If you can't change your product, your price, or influence marketing decisions, are you the boss?

Decades ago, I joined a network marketing company. I had a friend who earned good money. Ultimately, the company changed its product line and compensation structure. My friend's income stream was disrupted and eventually disappeared. The asset he created (his downline and cash-flow stream) vaporized in a matter of months. My friend had no control despite claiming that he "owned his own business." His mistake was to violate the Commandment of Control. He never had the keys to his business, and his empire was nothing but a mirage founded on false foundations governed by a political party in which he had no voice.

When drivers make radical turns and change terms, you have no choice but to go with them. If it's bankruptcy or criminal neglect, their sinking ship becomes yours. Do you really want to partake in a business relationship like this?

THINK SHARK, NOT GUPPY

If you lived in an aquarium, would you rather be the shark or the guppy?

Sharks eat . . . guppies get eaten.

Business is a fierce competition for the consumer's mind and their money. It's an expansive ocean where multiple species wage war over sustenance: money. In this oceanic game, you want to be at the top of the food chain, not at the bottom fighting to the top.

Build corporate ladders—don't join them.

Build pyramid organizations—don't join them.

Think manufacture, not retail.

To become a shark, you have to think like one. Sharks think big and guppies think small. As a shark, you have to drill into your belief system and change your mindset.

Think globally, not locally.

Think to lead, not to follow.

Think to innovate, not to copy.

The change and transformation from guppy to shark starts with your thoughts as your focus moves from the few to the many.

When you engage your Fastlane road, be the shark and use the entire ocean as your playground. Ever watch a school of fish? Each fish doesn't act individually. They act as a collective. Unfortunately, most people can't see the danger of this analogy. They're just one fish immersed in a collective controlled by a force greater than themselves. And who is attracted to these schools of fish? The sharks. Be the shark, the predator, not the guppy. Be a driver, not a hitchhiker.

INVEST IN YOUR BRAND ONLY!

Whose money tree are you growing? Are you investing in your brand or in someone else's?

Ever sit in traffic and spot a car plastered with some company's decals and stickers? From network marketing jigs selling acai drinks to the country's largest makeup company, these decals are official announcements from the driver: "Yes folks, my life is invested in someone else's brand."

They are guppies in a shark-infested ocean.

I recently had an older woman approach me in my gym's parking lot. She stopped her car and asked me about my Lamborghini and its vanity license plate. Then she opened a Pandora's box and asked, "Do you do any network marketing?" Before I unloaded, I glanced at her car. She drove a rusty old Hyundai that needed new tires and a paint job. The rear window was missing (unless duct tape and plastic counts). The side doors were plastered with magnetized signs exclaiming the greatness of her network marketing company.

"Make a huge income from home, call 555-555-5555!"

I wondered if her company (and her road) were so great, why was she driving a POS Hyundai that costs less than the front left tire on my Lambo? How can she advertise "Make a huge income from home!" when obviously, she wasn't? I respectfully asked her why she invests in a business that she doesn't control. Why are you painting someone else's "big picture" when you should be painting your own?

She smiled, raised her "dream-stealer" defenses, and rejected my analysis. As if what she was doing was working and reasonable, her mind was closed to my suggestions. That's fine. Keep doing what you're doing and see if that wins you real freedom. Don't listen to me; you approached me and I'm the one who's retired and living the dream. I know that sounds arrogant and pretentious, and I apologize, but logic eludes most people.

When you blindly invest your life and time into someone else's brand, you become a part of their marketing plan. You become a swab of paint in their big picture. You resign yourself to the slim possibility of making good money versus big money. Not investing in my own brand was my serious mistake as a young entrepreneur. Hitchhiking a Fastlane is an epidemic that deceives many would-be entrepreneurs. I say "would-be" because hitchhiking isn't entrepreneurial, because at the heart of entrepreneurship is creation and innovation. Hitchhikers aren't pioneers; they don't create or innovate. They sell, operate, and manage.

If the driver closes shop, you're out of luck. If the driver discontinues a product and it's your sole source of income, you're out of luck. Fastlaners control their brands, their properties, and their financial plans. They don't blindly give it to others and hope for the best.

NETWORK MARKETING AS A FASTLANE . . . ONLY IF . . .

Network marketing is a Fastlane but only if you *own* the network marketing company. As a Fastlaner, you want to create these companies, not join them.

Before I purged them, I had a lot of Facebook friends who were spiritedly engrossed in network marketing. I never publicized my views because ultimately, they have to see it for themselves. If they believe $20,000/month is a great income, let them believe it. If they believe their income stream will be passive forever, let them believe it. If they believe they're in control, let them believe it. These folks can't be told the fire is hot, they need to feel the burn for themselves.

It took me four network marketing companies to expose the truth. And that truth? The only people in the company who live on the Pacific coast with a garage full of exotic cars were the founders and inner circle—not the distributors who signed up years later.

I don't hide my discontent for network marketing, although the reason is misconstrued. Network marketing is a hitchhiking strategy that disguises itself as entrepreneurship. My discontent lies in the misconception; millions fall for the pitches such as "Be your own boss!" "Own your own company!" or "Passive residual income!"

While there is a small sliver of validity to these claims, they cloud the real essence of MLM, which is sales, distribution, and training—not entrepreneurship.

I was involved in four MLM companies. Not once do I remember dictating product decisions, research and development, marketing restrictions, rules, cost analysis, or any other activity fundamental to owning a business. As a network marketer, you don't own a business—you own a job managing and creating a sales organization. That's like stuffing money under the mattress and calling it an investment.

Years ago, I had friends who did well in MLM, and some of them still do. Heck, even I did OK. But two things nagged at me. First, I had no control. I was at the company's mercy, its policies, its procedures, its product line, its cost structure—and whatever mandate put forth, I'd be stuck with it. When my company discontinued its best product, I remember my income plummeted through no fault of my own.

My friend who was making a nice living at MLM? He quit due to opposition over corporate decisions, and from what I hear, he jumps from opportunity to opportunity every few years. He repeats the cycle: Climb aboard some hot opportunity, run it dry, and move to the next. Last I checked, he isn't rich, nor is he retired. He's not stuck in a rat race, but a rabbit race from one carrot to the next.

The second nag at my mind was clear: I didn't feel like an entrepreneur. I felt like a worker bee stuck in a chaotic hive. I felt like an employee of a large company that was benefiting from my hard work, even when that work yielded few dollars. My subconscious knew I was violating a multitude of commandments and unspoken rules, the Commandment of Entry, the Commandment of Control, and the rule of "everyone"(Chapter 31).

My dislike for the model lies in the misdirection conveyed to would-be participants; they think they're entrepreneurs when they're just sales managers in a Fastlaner's plan.

Can these folks make a huge chunk of change? Of course, I don't argue that fact. Top salespeople in *Fortune 500* companies also make a lot of money. Lottery winners also make lots of money. We're talking odds here, not absolutes. MLM distributors are commissioned employees disguised as entrepreneurs and working for a Fastlaner in a regime they don't control, but the Fastlaner does. *Network marketers are soldiers in the Fastlaner's army.*

So let me be clear to all those MLM folks out there ready to hang me: I love network marketing as an entrepreneur. If I ever invent a product that needs distribution, network marketing would be my first consideration. Furthermore, MLM has excellent educational value: sales, motivation, team-building, and networking. I believe if you can succeed at network marketing, you can succeed at anything.

As for my friend, he is a hitchhiker of a Fastlane. What he doesn't realize is that Fastlane wealth rarely comes from joining a network marketing company, it comes from creating it. You must create the company people are dying to join. You must control the product and the policy. Take the producer's role.

The Fastlaner creates and invests in his own brand; the hitchhiker climbs aboard someone else's and hopes to piggyback. If you don't control your system, your money tree, and your brand, you control nothing. You must sit atop the pyramid and serve the masses. *Stop climbing pyramids and start building them.*

CHAPTER SUMMARY: FASTLANE DISTINCTIONS

- Hitchhikers relinquish control of their business to a Fastlaner.
- There is a difference between "good" money and "big" money. Hitchhikers can make good money while Fastlaners make big money. Sometimes legendary money.
- In a driver/hitchhiker relationship, the driver retains control and the hitchhiker is at the driver's mercy.
- Hitchhikers are subordinated to someone else's Fastlane plan.
- Make the world your habitat of play in an organization you control.

- Network marketing has little to do with entrepreneurship but more to do with sales, networking, training, and motivation.
- Network marketing fails both the Commandments of Control and Entry, and sometimes, Need.
- Network marketers are soldiers in a Fastlaner's army.
- Network marketing is a powerful distribution system. As a Fastlaner, seek to own one, not join one.
- Network marketing can have some excellent education value in the realm of sales, motivation, and team building.
- If you can succeed at network marketing, you should be able to succeed in a Fastlane venture.

The Commandment of Entry

*Our plans miscarry because they have no aim.
When a man does not know what harbor he is making for,
no wind is the right wind.*

~ SENECA

YOU CAN BE THE SHEEP OR THE SHEEPHERDER

It was 1994 and I was stuffed in a hot auditorium, tucked away in a chaotic horde of people—an ant within an anthill. Months earlier, I got involved in a network marketing company, and this was their monthly motivational meeting. The crowd was excited, anxious, and revved up.

I wasn't. I looked around and didn't see a business, I saw a religion. I saw an army of drones clutching onto whatever was said, critical reasoning cast aside, and myself about to be indoctrinated. I didn't go so easy. I asked questions. I was persistent, nosy, and curious about the road I was about to take.

"How much money are you making?" I asked early and often. Like politicians, the answer was sideswiped and deflected to a default person in the organization, but I wasn't fooled. OK, you've already told me that Bill Hanson makes $30,000 a month, but how much do *you* make? And you? And you? And the other 3,000 people in this room?

The fact is, few of them made any money at all.

Why?

They were stuck driving a congested road full of traffic that failed the Commandment of Entry. Crowded, jammed roads move slowly, if at all.

I failed networking marketing four times because subconsciously I possessed the truth: The road violated the Commandment of Entry.

C - (ENTRY)- N - T - S

The Commandment of Entry states that *as entry barriers to any business road fall, or lessen, the effectiveness of that road declines while competition in that field subsequently strengthens.* Higher entry barriers equate to stronger, more powerful roads with less competition and need for exceptionality.

Low-barrier-entry businesses are weak roads because easy entry creates high competition and high traffic, all of which share the same pie. And where there is traffic, there is no movement.

In other words, if "getting into business" is as simple as paying $200 for a distributor kit, there are no entry barriers, and the opportunity should be passed. If any Joe Blow alley-napping next to a dumpster behind Chan's Chinese restaurant can start *your* business in minutes, it isn't a business you want to be doing! The world is littered with so-called businesses that have no entry barriers. And that is why they suck and the people who follow them aren't rich.

A decade ago the big buzz was "Make millions on eBay!" It didn't last long because this opportunity eventually violated the Commandment of Entry. If you could create an eBay business in 10 minutes, guess what? So could millions of other people. And who made the millions? The early adopters, eBay, and eBay's founders. They drove the Fastlane and picked up millions of hitchhikers along the way. Few did well, while millions did not.

Another big buzz years ago was Internet blogging. Bloggers are making thousands! True, but nowadays, the multimillionaire blogger is now the exception. Why? The opportunity has been beaten down by easy entry, causing traffic, competition, and saturation. Saturation causes declining sales volumes. Declining sales volumes cause profit erosion. If anyone can start a business in one day or less doing what you do, you probably are violating the Commandment of Entry and tough odds are ahead. This is why there are more dead blogs, than active ones.

Network marketing, or multi-level marketing (MLM), always fails the Commandment of Entry—unless you own and create the MLM company yourself. If you're in a room with 2,000 other people who do exactly what you do, you're fighting stiff odds. Who is the innovator, the leader, and the one standing on a cliff parting the Red Sea? The guy on stage who founded the MLM company is the Fastlaner. And you? Sorry, but you're just another soldier in his Fastlane army, a cog in his marketing strategy. The MLM founder doesn't need to climb the pyramid, because *he built the pyramid*! You can be a pyramid builder or a pyramid climber. You can be the sheep or the sheepherder.

"EXCEPTIONALISM" IS REQUIRED TO OVERCOME WEAK ENTRY

If you violate the Commandment of Entry, be prepared to be *exceptional*. Exceptionality breaks the odds of entry. Unfortunately, exceptionality is a long shot, much like an above-average high school athlete going pro.

For example, when I sat in that auditorium with thousands of other network marketers, I realized that success among thousands doing the same thing, I had to be exceptional. I had to be the best. Honest with myself, I knew I couldn't be exceptional in that construct. Could I be exceptional among 50,000 like-minded "distributors"? I was doubtful. Conversely, when I started my Internet business I had roughly 12 competitors. Could I be exceptional among 12? Absolutely.

Another example of exceptionality is playing professional poker and financial trading, like stocks, futures, and currency trading. Both disciplines violate entry and have little access restrictions. I can go to Vegas with $10,000 and enter a poker tournament at any time. I can deposit $10,000 in a brokerage account and start trading currency. *Lack of entry itself creates the marketplace*, and to succeed in that marketplace, you have to be exceptional. The best (and the richest) poker players in the world are exceptional and take advantage of the weakest lured by weak entry. The pros call these folks "dead money."

The same playing field exists in the currency markets. Newbies come and go, trading currencies, expecting to make a fortune, while the only folks making the millions are the exceptional participants and the purveyors of the field, like the currency platforms, brokerage houses, and poker websites.

There's an old saying, "In a gold rush, don't dig for gold, sell shovels!" When it comes to entry, your industry and your business should not be available to everyone, because if it is, you need to be exceptional. And if you are exceptional, easy entry becomes not a liability, but an asset.

ENTRY IS A PROCESS, NOT AN EVENT

Want to know if your business violates entry? The answer is simple: Is getting into business an *event* or a *process*? Real business startups are processes, not events. If you're suddenly in business because you bought a distributor kit, or completed an online form, you're violating entry. If you're suddenly in business because you took one or two actions, you violate entry. Conversely, if I wanted to start a bed-and-breakfast in Sedona Arizona, I'd have to find a property, fix it, finance it, insure it, get licensing and permits, hire a staff, and perform about 10 other steps. Entry is a detailed process.

Starting a business, like wealth, is a concerted series of choices that form process. Founders of network marketing companies do spectacularly well because they know that people love events, and what better event is there than "Complete this application and you're in business!" *They leverage entry ease as an advantage.*

As entrepreneurs, we want to start companies that others can join as an event. Don't fool yourself. Mailing a check to some address listed in the back of an entrepreneur magazine isn't a business launch. Any business that takes 10 minutes to do/join/participate violates entry. Violate entry and you stamp your ticket into the world of everyone and become a screw in someone else's Fastlane plan.

EVERYONE IS DOING IT!

Ever get stuck in traffic on the expressway and go nowhere for hours? Welcome to "everyone is doing it." A road full of traffic is a road full of everyone. If everyone is doing it, I won't be doing it. I'll exit the road, and you should too.

Why?

Because everyone isn't wealthy. If everyone were wealthy, "everybody is doing it" would work.

When it comes to money, the best warning flag is "everyone." Everyone is a red flag that the Commandment of Entry has been violated. If everyone is bewitched by the same activity, it surely will fail.

While "everyone" was buying houses like crazy during the housing boom, I did the opposite. I sat on the sidelines and sold. When the frenzy is buying, you should be selling. When the frenzy is selling, you should be buying or staying pat.

History is littered with "everyone is doing it" booms and busts. The tech stock boom of the late 1990s, the great oil price explosion thereafter, the housing crash that led to the worldwide financial meltdown, and even recently, the bitcoin / cryptocurrency rise into the mainstream vernacular. All exemplify "everyone is doing it"—a heavily trafficked road that usually crawls toward impending doom, like a herd of lambs heading for slaughter..

THE WARNING SIGNS OF "EVERYONE"

In the late 1990s when tech stocks were skyrocketing, I lost money because I followed everyone. I learned. During the latest housing boom, I didn't buy a house. No, this time I sold three properties before the decline. While the housing market collapsed and stocks soon followed, I was long gone and sitting in cash. How did I know?

I spotted the signs of "everyone is doing it," because if everyone were rich, "everybody is doing it" would work. While this logic might seem spurious, it has never failed me. How do I know when "everyone is doing it?" Simple. When there is irrational exuberance about any investment that pervades to Team Consumer—the general populous—that's when I know it is time to GET OUT AND STAY OUT.

When the plumber comes over to fix the toilet and raves about his three rental properties that have appreciated 15% in the last three months, it's time to get out and stay out.

When your personal trainer raves about his Internet stock portfolio that earned 40% in two months, it's time to get out and stay out.

When your truck-driving cousin says you need to invest in this great crypto-currency altcoin because it's up 250%, it's time to get out and stay out.

Dumb money—EVERYONE—always shows up at the end of a boom.

Who is dumb money? Consumers! Money chasers!

But some shrewd people have mastered the Rule of Everyone. Instead of getting out, they short the other side and profit from the downfall. With every busted boom, new millionaires and billionaires are created because they saw the impending collapse inevitable in every meteoric irrational ascension.

While the stock market imploded in early 2009, who was buying and who was selling? Everyone was selling. I was long gone and sold a year earlier. Warren Buffet was buying. Everyone sells and the richest man in the world buys. Hmmm. Could it be that everyone is wrong? Yes it could.

If you want to live unlike everyone, you can't be like everyone. Don't confuse that with exceptionality. You have to lead the pack and have "everyone" follow. When the sheep are lining up single-file for slaughter, you want to own the slaughterhouse.

CHAPTER SUMMARY: FASTLANE DISTINCTIONS

- The Commandment of Entry states that as entry barriers fall, competition rises and the road weakens.
- Easy access roads carry more traffic. More traffic generates higher competition, and higher competition creates lower margins for the participants.
- Businesses with weak entry often lack control and operate in saturated marketplaces.
- Exceptionalism is required to overcome weak entry barriers.
- Access to a business road should be a process with a toll, not an event.
- "Everyone" consists of the general populous and is served by the mainstream media.
- If everyone were wealthy, "everybody is doing it" would work. And if everyone is wealthy, then no one is wealthy.
- "Everyone is doing it" is a signal to overbought conditions and the entrance of "dumb money."

The Commandment of Need

What do we live for, if not to make life less difficult for each other?

~ GEORGE ELIOT

SAND FOUNDATIONS CRUMBLE HOUSES

Ninety percent of all new businesses fail within five years, and I know why they fail. They fail because they fail the Commandment of Need.

C – E – (NEED) – T – S

When you build a business on a flawed foundation, it will fail. Sand foundations crumble houses. Businesses which violate the Commandment of Need enter the 90% failure category or masquerade as a job. The winning business premise is a simple and often forgotten concept that should be ridiculously obvious, but it isn't. *Businesses that solve needs and provide value win.* Businesses that solve problems win profits. Selfish, narcissistic motives do not make good, long-term business models.

Think about the purpose of businesses. Why do they exist? To satisfy your selfish desire to "do what you love?" To satisfy your craving for wealth and financial freedom? Seriously, no one cares about your desires, your dreams, your passions, your "whys" or your reasons for wanting to be rich. No one cares that you want to own a Ferrari and prove your parents wrong. No one cares that corporate America wronged you. No one cares! Yes, the world is a selfish place and nobody gives two shits about your motives to "go Fastlane."

So what do people care about?

People care about what your business can do for them. How will it help them?

What's in it for them? Will it solve their problem? Make their life easier? Provide them with shelter? Save them money? Educate them? Make them feel something? Tell me, why on God's green Earth should I give your business money? What value are you adding to my life?

Reflect back to our producer/consumer dichotomy. Consumers are selfish. They demand to know is "what's in it for me!" To succeed as a producer, *surrender your own selfishness and address the selfishness of others.*

STOP CHASING MONEY—CHASE NEEDS

Never start a business just to make money. *Stop chasing money and start chasing needs.* Let me repeat that, because it's the most important thing in this book: Stop thinking about business in terms of your selfish desires, whether it's money, dreams or "do what you love." Instead, chase needs, problems, pain points, service deficiencies, and emotions.

Entrepreneurs fail because they create businesses based on selfish premises, and selfish premises don't yield profitable businesses; they lead directly into the 90% failure wastebasket.

"I need a new income stream."
"I'm an expert in [blank] so I'll do that."
"I read a 'get rich' book and it says to start a business."

Wrong. Wrong. And wrong.

Again, selfish, narcissistic premises are VIP invitations to violate the Commandment of Need.

You and your business attract money when you stop being selfish and turn your business's focus from the needs of yourself to the needs of other people. Give first, take second. Needs come first, not money! Charm the marketplace with your own selfish needs and my bet is placed on your failure.

> *Joe was a martial arts expert and he loved his craft. Following the advice of gurus, he set out to "do what you love" and opened a martial arts studio. Within 10 months, his studio closed, as he could no longer support his family on his $21,000-per-year business profit.*

Before Joe started, he was destined for failure. He got into business based on a faulty entrepreneurial road paved with sand, a premise based on selfish needs and selfish desires: "I'm an expert in martial arts and love the art, therefore I should open a studio." The correct foundation is externally based on market needs, not internal selfish needs. Instead of selfish motives, what should have Joe been thinking?

- Is there a NEED in my neighborhood for a martial arts studio?
- What are existing martial arts studios doing wrong that I could do BETTER?
- What improved VALUE do I offer the martial arts student?
- What ASSETS do I bring to this community?

Joe failed because there wasn't a genuine need in the marketplace and his motives were selfish. Had Joe analyzed these questions foremost, his odds of driving a successful road would have dramatically improved.

Several years ago, during the economic expansion, I noticed a standalone storefront being built in my mother's neighborhood of Chandler, Arizona, a suburban bedroom community south of Phoenix. As the building went up and the store tenant moved in, the heat of failure percolated. How did I know?

This new store was a hip-hop apparel boutique. Fasten your seat belt here comes failure! Why? The store violates the Commandment of Need. The neighborhood *doesn't need* a hip-hop store. The area isn't urban, there are no dance clubs nearby, and nothing looks remotely hip-hop. In fact, not 100 yards away there is an elder care retirement home. Is a 91-year-old grandpa the target market for hip-hop gear? The obvious problem here is selfishness. The owner is following his passions, and his love for hip-hop music and culture. Maybe a life coach told him to "do what you love." Whatever the motive, the need is internal and not externally based on the marketplace. I predicted the business would last 12 months. After 18 months, the business disappeared. The road was paved with sand because no need existed.

MONEY CHASERS CHASE MONEY, NOT NEEDS

Frequently I read posts from aspiring entrepreneurs with grandiose goals of making a fortune by starting a business. Hang out at any business forum and you will see the misdirected, selfish foundation poisoning the well.

- How can I make money starting a business?
- What business can I start with $200 and still make $5K per month?
- What home-based business can I start?
- I have a friend who manufacturers widgets; you think I can make money selling them?
- What can I sell on Amazon so I can get passive income?
- What's a good product to import from China and sell on eBay?
- What's the best business to start on a shoestring?

If you sit around and ask yourself these types of questions, you'll likely fail because these dialogues expose your preoccupation with money, and not needs or value. You've got it backward! I call these entrepreneurs "money-chasers." They hop from one business to the next, scalping and arbitraging market imbalances, rarely solving needs or creating momentum. Sometimes these selfish business owners use questionable business practices as customer needs are neglected and money is pursued with disturbing zealotry.

Money chasers are consumers who haven't quite made the transition to producer. They want to be producers, but they selfishly think like consumers.

For example, in the housing boom, money chasers became mortgage brokers and real estate agents. The burst of the bubble purged the industry clean of the excess. When foreclosures hit an all-time high, "loan modifiers" became the newest money chasers. Every boom attracts money chasers who hop aboard the trend train to solely serve themselves. With plenty of selfish consumers to prey upon, money chasers survive and sometimes thrive. At least until they're exposed for fraud or a new bust rolls in. In times of excess, scams, schemes, and rip-offs pervade because money chasers invade and imbalances occur.

TO ATTRACT MONEY IS TO FORGET ABOUT MONEY

Want to make big bucks? Then start attracting money instead of chasing it.

Money is like a mischievous cat; if you chase it around the neighborhood, it eludes you. It hides up a tree, behind the rose bush, or in the garden. However, if you ignore it and focus on what *attracts* the cat, it comes to you and sits in your lap.

Money isn't attracted to selfish people. It is attracted to businesses that solve problems. It's attracted to people who fill needs and add value. *Solve needs massively and money massively attracts.*

The *amount of money* in your life is merely a reflection to the *amount of value* you have given to others. Ignore this symbiosis and money will ignore you. Successful businesses share one common trait: The satisfaction of consumer needs as reflected by sales in the marketplace. The marketplaces and consumers, not you, determine if your business is viable. If you sell 10 million anything, 10 million people have VOTED that your product will help them, or satisfy one of their needs.

The only Fastlane road that works is a road paved with cement—rock hard needs, wants, and solutions—not sand. A rock hard pavement gives you the unfair odds. Solve needs on a massive scale or in magnitude. It could be as fantastic as starting a software company as Bill Gates did, or something seemingly minute like putting a new spin on something old. If you own a website that services 10,000 people daily, you're making an impact. If you own a real estate company that provides housing to 1,000 people, you're making an impact.

Make a freaking impact and start providing value! Let money come to you! Look around outside your world, stop being selfish, and help your fellow humans solve their problems. In a world of selfishness, become unselfish.

Need something more concrete? No problem. Make 1 million people achieve any of the following:

1) Make them feel better. (entertainment, music, video games)
2) Help them solve a problem.
3) Educate them.
4) Make them look better (health, nutrition, clothing, makeup).
5) Give them security (housing, safety, health).
6) Raise a positive emotion (love, happiness, laughter, self-confidence).
7) Satisfy appetites, from basic (food) to the risqué (sexual).
8) Make things easier.
9) Enhance their dreams and give hope.

. . . and I guarantee, *you will be worth millions.*

So the next time you're trolling the web looking to make money, sit back and ask yourself, "What do I have to offer the world?" Offer the world value, and money becomes magnetized to you!

"DO WHAT YOU LOVE" AND DIE AS YOU DO

Beware of another guru-speak: "Do what you love and the money will follow!" Bullshit. That is, unless you want to violate the Commandment of Need. "Do what you love" is another mythical decree perpetrated by hypocritical gurus and so-called life coaches who are probably three clients from broke. Sadly, the road of "do what you love" rarely converges with wealth. In fact, it might lead you down a road to destructive love.

If you're like me, "do what you love" was never an option. Think about what you love and then think, will someone pay for it? Is it going to solve a need? Are you good enough to make money doing it? Most likely, you aren't.

For "do what you love" to work, you need two things: 1) Your love must solve a need and 2) You must be exceptional at it.

I love to play basketball, but I suck at it. I can't parlay my love of basketball into a career. I love to play piano, but again, I suck at it. I love many things, but I suck at them! If I wanted a career in any of these "loves," I'd need unlimited time and money because no one would pay me a dime to do it. Who wants to endure that ineptness?

Consider this book. I love to write. The book represents a dream of "doing what I love," and that dream was made possible by the Fastlane. If I needed this book to pay for a mortgage (don't have one!) I'm not sure it would. I have no clue if this book will sell 10 copies or 10 million. Therefore I can't rely on it.

"Doing what you love" for money often isn't good enough because we aren't good enough. Additionally, so many people are "doing what they love" that their markets get crowded and margins deflate. Heavy competition reigns.

Authoring a book is a crowded space. Just because I love to write doesn't guarantee money will follow. In fact, no one cares that I love to write. Do you? Of course not! *You want to know if my writing will help you.*

In a magazine interview, billionaire RJ Kirk was asked about the benchmark to his success. He replied, "It is for others to say whether I am useful or not."

It isn't for you to decide whether you are useful. The marketplace makes that determination.

People pay for their satisfaction; they don't pay to satisfy your need of "do what you love."

People pay for solutions, not for your enjoyment.

People pay for solved problems.

People don't give a rats-ass about your love for whatever. If "do what you love" doesn't fill a need spectacularly, no one will pay for it!

This book is possible because I didn't need the confirmation of money to authenticate my skill. If that sentence is too complicated, you confirm my point. Maybe I'm just not good enough. Regardless of sales, my book is a testament to "do what I love" whether I'm good or not. The Fastlane allowed money to be removed from the equation.

Now, I don't need to get paid to "do what I love." I just do it.

In other words, money led to "do what you love," it didn't follow. How's that for irony?

Lebron James gets paid to play basketball because he is good. One of the many destinations of the Fastlane is to remove the confirmation of money from your "do what you love" activity. Fastlane success means I could play basketball seven days a week. I can play video games all day. I don't need to get paid to "do what I love" because I can now do it for FREE.

If you are one of the lucky few who can earn an income from a specific activity that you love AND are good enough, kudos to you. And congratulations—you might not need a Fastlane. A Slowlane just might suffice. No worries. But for those of us who can't transform our loves into income, there are other alternatives paved by the Fastlane.

"DOING WHAT YOU LOVE" FAKES AND DERIVATIVES

If you can't work a job or a business doing what you love, you're likely to fall into a trap. Your natural reaction is to make a deal with the devil—the Slowlane. You trade your life away, doing things you hate, in exchange for doing things you love. You say, "I'll do five days of work I hate so I can enjoy two weekend days doing something I love." Does this barter sound like rational thinking?

For example, my friend Andy is a bank collections agent and hates his job. At beer time, I hear the complaints, the frustration, and the BS about the job: the Nazi-like micro-management, the incompetent boss, and his psychotic coworkers. He's on the firing line from all fronts. He numbs himself to this suffering five days a week. His salvation? His weekend. He pays "do what you hate" with a weekend of "do what you love"—boating.

Then other people negotiate with "do what you love" into an alternative, or a derivative. For example, Pauline loves to knit, so she sells her knitting online. Jose loves automotive audio so he opens a car stereo shop. Janice loves to sculpt and sells her works at the local gallery. Gary is an avid bodybuilder so he becomes a personal trainer.

There are two dangers to derivatives:

1) They don't make money fast.
2) They endanger the love.

First, "do what you love" rarely creates money fast because more than likely, not only are YOU doing what you love but thousands of others are too (just tune into the first-week auditions for *American Idol* for proof). The need is weak. This saturates markets and makes profit margins shallow.

At my gym, a personal trainer acquaintance told me he is struggling to make ends meet. When I asked why, he responded that personal training is so competitive that he can't charge a price worth his time. His service fees are deflationary, caused by an abundant supply of trainers, and when supply exceeds demand (need) prices move down. Not enough need, too much supply.

So why is the field for personal trainers so saturated? Simple. People follow the espoused guru-esque advice without reflection on need: "Do what you love." Unfortunately, if you LOVE doing it, bet on thousands of others loving it too. When you "do what you love," prepare to face stiff competition. Who enjoys higher margins? The personal trainer? Or the guy who starts a company to clean up crime scenes?

The second danger of derivatives is that your love becomes vulnerable to contamination when you do it for money. If you are forced to do anything, even something you purport to love, in exchange for a paycheck, that love is put in danger.

Decades ago, I took a job as a limo driver because I loved to drive. By the time that job ended, I hated to drive. After work, I'd stay home because I was so sick of driving. My love was contaminated.

I once had a friend who created fantastic paintings as a hobby. When I asked her why she doesn't paint full time for a living, her answer was simple: I paint when I am impassioned to paint. The few times when she painted for money, it stunted her artistic creativity because a different force fueled the motivation—money, not emotion from the moment.

"Do what you love" is left to professional athletes, because they are at the pinnacle of their games. And yet, even after making millions, many of these athletes suffer the same fate. They lose their love of the game. Dancers lose their love for dance. Artists lose their love for art. Money and the demands of life cast a cloud over the love and darken it into a burden.

While derivatives of "do what you love" might yield a figment of happiness, they operate in saturated marketplaces and, more importantly, they could jeopardize your natural love for the activity.

YOUR IGNITION: MOVING FROM LOVE TO PASSION

The motivational fuel for the Fastlane is not love, but passion—passion for your future vision and a passion for personal growth. If you have a passion for a specific goal, you'll do anything for it. I had a passion for Lamborghinis and was willing to do anything for it. Pick up dog shit, mop floors, work at 3 a.m.—whatever it was going to take, I had the motivation to do it. Did I have a passion or a love for driving limos? Hell no. But I had a passion for my future goals and what I expected from life. It motivated me to act and then repeat.

Your vehicle needs an ignition, a starter, something that compels you to jump out of bed in the morning challenged to tackle the day. That ignition is passion. Other people might call this a meaning, a purpose, or a "why". You need to want something greater for you, your family, or something else. It is different for everybody, but when you find it, you will do anything for it.

When you put your goals on a road that actually leads to a dreamy destination, it impassions daily action. If you can't get paid doing some activity, identify a specific "why" or "end goal" that ignites your passion to act.

What is your WHY? Why are you doing this? Why go Fastlane? Whom do you want to prove wrong? My "WHYS" read like this:

"I want to pay off my mother's mortgage."
"I want to wake up without an alarm clock."
"I want to write a book without the pressure of money."
"I want a big house on a mountainside with a pool."
"I want a Lamborghini."
"I want to make a difference."
"I want to prove him wrong."

Passion beats "do what you love," because passion is generalized and can be laser focused toward any goal. When the focus is "doing what you love," the focus becomes industry-specific and you're likely to violate the Commandment of Need.

Why are you starting this business?

Because you love it?

Or because there is a real market need?

I repeat: Passion for an end goal, a why, drives Fastlane action.

Mike Rowe, host of the cable television show Dirty Jobs, profiled several owners of businesses who had less than lovable duties. From testing bovine manure to cleaning up pigeon goop, the owners were passionate. None of them "loved" what they did, but they had passionate "whys" and very deep bank accounts. Competition was sparse because everyone else was busy chasing "do what you love."

A formidable "why" is all you need to turn your daily activities into passionate motivation —the "get up in the morning" metamorphosis to bust open a Fastlane road. What are your WHYS, and are they strong enough to motivate you into process?

PASSION ERASES THE SUFFERING OF WORK

When I was in startup mode with my company, I worked long hours. Was I suffering? No. I enjoyed it, because I had my "whys" and I was moving toward them. The journey hardened me, challenged me, and yes, it was even fun! I was passionate about what I wanted and I was going to get it. *The Fastlane isn't a destination but a personal journey.*

Writing this book has been an enduring journey, and I admit that I gave up three times. Why? After a year of writing and not finishing, my love for writing evaporated. My love became a hate. I was "doing what I love" and suddenly that love faded because people started to expect a book. I confided to a friend, "I quit. I no longer enjoy it and I don't need to finish it."

So how did I finish if my love for writing evaporated? I found my passion, which compelled me to finish: I love to see the dreams of others become reality. When a dead dream is given sudden life, I feel invigorated. Any time I wanted to give up, I'd receive an email that applauded me: "Your forum changed my life" or "Thank you, my life has turned for the better." That is passionate currency that repositioned my writing effort into action. I went from love, to suffering, to passion.

GET YOUR ROAD TO CONVERGE WITH A FANTASTIC DREAM

A road that doesn't converge with your dreams is a dead end. When you concede dreams, life withers. Reflect back to childhood, when you heard: "What do you want to be when you grow up?" Underneath this question, what's it really asking? It's a probe to find the road to your dreams, and it was usually answered in a phantasmal vision. For me, I wanted to be an astronaut (blame Han Solo) a filmmaker (blame George Lucas) and an author (blame Isaac Asimov).

How about you? What is your outrageous, fantastic dream? And the real question of concern: Is there any chance you are doing it, or will be doing it? More than likely, you're not, because the Slowlane has killed it.

I asked my friend Rick this question. Guess what. He didn't answer this question with "I want to be a sales representative at Verizon Wireless." Nope. He answered with "I wanted to be a race car driver." So, why is Rick selling cell phones today? Is there any chance in hell he will actually become his dream, a race car driver?

There isn't. The dream is dead and the road is derelict. Nonetheless, as Rick sticks to his job and waits for a promotion, he wonders, "There's got to be more than this."

And then there's Sarah. She didn't answer this question with, "I want to be a shift manager at Taco Bell." Nope, she wanted to be an artist. But today, Sarah finds herself working the graveyard shift, mopping up the floors in the dining room from slobs who have mistaken sour cream for finger paint. As she slams the mop-head in the wringer, Sarah has a moment of disquiet. "Is this what my life has become?"

The problem with these people is not their jobs. We've all had crappy, embarrassing jobs that we hate. The problem is their dead-end road will never converge with dreams. Dreams are forsaken to pay the bills. Instead of a convergent road to dreams (or a chance of a dream), their road goes through an inescapable hell. Life becomes suffering. There is nothing wrong with working at Verizon or Taco Bell. Heck, these jobs would have been promotions compared to the meaningless jobs I've held. But please, don't make these jobs your end, your final road, because the "end" most likely will never come.

You see, if your dream is dead, so is your passion. "No passion" numbs you to the greatest violinist in the world while he plays in the train depot. "No passion" leads to mediocrity and the land of everybody. "No passion" leads to unhappiness. "No passion" equals no wealth.

If you're struggling for motivation, re-energize your dream and align it with a road capable of burning a trail to its reality. Dead dreams can't burn trails of passion. Passion fires your will to do what is necessary beyond what others can't. Fastlaners work unlike everyone else so they can live unlike anyone else. Take four years of hard work in exchange for 40 years of freedom. Unfortunately, most people take 40 years of hard work for four weeks of freedom, or however long their paid vacation lasts.

FIND YOUR "SNOW IN THE TOILET"

How do you find your passion, a meaning or a why? It comes from either excitement or discontent. Take this story posted on the Fastlane Forum (TheFastlaneForum.com):

> *I grew up in a poor family and lived in an old run-down barn that had been converted into a home. One of the worst times of the year was the winter, because our water pipes would freeze and we would have no running water. The only way to flush the toilet was to bring snow into the barn, pack it into the tank behind the toilet, and wait for it to melt. I saw my mom putting snow in the toilet bowl just for us to flush. The worst part was that it had to be refilled every time someone did their business. I thought to myself, "I never want to live like this again!"*

What is your passion—your perennial "snow in the toilet?"

Leslie Walburn is passionate about animals. Disillusioned by county-owned shelters that euthanize dogs, her dream is to own a no-kill dog rescue shelter. While she can "do what she loves" and get a job at a shelter, it doesn't bring her closer to her dreams, nor will the job help her amass the wealth needed to pursue the dream. Yes, dog shelters are expensive. Instead, Leslie allows her passion to fuel her motivation—she starts a Fastlane business (unrelated to animals) that eventually funds her dream. Her passion leads to a dream without the crucible of money.

Reflect on a time when your life was turned upside down with excitement and/or discontent.

That is your passion. For me, excited passion was when I saw my first Lamborghini as a teenager and I decided "One day, I will own a Lamborghini." For me, discontented passion was watching my mother struggle in dead-end jobs, trying to raise three kids without a husband. Both fueled my passion; I wanted a Lamborghini and I wanted to help ease the burden for my mother. Excitement (wants and desires) serves as passionate fuel, as does discontent (undesirable situations).

Both allowed me to do what others wouldn't.

If you find yours, you will too.

CHAPTER SUMMARY: FASTLANE DISTINCTIONS

- The Commandment of Need states that businesses that solve needs win. Needs can be pain points, service gaps, unsolved problems, or emotional disconnects.
- Ninety percent of all new businesses fail because they are based on selfish internal needs, not external market needs.
- No one cares about your selfish desires for dreams or money; people only want to know what your business can do for them.
- Money chasers haven't broken free from selfishness, and their businesses often follow their own selfish needs.
- People vote for your business with their money.
- Chase money and it will elude you. However, if you ignore it and focus on what attracts money, you will draw it to yourself.
- Help one million people and you will be a millionaire.
- For money to follow "Do what you love," your love must solve a need and you must be exceptional at it.
- "Do what you love" sets the stage for crowded marketplaces with depressed margins.

- When you have the financial resources, you can "do what you love" and not get paid for it, nor do you have to be good at it.
- Slowlaners feed "do what you love" with "do what you hate." Five days of hate for two days of love.
- "Doing what you love" for money can endanger your love.
- Passion for an end goal, a why, drives Fastlane success.
- Having a passionate "why" can transform work into joy.
- "Doing what you love" usually leads to the violation of the Commandment of Need.
- The right road for you is one that will converge with your dreams.

The Commandment of Time

The cost of a thing is the amount of what I will call life which is required to be exchanged for it, immediately or in the long run.

~ HENRY DAVID THOREAU

BREAK THE BINDS THAT TIE

The most loved (and misinterpreted) commandment is the Commandment of Time. The Commandment of Time requires that your business and its income detach from your time. Can your business work for you while you aren't? The Commandment of Time's objective is passive income and a vibrant money tree.

C – E – N – (TIME) – S

A profitable business doesn't guarantee wealth or time detachment. Some business owners are married to their businesses. Their business ostensibly is a job and a lifelong prison sentence.

While giving up your heart and soul for a business is perfectly normal in the startup, growth, and maturation stage, it isn't a prescription I'd want to endure for 40 years. The Commandment of Time asks:

- Can this business be automated and systematized to operate while I'm absent?
- Are my margins thick enough to hire human resource seedlings?
- Can my operation benefit from the introduction of a money tree seedling?
- How can I get this business to operate exclusive of my time?

Jobs are time trades for income, and yes, so are some businesses. The goal of the Fastlane is a disconnection of your time from income, even if that income isn't millions. Would you rather work 10 hours a week and earn $60,000, or work 70 hours a week for $140,000? I'd take the former over the latter every time.

Ashlyn Gardner loves the arts and literature. Following the prophetic advice of gurus, she sets off to "do what she loves"—she opens a coffee shop featuring local artisans and hosts weekly literature readings. Like a new love relationship, her new business starts with a bang and is the source of excitement and eagerness. However, after two years, her business normalizes and the luster fades into hardship. Ashlyn realizes that she doesn't own her business; it owns her.

She is up at 4 a.m. to open and has to be there at 8 p.m. to close. The 24/7 of business is a perpetual nag. Employees come and go, and the good ones demand pay she can't afford. Her social life dies and her boyfriend breaks up with her because she never has time. Her gym membership expires and, with it, her weekly yoga class. Seeking to reclaim her time and her life, Ashlyn considers hiring a general manager. Unfortunately, hiring a GM would put her margins in the red. She won't work the business for free and the cost to her life isn't worth the profit she makes. Three years into the business, she closes up shop and looks to return to the ranks of employee over employer.

Ashlyn didn't fail at business. Her coffee shop was successful and earned her a modest living. Where did she fail? She failed the Commandment of Time and like most business owners, didn't think beyond the excitement.

A MONEY TREE THAT NEVER GROWS

A successful business isn't fun and games, especially one that violates the Commandment of Time. Often people get into business with the wrong idea of what it will be like. Fueled by gurus and life coaches, many are misled, believing that "be your own boss" and "do what you love" is enough motivational fire to sprout success. Unfortunately, these would-be business owners merge onto roads that may as well trail through desert. And sorry, money trees don't grow in the desert.

Think about Ashlyn and her quaint coffee shop. The coffee shop didn't necessarily fail, but it failed her. Was Ashlyn her own boss? Sure, but it wasn't enough. She was motivated by her passion for art and literature, and to be her own boss. While such dispositions are healthy, it doesn't change a deficient road. You can't sprout flowers from arid soil.

As a Fastlaner, you can start any business but eventually you must strive for automation. You want passivity and a living money tree. When you fail the commandment of time, the failure is cause by one of two obstacles. They are:

1) You don't have access to the seeds because your business road started with a deficiency.
2) The seeds won't grow in infertile soil.

If your business is based on a money-tree seedlings, it should be capable of growing a money tree. Content systems, computer systems, software systems, distribution systems, and human resource systems are all seedlings to money trees. If your business isn't based on one, can one be added to make it passive?

For Ashlyn's coffee shop, she recognized she needed a money tree seed—human resources—in the form of a general manager. She couldn't justify the cost, and the seed was inaccessible. Her road started deficient. If she ignores her finances and hires a general manager, hence planting the seed, the seed won't take because the margins aren't there. Infertile grounds cannot grow money trees. And the failure starts when you choose a business not based upon a money tree seedling.

The problem with most business roads is that they are inhospitable for money trees simply because they fail the Commandment of Time. The seeds aren't accessible and those seeds that are accessible, won't take to the soil.

CHAPTER SUMMARY: FASTLANE DISTINCTIONS

- A business attached to your time is a job.
- A business that earns income exclusive of your time satisfies the Commandment of Time.
- To satisfy the Commandment of Time, start with a business that uses a money-system seedling, or introduce one.

The Commandment of Scale

In business, to be a success
you only have to be right once.

~ MARK CUBAN

SPEED LIMIT—15 OR 150?

When your business road violates the Commandment of Scale, wealth acceleration is restricted. In other words, you're given a speed limit. Drive any road with a speed limit of 15 and you aren't going to get anywhere fast. Scale is about leverage and leverage is what gives the Fastlane wealth equation its power.

C - E - N - T - (SCALE)

Business leverage is like a playing field, or a habitat of water. You can choose to inhabit the ocean or a pool at the local park. There are six business habitats:

- Local/community (pool)
- County/city (pond)
- Statewide (lagoon)
- Regional (lake)
- National (sea)
- Worldwide (ocean)

Scale is difficult to find locally or in a pool that fits only a small number of people. Sure, it can be done, but it requires magnitude, and magnitude doesn't come cheap. If you own a tanning salon, your habitat is local. If you own an upscale restaurant, your habitat is county/city. If you own an Internet company, your habitat is worldwide. The larger the habitat, the greater the potential speed, or leverage, of your Fastlane.

SWING FOR HOME RUNS, NOT SINGLES

Billionaire Mark Cuban recently wrote on his blog that it doesn't matter how many times you strike out in business because you only have to be right once, and that "once" can set you up for life. In other words, *be in the business of home runs.*

Business is like baseball. Play on a field where you can hit home runs; don't play on a field where they're prohibited! For example, if you own a clothing boutique on Main Street, you violate the Commandment of Scale because your pool of customers is drawn from the local trading area. To break scale, the business owner needs to introduce leverage in the form of replication: Open more stores, sell franchises, or sell on the Internet.

Unfortunately, most entrepreneurs undertake "singles-only" businesses. Their playing field is stunted. Their road screams "Speed Limit: 15." The home run is impossible and their habitat shriveled. If you're a massage therapist, you'll never have 10,000 patrons outside your door. There is no leverage! And if you don't have leverage in the Fastlane equation, you don't have a chance! The Commandment of Scale is like a tollbooth on the road to the Law of Effection!

THE FASTLANE WEALTH EQUATION: DISARMED

When you violate the Commandment of Scale you disarm the Fastlane wealth equation and demote its power to Slowlane status. Recall the Fastlane wealth equation:

$$\textit{Wealth} = \textit{Net Profit} + \textit{Asset Value}$$

Asset value is predicated on net profit, which is predicated by unit profit multiplied by units sold.

$$\textit{Net Profit} = \textit{Units Sold} \times \textit{Unit Profit}$$

If "units sold" has a ceiling, you stifle leverage. Without leverage, you can't create wealth exponentially. When you travel a business road incapable of scale, you render the Fastlane wealth equation impotent.

My favorite example is the guy who buys a popular sandwich franchise in his local neighborhood. This business violates the Commandment of Scale because the variables—units sold and unit profit—are implicitly limited.

How many sandwiches can this guy humanly sell in one day?

Fifty? A hundred? How many hours are in the day? Twenty-four?

See the similarity? The objective of units sold is to have an upper limit greater than 100. How about 10,000? Or 100,000?

Is there anything this sandwich shop owner can do to sell more sandwiches in one day?

Under his current structure, there isn't.

He is limited in scale to his local trading area. He'll never sell a cold-cut combo to a man living in Australia, let alone the neighboring city. Scale is limited, causing this road to have a constricting speed limit, just like a Slowlane road.

To make matters worse, the other end of the equation is also limited: unit profit. What is the maximum unit profit on a sandwich and drink? Two bucks?

Again, we are operating under a ceiling of low numbers. *These numbers don't transcend wealth; they limit wealth.*

Now let me clarify before I'm hammered: I'm not suggesting that a local restaurant owner can't get rich. In fact, I know a few restaurant owners who do well except they operate a different class of restaurant—upscale establishments, where scale and magnitude have more reach. If your average dinner bill is $300 and patrons come citywide, not just the local neighborhood, you operate on a different scale. Unit profit isn't $2 per sandwich, but $80 per person, and with alcohol it climbs to $160.

REACH OR MAGNITUDE = SCALE

To achieve scale, *magnitude* or *reach* must increase. Magnitude is naturally increased with price or cost. If you sell Lamborghinis over Hyundais, you have greater magnitude simply by the implicit price of Lamborghinis. You are near Effection (Lamborghini owners most likely exploit the Law of Effection). If you are a real estate agent for the rich and sell multimillion dollar estates, you achieve magnitude implicit by price. Higher prices and cost implicitly drive magnitude. If you successfully sell the most expensive apartment building in Manhattan, you have had an effect of magnitude and realize scale. If you are operating with magnitude, you are near or at Effection.

Reach, exclusive of magnitude, also achieves scale. Reach is massive numbers. The more people you reach, the greater scale potential. Who does your business serve? The local neighborhood? Or the world? The bigger your pool of play, the bigger your potential for wealth.

The guy stuck on Main Street selling sandwiches has no scale and no magnitude. Is there anything this guy can do to turn his $40,000-per-year profit into $400,000? Nope. He's done before he even started. He didn't buy a franchise; he bought a job. He will never get rich until he wakes up and realizes that scale is not reached selling one-buck-margin sandwiches to 100 people a day.

SCALE IS LEVERAGE!

The Commandment of Scale demands a business that maximizes the Fastlane wealth equation. Give the Law of Effection a chance! Give wealth a chance! How do you know if your business (or potential business) honors the Commandment of Scale? Ask:

- Can the net income of this business scale limitlessly, say, from $2,000 per month to $200,000?
- Can the asset value of this business scale into the millions?
- Can this business impact millions? Or does it impact hundreds? Is its customer pool the world or a small community in the city?
- Can this business be replicated and expanded beyond the local trading area by franchising, chaining, or additional units?
- Best-case scenario, what is the units-sold potential? One hundred or one hundred million?
- Best-case scenario, how pliable is unit profit? Does it have magnitude?

If you can't affirm these questions, you might be stuck in a restrictive business where wealth creation is stifled.

Tiny habitats create tiny wealth. Scale is large numbers. Think big, nationally, and globally. Big numbers, or scale, is the inroad to The Law of Effection. To make millions, you must affect millions. That doesn't happen in a small store on Main Street, but in hundreds of stores across the country.

DRIVE EFFECTION'S NEIGHBORHOOD

A "wealth-seeking" friend of mine asked if I thought buying a coffee franchise was a good idea. I said, "No." My answer shocked him because he played the "be your own boss" drum. I didn't like the idea because the Law of Effection was barricaded.

The problem?

His goal was financial freedom.

If this was his goal, owning a coffee franchise in the local community wasn't going to do the trick. With a coffee shop, he has no access to the Law of Effection. Selling 100 lattes a day simply won't make an impact in either scale or magnitude. And since he didn't want to own 20 of these franchises, but just one, he was barricaded from the Law.

Road closed.

If you can't access the Law of Effection, you won't get rich. The conduit to all wealth is via the Law of Effection. For the Slowlaner, the LOE has to be hit by massive intrinsic value explosion: Sing in front of millions, entertain millions, play ball in front of millions. For the Fastlaner, the LOE is leveraged by scale or asset value explosion: Sell millions, help millions, serve millions, impact millions.

LAW OF EFFECTION BARRICADES

There are three barricades that prevent entrepreneurs from realizing the Law of Effection: Scale, Magnitude, and Source.

Effection's strongest barricade is scale. If you can't serve millions, you won't make millions. Returning to my friend's coffee shop, his "units sold" variable within the Fastlane wealth equation is restricted because his cafe is confined to a local community. His sales are mathematically caged to a stiff number—scale is absent. He will never sell coffee to someone in New Zealand. A business that lacks scale acts like a car with a speed governor that prevents acceleration.

My friend's only option to break scale would be to purchase more franchises in more locations. If he owned 29 franchises across the state, he suddenly would be serving 6,000 coffees per day. Scale becomes prevalent, and attached to scale is the Law of Effection. Of course, the optimum Fastlane strategy is not buying franchises, but selling them.

If my friend doesn't want to own multiple franchises he can't break the barricade of scale. Without scale (units sold) or magnitude (high unit profit) he drives a business that will produce a weak asset value. His wealth equation becomes retarded and the Law of Effection quarantined, remanding him to a middle-class work-life existence. With a middle-class income and a weak asset valuation, he defects to a wealth equation emblematic of the Slowlane.

The other barricade to Effection is Magnitude.

Because our coffee shop owner is restricted in scale, his other option is scale by magnitude. Unfortunately, the magnitude road is also closed. Unit profit cannot be manipulated. Every sale won't generate a profit of greater than a few bucks and raising prices reduces units sold. A $100,000 profit on each coffee sold is impossible.

While direct access to the Law of Effection is a foolproof road to wealth, indirect access isn't so clear, since Effection always trickles up to owners and producers, not down to employees or consumers.

For example, if you work as a doctor at a private-care facility, you could argue that you have magnitude and therefore, you should be rich. In fact, all doctors should be rich since they have magnitude, right? Not exactly. The fault in this presumption is that *the Law of Effection honors only those in control.*

That private health-care facility? The facility's owner receives the full benefit of Effection, not the doctors he hired. The doctors on staff aren't guaranteed access to Effection, because they don't control the system. Can they be rich anyway? Sure, but that decision is left to intrinsic value evaluations made by the owner of the system.

Doctors who own practices and hire other doctors get full access to Effection and get rich. *Effection always is biased toward the architect of the system.*

HOW TO ACCESS THE LAW

If you want access to the Law of Effection, drive a road that can break through scale or magnitude while controlling its source. If you can't be the source, *serve the source.*

Thankfully, you can easily determine which roads run parallel to the Law of Effection. Whatever your road, regardless of roadmap, can it directly scale to impact millions (scale)? Can it tremendously impact a few (magnitude)?

- If you invent a gadget that millions can use, you have direct scale and the Law is accessible. Fast wealth is a possible.
- If you are chosen as a finalist for *American Idol*, you have direct scale and the Law is accessible. Fast wealth is possible.
- If you build a website that serves single moms, you have direct scale and the law is accessible. Fast wealth is possible.
- If you are two management positions away from a CFO position at a *Fortune 100* Company, you have indirect scale and the law is accessible. Fast wealth is possible.
- If you are an attorney and take cases that involve wrongful deaths, you have indirect magnitude and the law is accessible. Fast wealth is possible.
- If you create a successful retail store and franchise it to 300 entrepreneurs around the country, you have both scale and magnitude and the law is accessible. Fast wealth is possible.
- If you invent a machine that detects skin cancer, you have magnitude and scale and the law is accessible. Fast wealth is possible.

Think big, but think scale and/or magnitude.

Analyze your Fastlane equation and examine the variables. What are your maximum units sold and maximum profit per unit?

What is the size of your customer pool?

For example, as an author, I have scale, and with scale, the Law of Effection is accessible. Who is my audience? The whole English-speaking world, tens of millions of people! I'm reminded of scale any time this book is ordered from Australia or New Zealand. My upper limit is the world. My road has no speed limit and that grants access to the Law of Effection.

CHAPTER SUMMARY: FASTLANE DISTINCTIONS

- Your total pool of customers determines your habitat. The larger the habitat, the greater the potential for wealth.
- A business can be a singles or a home-run-based business. Its strength is determined by scale, which is derived by habitat.

- The Fastlane wealth equation is disarmed when you violate the Commandment of Scale.
- Scale is achieved in reach (units sold) and/or magnitude (unit profit).
- The Law of Effection is the primary conduit to wealth, which can be roadblocked by scale, magnitude, or source.
- Effection consequences trickle up to owners and producers. Breaking scale or magnitude indirectly in an uncontrolled entity is not a guarantee of wealth.
- To gain access to Effection, you have to break the barrier of scale or magnitude in an entity you control.
- Scale, magnitude, or source deficiencies create governors on the speed of wealth creation.

Rapid Wealth: The Interstates

You can't live a perfect day without doing something for someone who will never be able to repay you.

~ JOHN WOODEN

THE CROSSROADS

If you want to get across the country, drive the fastest roads, not the slowest. Seems logical, except when it comes to financial independence. Instead of driving the fastest roads, most people drive the slowest, and in some cases, a road that won't even get them there.

Starting a business is a big decision. Treat it with cursory interest, and your business resembles a hobby. And businesses run like hobbies pay like hobbies.

Back in my mid-20s, I dabbled in a variety of businesses with no lasting success. It was the crossroads of my life and my latest job-flavor-of-the-month was driving limousines. Sure, I took the job because I had bills to pay, but I had other motives: infiltration.

I thought I wanted to own a limousine company.

Having never been involved in the limo business, I figured I'd get a job in the business and learn the ropes. After a year in the business, my opportunity—my crossroads—arrived. The owner of the limousine company put the company up for sale and offered it to me for no money down. Here was my opportunity—a chance to own a limousine service! Except there was one problem.

I was torn.

Just weeks earlier, I decided to move to Phoenix and was preparing to move. Now this.

Should I stay?

Also, after watching the current owner dredge the constant demands of the business for over a year, I realized something very potent: I didn't enjoy it. The business was 24/7 with a lot of early mornings. Me? I'm one cranky bastard in the morning.

So I was faced with a choice that could be either treasonous or accelerative. Was this a road I wanted to take? Did I want to pass on this great "no money down" opportunity and forgo Phoenix?

What did I do?

I compiled my weighted average decision matrix (WADM) to give me clarity. Yes, I really use the stuff in this book! Obviously, Phoenix won and I didn't buy the limousine company. But what was in that decision matrix that helped me identify the right road and the right course of action?

I knew the five Fastlane commandments and which roads of business had "Fastlane Purity" . . . and I knew the odds of implementation of both.

FASTLANE PURITY: FIVE COMMANDMENTS

Thou shalt not invest in a needless business.

Thou shalt not trade time for money.

Thou shalt not operate on a limited scale.

Thou shalt not relinquish control.

Thou shalt not let a business startup be an event over process.

When I analyzed the limousine service as a potential business, it wasn't a pure Fastlane. The operation had satisfied the control and entry criterion, but it didn't have scale; it served the northwest suburbs of Chicago.

The operation didn't have time detachment; I would have had to log long hours, and the margins weren't thick enough to deploy human resources.

And it certainly didn't solve an unmet need; in Chicago, limo companies were a dime a dozen.

To "Fastlane" the business, it would have required a lot of time, effort, and money.

Deep down, I knew that I wanted to be involved in a business that was pure Fastlane from the start, not one that needed sculpting.

The purest Fastlanes have the best wealth potential, and I knew it. When you grace the Law of Effection, money moves your way. What are the purest Fastlane roads that possess super-fast speeds? Which roads can tap into the Law of Effection and start Fastlane?

THE THREE FASTLANE INTERSTATES

I call the most potent Fastlane roads "The Three I's," or "The Three Interstates," because they possess the fastest upper speed limits and meet, or can meet, all five Fastlane commandments. The three Interstates are:

1) Internet
2) Innovation
3) Intentional Iteration

Each interstate road is an umbrella for dozens of other roads. Put all three together and you have hundreds of roads available for your travel.

Potent Fastlane #1: The Internet

The most potent interstate is an Internet business. The Internet has made more millionaires in the last decade than any other medium out there. The Internet has, and is, destroying old hard-line industries such as travel agents, stockbrokers, newspapers, and magazines. The Internet is the Fastlane shark.

The Internet is where I found my fortune and it is one reason why I declined the limousine opportunity. The Internet is the best Fastlane available, because it immediately obeys the Five Fastlane Commandments, assuming a need-based premise. It naturally scales to a worldwide audience, it systematizes to automation via computer systems, it is a medium you can control (unfortunately, most don't), and its barriers are still strong enough to prevent "everyone" from entry.

Internet business models (roads) fall into seven broad categories:

1) Subscription-based

Offer users access to data, information, or software (SAAS), and charge a monthly fee. Data can be leads, sales information, management services (social media dashboards), a proprietary database, or good old-fashioned pornography. When 10,000 people pay you $9.95 per month for your information, you're balling the Fastlane!

When I owned my company, I paid for many web services, all subscription-based. From data analytics (who is visiting my site?) to affiliate management (who wants to offer my service?).

One particular company ran a web-site-monitoring service that kept track of website uptime. On its home page it advertised how many clients it monitored. At the time, it listed "20,000 clients served," and I was paying $50 per month for service. Assuming my fee was average, 20,000 × $50 = $1,000,000 in gross revenue—PER MONTH. This is a perfect example of an Internet business system in which the business is the system. No products. No shipping. No headaches.

I'd speculate that this website enjoys margins of 75% and nets in the $750,000 range, per month. How quickly would you become a millionaire earning $750,000/month? Or, would you rather save $200/month from your $45K/year salary? The disparaging field of play is laughable.

Examples of subscription sites are Buffer.com, Adobe, and yes, even my own Fastlane Forum (which is FREE but has a subscription upgrade).

2) Content-based

Content-based models are online news magazines and blogs that disseminate information to a particular niche or industry. These services provide content for free consumption and sell advertising to parties who want to reach those eyeballs. My Fastlane Forum is partly a content-based revenue model. Succeeding at a content-based revenue model is difficult because entry barriers have significantly declined and they're dependent on high traffic. Also, content systems heavily use affiliate programs, which is a hitchhiking structure.

3) Lead generation

Lead generation services often provide a service to consumers while simultaneously aggregating a non-homogeneous industry. This is what I did for the limousine industry. I pooled a highly fragmented industry into one centralized source, brought consumers into the mix, and sold that consumer information to limo companies. Lead generation is popular with fragmented industries, where the industry players consist of mostly small to medium-sized businesses. Lead generation in the airline business probably wouldn't work while lead generation for plastic surgeons would. Lead generation solves two needs: 1) The consumer's desire to save time and money and 2) The business owner's need to find new customers inexpensively.

4) Social Networks / Communities / Forums

Community building is a cousin of content systems. Instead of pooling content for eyeballs, people are pulled into groups, or tribes. Facebook started off as a pool for college-aged students and evolved into a generic social network for all ages. LinkedIn hits the upwardly mobile professional. Social networks are mere aggregators of like-minded communities, from mystery novel writers to gear heads who like to rebuild engines on the weekend. Community building, however, is not limited to gigantic corporations. If you have 500,000 subscribers on your YouTube or Instagram account, you are community building.

5) Brokerage Systems

Brokers bring buyers and sellers together and facilitate transactions. They are market-makers for a particular industry and earn money typically on each transaction. For instance, my website used to take limousine reservations and take a percentage cut of the fare price. Examples of known brokers are PayPal, Upwork, CarsDirect, and Travelocity.com.

6) Advertising

Similar to brokerages, advertisers merge buyers and sellers together and accept advertising fees in lieu of transaction fees. I also owned a niche website that listed limousines for sale. The site accepted advertising fees for each limousine placed for sale. I introduced buyers and sellers. Some services leverage both brokerage and advertising together, such as eBay. Search engines like Google and Yahoo operate both advertising and brokerage models.

7) E-Commerce

E-commerce is the act of selling goods, services, and information over the Internet. Amazon, Target, and Rakuten are examples of large-scale e-commerce providers. However, many small local stores have expanded and created scale with the e-commerce model. In my backyard, I have 24 solar lights that I bought online from a small retailer in Minnesota that operates an e-commerce store. Just years ago, that store was local with no scale—now with an e-commerce presence, they are worldwide and are selling products to retired farts in Phoenix.

E-commerce also can be information. E-books are the most popular form of information distribution on the Internet. When I sell my book in e-book form on the Internet, I'm participating in eCommerce. I can sell books out of my trunk by sitting in the parking lot at Arizona State University, or I can set up a website and sell books to folks in Europe.

When you look at the Internet as a Fastlane road, it is immensely powerful when examined against our Fastlane Wealth Equation.

Wealth = Net Profit + Asset Value

Within the units sold variable (within net income), the world becomes your upper limit when dealing on the Internet. Additionally, asset value, a component of the Fastlane wealth equation, is not only determined by net income, but by traffic metrics. Many websites are sold for billions and don't have a penny of profit. Traffic, or visitors to a website, also has a boundless upside scale. The Fastlane variables of net profit and asset value have a virtually limitless upside.

Potent Fastlane #2: Innovation

Innovation is another broad stroke of Fastlane purity and encompasses many roads. It is the good old-fashioned way to get rich: Invent a product, service, or piece of information, manufacture it, and then distribute it.

Innovation covers any act of creation followed by distribution. Let me repeat that: Innovation involves two acts:

1) Manufacture and
2) Distribution.

Invent a product, then sell it by infomercial, sell it on the Internet, sell it on QVC, sell through 10,000 network marketing distributors, or sell it to 20 wholesalers that then sell it to 20,000 retailers.

What is the product of innovation?

Virtually anything that solves a need or fulfills a desire.

- Food (beer, barbecue sauce, cookies, secret recipes)
- Household (robots that vacuum, tools, hangers)
- Health and vitality (vitamins, herbs, energy drinks, bars, "male enhancement formulas")
- Information (books, magazines, subscription newsletters)
- Personal (clothing, purses, shoes, gloves)
- Automotive (accessories, add-ons, stick-ons)
- Games or toys

Inventing is still recognized as the default get-rich-quick method out there, and yes, it is alive and well. However, don't be fooled. Inventing isn't really about inventing the vehicle, the telephone, or the goofy Segway—the core inventing activity is just taking something and improving or modifying it. Take something old and stale and make it better. Take an underexposed product, make it your own, and reintroduce it to the world. Take something unconventional and make it conventional.

On TV I saw an inventor who repackaged vodka from boring clear bottles to colorful bottles with razzle-dazzle. In fact, I received a skull-shaped bottle of vodka for my birthday. Vodka has been around for centuries, yet an entrepreneur took a stale product and added an element of uniqueness and differentiation. Sometimes it's that simple.

My favorite example is the Snuggie, an oversized mass-marketed blanket with arms. The product concept has been around for years, but they took the concept, repackaged it, remarketed it, and wham, 40 million sold later, they had a blockbuster.

Innovation is a dual challenged process: *manufacture* and *distribution.*

Inventing a product that solves a need is half the battle. The other half is getting your invention into the hands of millions, which involves a variety of distribution channels: infomercial (sell via mass media), retail (sell to distributors and wholesalers), and direct marketing (sell via print media, postal mail, Internet).

For example, when I wrote this book, I was the manufacturer. I wrote it, put it together, edited it, and had it physically published. I practiced innovation. However, like all innovation roads, manufacture is one tiny battle in a larger war.

Distribution is where the war is won.

A great product is worthless if it doesn't get into the hands of people, and that requires distribution. For my book, I will need to leverage Amazon (a distribution system), book distributors (wholesalers), and the Internet (another distribution system) if I am to succeed.

Yes, your product invention can be something you invent yet is manufactured in China, or an e-book you write in a weekend. Innovation—from books to products—is Fastlane. Have you ever wondered why people sell get-rich-quick books and yet the content is just regurgitated blather from 30 prior books? The authors know that authoring is a potent Fastlane.

The challenge of any authoring Fastlane is never the book or the words themselves. Some of the greatest books in the world go unread, while the mediocre stuff sells millions. The difference lies in marketing, public relations, and just good old-fashioned business know-how. *Writing a book is not a business; selling the book is.*

If I'm obsessively intent on selling this book to millions, I have to manufacture, then distribute. I have to sell, market, promote, appear, speak, interview, and write; I have to invest in the business of distribution. To leverage the Fastlane wealth equation and get near the Law of Effection, I have to strap on my commitment helmet and work, work, work…

Potent Fastlane #3: Intentional Iteration (II)

The final Fastlane Interstate is "Intentional Iteration" (II). Iteration is: "the means or act of repeating a process, usually with the aim of approaching a desired goal or target or result."

Intentional iteration is a potent Fastlane but it offers the greatest challenge because it really doesn't satisfy all five commandments, but four.

The process of intentional iteration is the act of satisfying the final commandment, scale. Scale is achieved either through human resource systems or repeated successes.

For example, when a real estate investor buys a single-family home at a bank auction and later rents it, there is no scale, and with that one act, nothing can create scale. The investor has little wiggle room in his Fastlane wealth equation: Net income is derived from rent and asset value is derived by the home's market value.

To solve that challenge, the investor deploys II and repeats the process. Instead of buying one home, he buys 50. Yes, easier said than done, and it can be incredibly slow. In effect, the investor has chosen to play on a field of "singles," and to hit the home run, II needs to become the strategy.

Iteration is a profitable, singles-based business scaled to home runs.

Franchising is another example of II.

If you build a small store with intentional iteration in mind, your goal isn't one store, but hundreds, perhaps thousands, through the act of chaining or franchising.

The intentional iterator goes into business to cookie-cut his system across many successes. A small store often starts out as a violation of four commandments but can quickly transfigure into a full-fledged Fastlane venture with iteration. The Fastlane franchising premise is to build a local business defined by systematic processes, then franchise the concept nationally or worldwide. The iterator's goal is to replicate and sell a concept, a brand, and a system and remove himself from operations. While your little deli might not be particularly Fastlane it could be turned Fastlane by the process of II, through franchise or chaining replication.

A popular thread at my forum is titled "Is a candy kiosk Fastlane?" A forum user wanted to know if having automated candy kiosks in the mall constitutes a Fastlane plan. As a standalone, no. But with II? Maybe, assuming online retail doesn't kill every mall in America. One kiosk in one mall isn't going to make you rich because it's a singles-based business. However, 200 kiosks in 50 malls might, because it creates net income, scales asset value, and makes a bigger impact of magnitude.

Intentional iteration is the Fastlaner's response to limited scale.

CHAPTER SUMMARY: FASTLANE DISTINCTIONS

- The best Fastlanes satisfy all five Commandments: Control, Entry, Need, Time, and Scale.
- Assuming a need-based premise, the Internet is the fastest interstate, because it overwhelmingly satisfies all Commandments.
- Innovation can be any variety of open roads: authoring, inventing, or services.
- Inventing success needs coupling with distribution.
- A singles-based business is scaled to a home-run business by intentional iteration. With iteration, scale is conquered.

Find Your Open Road

At first, people refuse to believe that a strange new thing can be done, then they begin to hope it can be done, then they see it can be done—then it is done, and all the world wonders why it was not done centuries ago.

~ FRANCES HODGSON BURNETT

NEEDS, IDEAS, OPPORTUNITY, AND THE OPEN ROAD

Opportunities, and the open roads they represent, are everywhere. Look around. That person complaining at the store counter. Opportunity. That stupid voicemail maze you hate navigating when you call the bank. Opportunity. That unsold house that languishes on the market. Opportunity. That trash on the side of the road. Opportunity. The rotting salad that lasted only two days in the refrigerator. Opportunity. Those people bitching on that online forum. Opportunity.

If you can't see the opportunities that surround you, you haven't tuned your Fastlane frequency to them. When you make a few minor mental adjustments, roads seemingly closed are suddenly opened. Many entrepreneurs misinterpret opportunity because they associate opportunity with breakthrough, legendary ideas. They seek virgin ideas, perfect and new; ones that would be unveiled to the world in grandiose events. Rarely does that happen.

Opportunity is rarely about some blockbuster breakthrough like the light bulb or the car, but as simple as an unmet need, or a need not met adequately. Opportunity is a solution to an inconvenience. Opportunity is simplification. Opportunity is a feeling. Opportunity is comfort. Opportunity is better service. Opportunity is fixing pain. Opportunity is putting weak companies out of business.

SOMEONE IS DOING IT

You've got a great idea, but someone is already doing it? So what. Do it better.

"Someone is doing it" is a monumental illusion imposing as an impassable obstacle. *Someone is always already doing it.* The bigger question is, can you do it better? Can you fill the need better, offer greater value, or be a better marketer? When I was struck with my idea to start a limousine portal on the Internet, I thought it was a legendary idea . . . that is, until I went on the web and searched. There were already a dozen companies doing what I thought was a pristine, unmolested idea. At the time, my frequency wasn't tuned. I was going to drop the idea and start a new brainstorm session in search of that infamous blockbuster idea, one that no one among 7 billion people on planet Earth had ever thought of. But a friend interrupted my perception and kicked my antennae into a proper tune. She said, "Competition is everywhere. Just do it and do it better."

She was right. Competition is a staple of business. This opportunity was an open road, not a closed one. These existing web directories weren't easily found and, for the most part, weren't user friendly. I recognized a poorly met need and I decided to drive this road of opportunity, despite the numerous barricades that warned "Road Closed." A decade later, every one of those companies I feared disappeared or became insignificant. In fact, the industry leader, unable to respond to my domination, diverted into an alternative service.

FORGET THE BIG IDEA; GO FOR BETTER

Successful businesses rarely evolve from some legendary idea. Nope, successful entrepreneurs take existing concepts and improve them. They take poorly met needs and solve them better. *Skip the big idea and go for the big execution.* You don't need an idea that has never been done before. Old ideas suffice; just take it and do it better! Execute like no one has!

Years ago, what if Sergey Brin and Larry Page looked at the Internet landscape and said "Gee, there are plenty of search engines out there—Yahoo, Snap, Alta Vista—why start Google? It's being done!" Thankfully, they didn't, and now Google is the most used search engine, and because of it, Brin and Page are now billionaires. A brand-spanking new idea? Nope, a need solved better with big execution.

Department stores have been around for decades, but that didn't stop Sam Walton from creating Wal-Mart. It was an open road when the road seemed closed.

Hamburgers were around for decades, but that didn't stop Ray Kroc from blowing up McDonalds after joining the company. It was an open road when the road seemed closed.

Coffee had been around for a thousand years when Howard Schultz bought into the Starbucks concept. A new idea? Nope, Starbucks made coffee fashionable and invented a brand, an ambiance, and an emotion and attached it to coffee. It was an open road when the road seemed closed.

DVD rental stores were around for a long time, but that didn't stop NetFlix or RedBox from starting a company and adding "convenience" to the need equation. It was an open road when the road seemed closed.

Beer has been brewed for thousands of years, but that didn't stop Jim Koch from starting Sam Adams or Sam Calagione from starting Dogfish Head Craft Brewery, now the fastest growing brewery in America. Dogfish was started back in 1995 with a 10-gallon home brew kit and little cash. There was an open road when the road seemed closed.

Garbage has been around since men have walked the planet. Yet that didn't stop Brian Scudamore from starting and then franchising 1-800-GOT-JUNK, nor did it stop Wayne Huizinga from founding Waste Management with just one truck and a handful of customers. He later built Waste Management into a *Fortune 500* company. Is garbage a new need? Or a need that needed better fulfillment? It was an open road when the road seemed closed.

A blanket with arms? It's been around for years, but that didn't stop Snuggie from selling 40 million blankets via infomercial marketing. An old idea better marketed and better executed. It was an open road when the road seemed closed.

MySpace was thriving well before Facebook, but that didn't stop Mark Zuckerberg. He saw a niche need and solved it. And then adjusted as growth followed. It was an open road when the road seemed closed.

Poorly met needs are open roads often appearing closed. Successful businesses take existing ideas, services, and products and simply make them better, or spin them in new directions.

HOW TO SPOT OPEN ROADS

Not a day goes by when I don't spot a need that can be exploited for Fastlane opportunity. My mind is tuned because I see opportunity's terrain through heightened senses. I see and hear what most people don't. How can you tune your eyes and ears to the same attuned frequency? With a little practice, it's easy.

Open roads, needs and opportunity come prefaced with "code words" or phrases that scream "This is an opportunity!" When you catch yourself (or someone else) in these words, you've just uncovered a possible opportunity. Here are the most common phrases:

"I hate . . ."
What do you hate? Solve the hate, and there's your open road.

"I don't like . . ."
What don't you like? Remove the dislike, and there's your open road.

"This frustrates me . . ."
What is frustrating? Remove the frustration, and there's your open road.

"Why is this like this?"
I don't know, why is it? Remove the "why," and there's your open road.

"Do I have to?"
Do you? Remove the "have to." There's your open road.

"I wish there was . . ."
What do you wish? If you wish, others wish too. Make wishes come true, and there's your open road.

"I'm tired of . . ."
What are you tired of? Fix someone's tiresomeness, and there's your open road.

"This sucks . . ."
What sucks? Remove or reduce suckage, and there's your open road.

Opportunity is dressed in predictable code words that spotlight its presence. For example, I'm a sloppy eater. A white shirt plus spaghetti and forget it. Aside from the slop, I have a nasty knack of biting my lip on the inside of my mouth. When I bite myself, a canker sore forms every time. I've had canker sore issues since grade school. The last canker sore I had lasted a week and was excruciatingly painful. "I'm tired of these canker sores!" I bellyached. Notice the language "I'm tired . . ." Ring ring, opportunity!

My discomfort led me to the Internet for canker sore research. I found some conflicting conjecture and information on how to prevent them. Some people recommended Vitamin X while others recommended Herb Y. (Vitamin X and Herb Y is not the real name because I'm protecting my formula!) So, I bought Vitamin X and Herb Y and waited until my next chewing mistake.

Then it happened. While eating some oatmeal, I bit my lip. A few days later I felt a canker sore brewing at the bite location. I loaded up on Vitamin X and Herb Y. Remarkably, the canker sore never formed, and it appeared that Vitamin X and Herb Y worked as a canker sore preventive. Now, anytime I feel a canker sore brewing from an earlier bite wound, I repeat this process, and each time, the sore does not form. I haven't had a canker sore in nearly three years! I went from one every other month to none. My opportunity is clear. I could market my special "canker formula" to the masses. I have control, decent entry barriers, scale, and time. How many people suffer from canker sores? How many canker prevention formulas are out there? A few, but are they being marketed well? Can I execute better? (Note: Fixing my diet ultimately ended my canker sores and the need for my formula!)

The opportunities of open roads come in easily painted language: Discomfort, distress, inconvenience, complaints, problems, and performance gaps. You must attack these challenges and introduce solutions—offer solutions to the masses and I guarantee money will follow! Moral: Solve other people's problems and you will solve your own money problems!

FAILURE CRACKS ROADS OPEN

Unfortunately, the least-traveled Fastlane roads are paved in failure, not smooth asphalt. This means stalls are guaranteed. *Everyone fails on the road to success.* What separates the winners from the losers is what happens when failure arises. How are you going to react? Will your road trip end with the verdict being, "This Fastlane shit don't work," or will you switch roads? Or keep going?

Failures that drive you into new directions are often the most productive forces for invention. The heart pacemaker, microwave ovens, penicillin, and vulcanized rubber are all inventions that are the profound results of failures and accidents. Failure cracked the road open, and in that failure, the inventors had the fortitude to recognize it.

Yes, quitting your road and changing directions is sometimes the best choice. But be mindful of the distinction between "quitting" and "quitting your road." Quitting is leaving your dreams for dead and putting them into the bin of impossibility. "Quitting your road" is changing course and turning down a new road. If you end your career as a teacher to start a private tutoring company, you have switched roads. If you sell your tanning salon and start an Internet company, you have turned off one road onto another. If you quit that network marketing company and decide to start your own, you have switched roads.

I made many road changes, but I didn't give up on the dream. If your road doesn't converge with your dreams, it might be time to quit your road.

CHAPTER SUMMARY: FASTLANE DISTINCTIONS

- Opportunities are rarely about inventing breakthroughs, but about performance gaps, small inconveniences, and pain points.
- Competition should not impede your road. Competition is everywhere, and your objective should be to "do it better."
- Fastlane success resides in execution, not in the idea.
- The world's most successful entrepreneurs didn't have blockbuster ideas; they just took existing concepts and made them better, or exposed them to more people.
- Opportunity is exposed in your language and your thought processes, as well as other people's language.
- Failure cracks open new roads.
- Quitting only happens when you give up on your dream.

Give Your Road a Destination

The tragedy of life doesn't lie in not reaching your goal.
The tragedy lies in having no goal to reach.

~ BENJAMIN MAYS

WHAT IS YOUR END?

The Fastlane doesn't care about your ends; it just wants to be the means. Expensive Italian cars and luxury estates might not be important to you.

I get it.

Maybe you're altruistic and want to live modestly, spread the gospel, or contribute to charity and philanthropy. The end of the Fastlane road trip is to crown your happiness with freedom. Freedom from financial encumbrances, freedom freedom from bosses, alarm clocks, two-hour commutes; freedom from bad ratios (9-to-5, 5-for-2, 2 weeks every 52 weeks and 8% over 40 years) and freedom to enjoy the world as your playground.

THE PRICE OF FREEDOM: MONEY

Freedom has a price, and that price is money. Big dreams, from materialistic Ferraris to altruistic nonprofit foundations, cost money. You can't travel the world by swimming in the oceans. You have to pay your way, and if you think money is evil, you've already lost.

On the Fastlane Forum, a user posted this exchange that demonstrates how people want the fruit of the freedom tree but lack resolve to plant it.

I sat around a campfire talking to some people. The subject of money came up. One of the guys told me how life is not all about money, and that money isn't even real—just a socially accepted mirage—and that he wants to be poor and not some corporate asshole. This guy tells me that he's left his life behind in order to "find himself," so he's interning (for free) at this place in exchange for room and board.

Things have been hard since he had to leave his four-year-old son behind—but he needed to "find himself." After all, life isn't about money; and all he wants is a little house and a horse, like what the neighbors have down the hill. Everyone around the campfire is nodding and commending this guy for being so enlightened. First, I agree. Life is not about money, it's about time—so why are you throwing away 40 hours a week in pursuit of housing (not even money!)? Second, money doesn't change people; it just makes them more of what they already are. Third, that little house and horse down the hill are worth about $1.5 million. And most importantly, you abandoned your son to find yourself? And you aren't making a dime in the process? Who is subsidizing your journey of enlightenment, and the emotional and financial responsibility of your son you left behind? I've run into a series of people lately who hate money and everything having to do with money, but they still want the end result: Free time and the ability to live their dream. I won't even get into how this conversation went when he introduced his politics. Suffice to say, that we (not him) should pay for this guy to have a little house, a horse, and someone else to raise his son.

No matter how big or small, dreams have a price, and that price is money, responsibility, accountability, and commitment. Yes, it will cost you money, but how much?

SET YOUR DESTINATION: FOUR STEPS TO STARTING

Your destination is the lifestyle you want while having the freedom to enjoy it.

There are two strategies to hit your destination.

The first is a money system in which you save enough money that is large enough to support your lifestyle through monthly interest and dividends.

The second is a business system that spawns passive cash flow that supports your lifestyle AND simultaneously funds your money system.

To make this happen, you need targets. Specifically, how much money will you and your family need?

What is the price for the freedom and lifestyle you want?

Find out with this four-step process:

1) Define the Lifestyle: What do you want?
2) Assess the Cost: How much do your dreams cost?
3) Set the Targets: Set the money system and business income targets.
4) Make It Real: Fund it and open it!

Step 1: Define the Lifestyle

Define the lifestyle you want and its associated costs. Do you want the big house or the nonprofit foundation? What exactly do you want? Write everything down. For the purpose of this exercise, I will play along.

Three cars: a Mercedes, a hybrid, and a minivan
A 6,000-square-foot house with a fountain, pool, and waterfall
A small cabin in the mountains
The ability to travel three months a year
Private school for my children

Step 2: Assess the Cost

Determine the monthly cost for each, including all associated expenses; taxes, utilities, maintenance, insurance, etc. Don't forget life overhead, such as health insurance, food, etc.

Three cars: $2,000
House: $5,000
Cabin: $1,000
Travel: $1,000
Private School: $1,000

Lifestyle Cost = $10,000*/month*

Next, determine your monthly allowance and other unknowns. This is for stuff like clothes, gadgets, toys for the children, entertainment, etc. Add this to your Lifestyle Cost to arrive at your Gross Living Cost.

Gross Living Cost = $10,000/mo. (Lifestyle Cost) + $4,000/mo. (Allowances)
Gross Living Cost = $14,000/mo.

Next, determine your Net Living Cost by dividing Gross Living Cost by .60, or 60%. This will account for potential taxes.

Net Living Cost = $14,000 / .60 = $23,333/mo.

Step 3: Set the Targets

The goal of this step is to set your two targets: the *business system* income target and the *money system* target. To calculate your money system target, multiply your Net Living Cost by 12, then divide by .05, or 5%. Five percent is the minimum expected yield on a money system.

Money System Target = ($23,333 × 12) / .05 = $5,599,920

For your business system target, multiply your Gross Living Cost by 5, the required parameter to achieve a similar result by a money system.

Business System Target = ($14,000 × 5) = $70,000/mo.

These are your two targets.

First, seek to create a business system that generates $70,000/month in passive monthly income. Of this income, 40% goes to taxes, 40% goes to fund your money system, and 20% pays your lifestyle. This delivers your target lifestyle AND simultaneously funds your money system.

The other target is your passive income from a lump-sum money system. To enjoy your designated lifestyle supported by a money system, your target number is $5,599,920. Five percent interest on this amount is roughly $23,000 monthly, which covers lifestyle and taxes.

This dual-flanked attack builds a passive income stream from a business that funds a money system. The result is like warping the destination to you. You can experience retirement without being retired.

For example, my web business routinely earned $100,000 per month, month after month. Yet, in those instances, I didn't have $20,000,000 lying around, but the lifestyle was an option because *my business system cash-flowed the equivalent of that lump sum*. Excess income funded my money system.

Then, later, I liquidated the asset to arrive at my "money-system" number. If your business system generates passive income, you can use it to fund your lifestyle and your money system simultaneously.

Step 4: Make It Real

Get started today by looking three feet in front of you, not three miles. A long gaze at the mountain crest will overwhelm you, so stop looking at it.

The key to achieving enormous tasks is to break them down into their smallest parts. You can't run a 26-mile marathon by focusing on the 26th mile. You attack the first, then the second, third, and so forth.

I see this repeated at the Fastlane forum (TheFastlaneForum.com): "I'd like to make $5,000/month; how do I do this?" Aside from the flawed "money chasing" logic, the first step is to make $50/month. You can't make $5,000 per month until you learn how to make $50 per month! It's amazing how people love to skip process and want events.

To start your money system, find a quarter and drop it into a coffee can. Congratulations, you are 25 steps closer to your goal.

No, I'm not kidding.

Your goal isn't 5,600,000 dollars but 560,000,000 pennies.

Drop your loose change into your can at the end of each day. Find 60 cents there, 25 cents there, 115 cents there; it adds up and, albeit small, you move closer to your goal daily.

Ridiculous?

Nope, this is how I started, and yes, I still practice this today because this exercise has three conditioning purposes.

First, when you drop change into your bucket daily, you train yourself to visualize your goal moving closer. You get a daily reminder. Certainly you won't accumulate 560 million pennies in this fashion, but the objective is repetitive progress toward a seemingly distant goal.

Second, it forces you to evaluate: Have you applied pressure to that goal, or is your change bucket the only weapon in your arsenal? Are you pursuing a Fastlane business or still confined to a job?

The third purpose is to *change your relationship* with money. If you are serious about a money system, you're going to need a big shift in your beliefs about money. What is money to you? A medium to get the latest *Call of Duty* release? Or the soldiers for your army of freedom fighters?

The final step is to fund your money system at a brokerage firm. Designate an account that represents your money system. Typically, most brokerage accounts require a minimum $1,000 deposit. If you already have an account, pick an income fund that yields at least 5% yearly and move the funds there. Or alternatively, you can open a trading account and leverage cheaper and regularly traded Exchange Traded Funds (ETFS) instead of a traditional mutual fund. Here are the brokerage houses I recommend to fund your actual account.

1) Fidelity (Fidelity.com/1-800-FIDELITY)
2) Vanguard (Vanguard.com/1-877-662-7447)
3) T. Rowe Price (TRowePrice.com/1-800-638-5660)
4) TDAmeritrade (TDAmeritrade.com/1-800-454-9272)

If you don't have $1,000 to fund the account, you can do it once you hit the $1,000 milestone. Your change bucket should yield about $500 per year. With an actual account, you can witness the real-time passivity of your money system. If you have $50,000 in your passive money system (not leveraged in a Fastlane pursuit) you can literally see your passive income stream every month in the form of either interest or dividends. For example, if you invested in a world bond fund for your money system and it yielded 6.5%, from $50,000 you'd generate $270 per month in passive income, each and every month.

Now, I reiterate, Fastlane wealth is created by the net income and asset value—not by the stock market or compound interest. Your Fastlane business should fund this account, not savings from your paycheck.

THE RULES OF THE ROAD: FINANCIAL LITERACY

After my sister turned 21, she bought her first new car—a Nissan Pulsar. It was her first mistake in the world of finance and my first exposure to financial illiteracy. My sister had trouble making the car payments, and when I asked to read her loan documents, I was floored. I investigated and asked, "How did you buy this car? How did you negotiate?"

She replied, "I told the dealer I wanted a payment of $399 per month."

Her tragic mistake wasn't negotiating weakness, but financial illiteracy. The dealer gave her exactly what she requested, and by doing so, she got ripped off. She bought a car for thousands above sticker and borrowed at near illegal rates. The dealer gave my sister exactly what she wanted: a car payment at $399/month, and all they did was fill-in the blanks. Her loan was 60 months (when it should have been at 48) and at an interest rate of 18.8% (when it should have been 9%). Ultimately, she'd pay twice the cost of the car because of one error—the error of being financially illiterate.

MANAGING A MONEY SYSTEM DEMANDS FINANCIAL LITERACY

You can't build a financial empire if you're ignorant of basic finance and economics. These disciplines are the building blocks to a financial empire, and without them the Sidewalk becomes a danger.

Remember, more money doesn't solve money problems. If not educating yourself after graduation is one step on the Sidewalk, the other is not educating yourself on basic finance and economics.

The world is full of financial illiterates; they've failed driver's education and don't know the rules of the road.

As kids, we aren't taught money management or basic financial discipline. We're abandoned in a financial jungle swarming with predators. Many perfectly intelligent people lack rudimentary knowledge of basic financial concepts such as:

- Interest rates
- Taxable and non-taxable yields
- Amortization of mortgages
- The balancing of a check book
- Basic percentage calculations
- Calculating return on investment
- Why stocks rise and fall
- Why a guaranteed 15% return on a bank CD is screaming, "scam!"
- How stock options work, such as calls and puts
- Why insurance exists
- How a mutual fund works
- What bonds are and how they rise and fall
- Global currency

To successfully leverage a money system for passivity, you have to familiarize yourself with financial instruments that fuel the money system. Do you know how to calculate simple interest? Return on investment? Do you know what happens to the price of a bond when interest rates go up? Can you figure out the difference between a tax-free yield and a taxable yield?

Financial illiterates can't manage money systems. To succeed on your road trip, you have to know the rules of the road and pass wealth "driver's education"—basic finance and economics.

LIVE BELOW YOUR MEANS—SLOWLANE?

The first rule of financial literacy: "Live below your means." Yes, a pragmatic doctrine echoed from Slowlane dogmaticians that is an affable replacement for its mathematical equivalent of "Keep expenses under your income." Earn 10 bucks and don't spend 20.

But is it Fastlane relevant?

Absolutely, with one distinction: *Live below your means with the intent to expand your means.*

"Live below your means" is relevant at any income level. The key variable is the word "means." If Bill earns $50,000 and Jack earns $1 million, who has the greater means? Who will live the extravagant lifestyle? Both might be living "within their means," but Jack has a drastically different lifestyle.

Remember, *Slowlaners seek to minimize expenses while the Fastlaner seeks to maximize income and asset values.*

You can live richly and still live below your means, but for Fastlaners it's a big challenge because we get paid first, not last. Tax bills come long after the income is earned, and "live below your means" requires above-average discipline.

A FINANCIAL ADVISER DOESN'T FIX ILLITERACY

I am my own financial adviser because I don't like losing control. Hiring a financial adviser might make sense to you aside from one caveat: *Hiring a financial adviser doesn't fix financial illiteracy.* Yes, just because you had salad for lunch, doesn't mean you can eat doughnuts for dinner. If you hire a financial adviser, you need competency to assess his advisement. Is your adviser advising a bond in a rising interest rate environment? Is your adviser advising treasuries when they are overbought? Is your adviser advising an investment that seems "too good to be true?" *Literacy gives you the power to evaluate your adviser's advice.*

In October 2009, actor Nicolas Cage, who reportedly earned more than $40 million in 2008, sued his former business manager for $20 million, accusing him of poor advisement and leading him down a path toward financial ruin. Cage contended that his manager exposed him to a basket of risky investments resulting in catastrophic losses. In a countersuit filed later, Cage's former business manager blamed "lavish spending" on Cage's financial difficulties—not his advice.

Whatever the truth, if you can't audit your adviser, you don't have control. If you can't critique good advice from bad you don't have control. For those who hire financial planners, *literacy is insurance.* Financial advisers do not solve financial illiteracy just as more money doesn't solve poor money management.

Financial illiteracy exposes you to risk, and in the worst case scenario, fraud. Bernard Madoff's investment fund defrauded thousands, and billions were lost, but what's more shocking is that the whistle was blown years before. You see, when you are financially illiterate, you are deaf. And when you are deaf, *you can't hear the whistle.*

CHAPTER SUMMARY: FASTLANE DISTINCTIONS

- The Fastlane is the means to your end because dreams cost money.
- Conquer big goals by breaking them down to their smallest component.
- Daily saving reinforces your relationship with money; it is your passive system that buys freedom and another soldier added to your army.
- A money system isn't used to grow wealth but to grow income. Growing wealth should be left to your Fastlane road.
- You will struggle to build a financial empire if you are financially illiterate.
- "Live below your means" is relevant at any income level.
- For the Fastlaner, "Live below your means" means to expand your means.
- A financial adviser doesn't solve financial illiteracy and literacy is insurance.
- Financial illiteracy dilutes your control, especially when evaluating the advice of a financial adviser.

Part 8

Your Speed: Accelerate Wealth

The Speed of Success

Ideas are nothing but neurological flatulence.

~ MJ DEMARCO

"WOW—220 MPH!"

I hear the "220 comment" from youngsters who sneak a peek into my Lamborghini while it's parked in public. The top speed on its speedometer is 220 mph. Yet, despite all that implied power, the car has never been driven to 220 mph or even 150 mph. The "220 mph" is nothing but "potential speed," and everything you've read in this book is just that: idle, unrealized potential.

The Fastlane philosophy and its mathematics are potential speed.

You understand the Fastlane roadmap and its wealth equation. You've dumped the Sidewalk and the Slowlane. Your vehicle is primed and filled with fuel. You're committed, not merely interested. You're ready to undertake process, and know what you want and where you want to go. You've picked a road, and it's time to hit the accelerator.

DOING NOTHING IS EXPECTED

Do those late-night get-rich infomercial products really work? Can you really make millions trading foreign currency or buying real estate with no money down? The truth is you can—but these infomercial peddlers don't tell you their real revenue model: *planned obsolescence.*

Planned obsolescence is a marketer's expectation that whatever they're selling you, you won't use it. And if you don't use it, you're unlikely to ask for your money back.

Doing nothing is expected. Human nature plays a powerful role in the business models of producers. Get-rich systems sold on TV (or online via landing pages) take advantage of human nature because humans seek events and want to avoid process. The path of least resistance is to not do anything, or to try halfheartedly.

The fact is, most people—whether they agree with Fastlane strategy or not—will do nothing with the information. They'll stare at the roadmap and agree with the mathematics, but never hit the road and the accelerator. It's one thing to possess the treasure map; it's another to get out of the house and follow it. Doing nothing is normal when it's normalcy that you seek to avoid.

THE STRATEGY FOR SPEED: CHESS, NOT CHECKERS

Speed is not thinking about a Fastlane business, but creating it. Speed is turning off Playstation. Speed is uncovering a need and formulating a solution and a prototype. Speed is filing paperwork for your business entity. Speed is making contacts and forcing your process out into the world. Speed is approaching your business like a strategic game of chess while your opponents play checkers.

Chess is a complex game with complex maneuvers, and your business must be run similarly. Unfortunately, most business owners approach business one-dimensionally, like checkers. All the pieces move identically, while in chess, the action is multi-dimensional because each piece moves differently with different roles. The entrepreneur who tries to compete playing checkers puts themself in a winless game.

Why?

The checker-playing entrepreneur has one move in the playbook: *price*. Raise prices, lower prices, cut costs, cheaper suppliers: "Oh Lord, how can I be the cheapest so everyone buys from me?" This one-dimensional attack throws entrepreneurs into cyclical bidding wars, marginalizing their offers with one goal in mind: To be the cheapest.

In the limo industry, price wars dominated because owners commoditized their brands to a unidimensional attack: "If my offer is the cheapest, I will book more business."

Success requires that you drop the checkers and start strategizing multi-dimensionally like a chess player. How? You treat each business function like a chess piece. How they're played will fate your Fastlane for speed or aimless drifting.

- The King: *Your execution*
- The Queen: *Your marketing*
- The Bishop: *Your customer service*
- The Knight: *Your product*
- The Rook: *Your people*
- The Pawn: *Your ideas.*

While it isn't within this book's scope to dissect every nuance of each (Unscripted, the book I published in 2017 is more detailed) I will highlight the crucial momentum-building elements that explode speed. You've got a system to build!

EXECUTION IS KING. IDEAS ARE PAWNS.

Potential speed is a loose idea that needs an executioner. When a youngster sees 220 mph on a speedometer, they see an idea and a possibility. In business, ideas are pawns; they're 220-mph speedometers on idle, parked Lamborghinis. Actual speed is execution—pressure applied to an accelerator—and it's the king of the entire game.

Potential Speed —> An Idea
Actual Speed —> An Idea Accelerated and Executed

An idea trapped in your brain is like a supercar trapped in the garage with a dead battery. It accomplishes nothing and its purpose is untapped. Execution is making an idea real and giving the battery a charge. Execution is taking that speedster out of the garage and slamming the accelerator to the floor, with the wind giving you a temporary face-lift. Execution is getting that idea out of your mind and onto the roads of possibility.

Entrepreneurs struggle to differentiate between idea and execution.

They think ideas are worth millions, when success is never about the idea but about the *execution.*

"I had that idea!"

Oh yeah?

Who cares.

So did a thousand other people. What separates you from them? They executed. You didn't, and you did nothing. Instead, you spent hours playing fantasy football. You spent the morning sleeping. You spent five days at a job. You chose everything but that great idea. You see, ideas are nothing but a chemical reaction in your brain. It's an event that requires little effort.

An idea is the event, the execution is the process.

Successful entrepreneurs don't start in flashes of brilliance; no, they take that flash of an idea (the event) and transform it into massive execution (the process). Execution is the great divider separating winners and losers from their ideas.

If you want to retire 30 years early, you need a dominant, relentless king. Aloof and blasé kings lose games and don't win races.

IDEAS ARE WORTHLESS; EXECUTION IS PRICELESS

Spend 10 minutes at my forum and you'll discover most entrepreneurs love ideas but rarely discuss execution. They dabble with the pawns of the game.

I have this great idea!
Is anyone doing this?
I can't disclose this idea because it will be stolen!
Will you sign my non-disclosure agreement before I tell you my idea?

No, I won't sign your NDA, nor do I care about your idea. In the world of wealth, ideas are worthless yet treated like gold. I love how idea conjurers protect their ideas with great stewardship, careful they don't get into the hands of would be thieves, not knowing their ideas are already shared by hundreds of others.

The owner of an idea is not he who imagines it, but he who executes it.

According to entrepreneur Derek Sivers (Sivers.org) ideas are just multipliers while execution represents actual money. Within our Fastlane chess game, ideas (pawns) are potential speed, while execution (the king) is the pressure applied to the accelerator.

This relationship demonstrates how the coupling of a great idea (potential speed/strong pawns) is worthless when attached to weak execution (no acceleration pressure/weak king).

The Pawn: Idea (Potential Top Speed)
Awful idea = 1 mph
Weak idea = 5 mph
So-so idea = 35 mph
Good idea = 65 mph
Great idea = 100 mph
Brilliant idea = 200 mph

The King: Execution (Accelerator Pressure)
No execution = $1
Weak execution = $1,000
So-so execution = $10,000
Good execution = $100,000
Great execution = $1,000,000
Brilliant execution = $10,000,000

If you notice, a brilliant idea and no execution are worth all of 200 bucks. Awesome potential speed (idea) is married to weak accelerator pressure (execution).

Yet a so-so idea with brilliant execution could be worth $350 million.

You see, it isn't about your ideas and their potential speed, *but about your execution!*

When I started my web business, several other companies already had established websites. Instead of reasoning, "Someone is already doing it," I executed better and became the leader in my industry.

Was my idea spectacular?

No. It was an OK idea, but I executed better than the competition.

After my revenue model became successful and unmercifully copied, did my business decline and fail? No, because the idea wasn't the linchpin to success, *it was execution.*

Competitors who copied my idea didn't possess a powerful king to the wealth game, and that is execution. Chess isn't won by stealing pawns.

How did Instagram and Facebook become two of the most popular social networks when they weren't the owners of the original idea? Execution. Execution is taking the neurological fart that is an idea and making it smell like a rose.

Seriously, think about what I've been saying throughout this whole book: Why is execution so difficult, while ideas are so routine? Once again, we return to our wealth dichotomy: EVENT VERSUS PROCESS. Execution takes process: effort, sacrifice, discipline, and persistence. Ideas are just events.

If you need to travel 6 million miles and you move at 15 mph, you will get there in 45 years. This represents the Slowlane. If you move at 95 mph, you get there in seven years. This is the Fastlane. The business of speed is execution. The speed of the Fastlane is growing a business exponentially and taking advantage of exploding net income and asset value.

CHAPTER SUMMARY: FASTLANE DISTINCTIONS

- Speed is the transformation of ideas to execution.
- Most people let powerful information expire and become worthless.
- Successful Fastlane businesses are run multi-dimensionally, like a game of chess. One-dimensional businesses focus on price only.
- Execution divides winners and losers from their ideas.
- In business, execution is process. Ideas are events.
- Ideas are potential speed. Execution is actual speed.
- Others share your blockbuster idea. He who thinks the idea owns nothing. He who executes the idea owns everything.
- Real money and momentum is created when an idea (potential speed) is matched with execution (accelerator pressure).
- An idea is neurological flatulence. Execution makes it smell like a rose.

Burn the Business Plan, Ignite Execution

Having the world's best idea will do you no good unless you act on it. People who want milk shouldn't sit on a stool in the middle of the field in hopes that a cow will back up to them.

~ CURTIS GRANT

THE WORLD REACTS HOW IT REACTS

The world reacts how it reacts. If you think 1 + 1 = 2 and the world tells you it's 3, you have to let it be, despite what your brain tells you.

When it comes to your ideas, your plans, and your business, you NEVER know what works until you put it out to the world.

In business, I call this "putting it out into the box."

Anytime I launched a new service or feature at my website, it turned into an experiment to see how the world reacted. And with each experiment, I'd be surprised.

"This new site design is going to be a blockbuster!"

And then, wham, hundreds of emails pour in from disgruntled visitors who want to string you up on an oak tree and castrate you.

The ultimate judge-and-jury of ideas is the world and the marketplaces that serve them. If the world likes your offer, they vote by giving you their time, their thoughts, or their money.

If they don't like your offer, they withhold their money and look elsewhere. And the really pissed-off ones? They email or post a blog calling you an idiot.

THE TRIBE HAS SPOKEN

My website needed a redesign, and I spent six weeks creating a new look. I was excited, and the world was going to love this design—it was clean, user friendly, and showcased my design prowess.

And then I launched it.

And the world hated it.

Complaints poured in. My site's bounce rate (people who visit one page and immediately leave) skyrocketed. My conversion rate plummeted to virtually nothing. I went from 1,200 leads per day to barely 500.

The tribe had spoken.

Despite my investment in that redesign, I immediately reverted back to the old version and trashed six weeks of work. My golden child was a golden failure. The world heralded a sign, I read it, and then reacted.

You see, *the world tells you which direction you should be going at all times.* Heed the signs.

How do you get the world to tell you?

Put your executed ideas and concepts out into the world and let it tell you. Paint the world with your brush of genius so they can tell you how right or wrong you are.

Put your executed ideas out into the box.

DEAD COLLEGE PROFESSORS ROLL OVER

The world doesn't care about ideas; it only reacts to them. This simple fact pokes a hole in one of the sturdiest institutions of entrepreneurship—business plans. Academia will be outraged at the atrocity. Be prepared for the ultimate business sacrilege: *Business plans are useless.*

Yes, I said it.

Business plans are useless because they're ideas jacked-up on steroids.

Unless you count a barbecue-stained Hooters napkin, I never had a business plan. In fact, the best business plans are ad-hoc scribbles on notepads, old Arby's bags, Baby Ruth wrappers, and voice memos on your iPhone. The problem with business plans is that they're another manifestation of potential speed. Like super-charged garage queens, they aren't any more powerful than the lawn mowers that sit next to them. *Business plans are useless until they are married to execution.*

And guess what happens then?

The moment you execute, the world will tell you just what I told you: Your business plan is useless.

The market (the world) will steer your business in unimaginable places that will violate everything about your business plan. Interview any successful entrepreneur and they'll tell you that they started off with intention A and ended at intention B. They sell product X and ultimately end selling product Y.

The world tells you where you should be going, and no, the world doesn't give two pence about your 150-page PowerPoint business plan.

Instagram started as a check-in location application. After hearing the market, it pivoted into a mass-market social network that focuses with a photographic emphasis. I started my website as a directory, and it transformed into a lead-generation portal. The world has the incorrigible power to corrupt business plans the moment the idea is transformed to reality.

However, this does not exempt financial analysis.

A blind jump into a business without knowing the specific financial constraints that govern that business would be foolhardy. When I made the decision to create a limousine website over a limousine company, I did a financial analysis. However, I didn't get entangled in the intricacies and paralysis of planning, which is no substitute for execution.

Figure out what needs figuring and just go do it.

The world will do its job and tell you the directions to travel.

BUT I WANT VENTURE CAPITAL!

I know I know: I can hear the objections already. Without a business plan, how will you get venture capital? Or investors?

You can't.

Without a business plan, you won't get funding. But please, take heart, the issue isn't your business plan nor will it ever be your business plan.

The best business plan in the world will always be a track record of execution.

If you are a successful entrepreneur, suddenly people will want your business plan because they know you can execute. If I received a business plan from an entrepreneur who sold his company for $20 million just two years earlier, you can bet your sevens I'd read it. The value is not the plan, *but the person giving it* and his track record of execution.

Today, I know a circle of people who would read my business plan if I gave them one. They know I have a track record of execution that validates the business plan. If you don't have a track record of execution, the business plan is a worthless piece of Kinkos-bound pulp.

GET FUNDED WITH EXECUTION, NOT WITH BUSINESS PLANS

I started my company on a shoestring and 900 bucks. No investors, no funding, and no help. The fact is, had I wasted 150 hours on a 95-page business plan, no one would have read it because I was unseasoned: I had no money, no track record, no races entered, no finishes, and no races won.

However, as I built and grew my business, something miraculous happened. As my ideas crystallized into tangible assets that could be consumed by the world, suddenly I became the approachable asset.

Venture capitalists and angel investors called me—I didn't call them.

Suddenly, people wanted to see my business plan. Why the sudden change of heart? Wasn't I the same guy just years earlier?

Sure, but instead of an idea on paper, *I had a tangible concept that reflected execution.*

A common question on the Fastlane Forum is "How can I find investors for my idea?" It doesn't matter if the idea is an invention or a great new website, my answer is never what these people want to hear.

If you want investors, get out and execute.

Create a prototype.

Create a brand.

Create a track record that others can see or touch.

Dive into process.

When you have a physical manifestation of an idea, investors will open their wallets. Heck, be good enough and they will be fighting to give you money.

You see, when you have nothing except 120 pages of text, charts, and graphs, that shows organizational skills, not execution. Angels to private equity never invest in business plans—*they invest in people with track records of execution.* That is your best business plan!

So if you really want to get funding for your business, get out and make your idea tangible. Give investors something they can see, touch, and feel. Give investors a glimpse of your execution, because that is what creates speed on the Fastlane.

CHAPTER SUMMARY: FASTLANE DISTINCTIONS

- The world gives clues to the direction you should be moving.
- Business plans are useless because they are ideas on steroids.
- As soon as the world interacts with your ideas, your business plan is invalidated.
- The marketplace will steer you into directions that were previously unplanned for.
- The best business plan in the world is a track record of execution—it legitimizes the business plan.
- If you have a track record of execution, suddenly people will want to see your business plan.
- If you want your business to get funded, take action and create something that reflects tangible execution.
- Investors are more likely to invest in something tangible and real; not ideas dissected endlessly on paper.

Pedestrians Will Make You Rich!

If you do build a great experience, customers tell each other about that. Word of mouth is very powerful.

~ JEFF BEZOS

THE BISHOP IN YOUR CHESS MATCH

When life is tough, we seek the counsel of priests, rabbis, or pastors. They are the "go-to" guys of life's problems. Yet when it comes to your business, who is your go-to guy? Who is on the frontline with your customers? The bishop in business's chess match is how you treat your customers—customer service. Your customer service should serve one function, similar to our men of the cloth, and that is to "always be there": help, support, and resolve.

MY INTERNAL ROADMAP: MY BLACK BOOK

The Fastlane roadmap was my compass for wealth, but I also had an internal roadmap, and no, it wasn't my business plan.

It was my little black book.

Nope, my black book wasn't a treasure trove of telephone numbers from female hotties but a written record of all complaints, grievances, and issues my business experienced daily. This book has served as my guide for over a decade.

When business owners hear a complaint, most of them ignore it. Most of them pass the buck to an employee and pray the issue goes away.

Not in the Fastlane.

Complaints are a beautiful thing. They represent free feedback and expose unmet needs in your business. *They represent the journey's road noise.*

I logged my customers' complaints because they provided a kaleidoscope into the customer's mind. One complaint meant there were 10 others who felt the same way. When my black book accumulated similar complaints weekly, I had to evaluate the issue and take corrective action.

Complaints are the world's whispers hinting the direction you should be moving.

THE FOUR TYPES OF ROAD NOISE (COMPLAINTS)

When the world unleashes its opinion on your new website, product, or concept, what should you expect? What should be addressed and what should be ignored? There are four types of complaints:

1) Complaints of change
2) Complaints of expectation
3) Complaints of void and
4) Complaints of fraud.

Complaints of Change

Take anything that people love, change it, and you'll have a riot at the steps of your business. Remember when Coke changed its formula? Oh heavens! How dare they! Remember when HBO ended the gangster drama *Sopranos*? Dear God! The world hates change, and it's a natural human behavior to resist change.

Change endangers comfort, expectancy, and security.

When I redesigned my website and hundreds of complaints poured in, I expected a certain degree of resistance. It's normal. In fact, every redesign I've ever done in 10-plus years was met with resistance. The question for critique was, how much was normal? And how much was legitimate?

Complaints of change are the least informative and therefore are the ones most difficult to decipher. For my redesign failure, data confirmed that the complaints were substantial. Bounce rates tripled and my conversion ratio suffered. I had to suck up the failure, revert back, and start over.

When you change, there will be complaints. Guaranteed. And yes, not all of them are actionable simply because human psychology is in play, not the integrity of your work.

Complaints of Expectation

Complaints of expectation occur when you negatively violate customer expectations. You convince them to do business with you, they expect something, and what you provide doesn't meet that expectation. This happens because either your service failed or their expectation was malformed by a deceptive marketing strategy. Regardless of which, both expose a problem. And it's your problem, not the customer's. You either need to do a better job in fulfillment or a better job in managing their expectations.

"Your service sucks."

I heard that complaint hundreds of times and yet my company not only survived, it thrived. If my service sucked and I was told it sucked, how did my business succeed?

I dug into the claims.

Advertisers who complained, "Your service sucks," didn't use my service as designed. Their expectations were malformed. I owned a lead generation service that sent email leads to clients. The thing about leads is they must be followed. You don't book leads after they sit in your email box for three weeks and then answer them like a first-grader. You don't book leads when you log in to your account once every millennium. Yes indeed, my service sucks when it isn't used properly.

Instead of targeting my customer, I sought to better manage expectations.

I made it abundantly clear that leads are only as good as the person following them. Unfollowed leads go unbooked.

Also, because most of my customers weren't communicatively savvy, I launched educational campaigns to ensure professional responses. If I couldn't manage the complaints, I could manage the expectations.

I knew if my customers were making money, they'd keep paying me.

When you order halibut at a restaurant and it's served raw, your expectation of a well-cooked meal is violated. You complain. Yet, for the owner there is a bigger problem: Why was it raw? Is the chef incompetent? Does the kitchen process need retooling? Complaints of expectation expose operational issues, marketing misinformation, and/or product problems.

If you hire a home renovator who advertises "guaranteed bathroom remodels in two weeks" and the job takes two months, your expectations are violated and either the marketing campaign needs to reflect that truth, or the operation needs to be retooled to fit the expectation. Either way, operations or marketing needs change.

Complaints of Void

Complaints of void are when your customer continually requests something and you don't have it.

Complaints of void are extremely valuable, as they expose unmet needs.

Early in my lead generation days, one of the most common complaints I received from limousine service providers was, "I don't do weddings!" Customers would request limousines for weddings and some providers didn't offer wedding service. Likewise, many providers didn't do airport transfers.

The complaints piled in and a pattern emerged.

I added a website feature that allowed providers to specify the services they offered—problem solved.

By fixing the issue, I *raised the value* of my leads.

Higher value equals greater magnitude, higher profits, and growing asset values.

Complaints of void are gold mines of opportunity. People freely tell you exactly what they want and you don't have to pay for it! Unmet needs are served up on a silver platter.

Complaints of Fraud

In March 2005, a woman entered a Wendy's restaurant and claimed that a dismembered human finger was in her bowl of chili. Her intent was not only to complain, but to sue. Fortunately, the fraudulent complaint was thwarted after the woman's litigious past was exposed. The following month, Las Vegas police arrested the woman for grand larceny.

At the bottom of the barrel are fraudulent complaints.

Ask any business owner and they'll confirm fraudulent complaints are the most disheartening because they reflect society's worst: Illegitimate complaints designed to exploit the business owner.

I had to deal with fraudulent complaints almost weekly.

A customer typos a price and some idiot thinks that they are entitled to a limo for $5.00 an hour versus the $50.00 per hour. "You owe me or I will contact my attorney and sue!" Yes, I'm sure you have an attorney. Good luck with that, champ. You're going to pay a lawyer $250 an hour to fight over a typographical error amounting to 45 bucks? Do you know what kind of fool you sound like?

Unfortunately, when you deal with millions of customers, you will encounter hundreds of Sidewalkers determined to get theirs. Yes, it can make you cynical because exploitive complainers are low-class frauds. When you drop a fly in your soup hoping to get a free meal, sorry, you're a crook.

How do you deal with exploitive complainers?

You respond once with grace, explain your position, and move on.

PICK YOUR BATTLES

There's an old saying, "I don't know the key to success, but the key to failure is trying to please everybody."

I started my business with an overzealous goal to keep everyone happy.

That soon proved to be insanity.

Complaints need to be managed with a balance, which is why I kept records. I wanted to identify patterns that would enhance the value of my service. I knew better products produced better customers, and better customers paid more.

Nowadays it's easy to follow the complaints for your business. Twitter.com offers owners the ability to keep track of what customers say. Google alerts can notify you when a website mentions your company name. With social media, keeping track of feedback is easier, but deciphering the noise is difficult.

"I don't want to pay for your service."

Some complaints need to be ignored. If you try to make everyone happy, you'll drive yourself nuts.

Pick your battles.

Solve complaints that add the most value while helping the most. As a business owner you must remember that, while you don't have a boss, the person who pays your rent is your customer and they always should be heard—but sometimes ignored.

USE "SUCKS" TO YOUR ADVANTAGE

No need to sugarcoat it. Customer service in the modern age sucks. We have become so swamped by poor customer experiences from the world's businesses that we now expect crappy customer service as a standard.

Have you ever called a computer manufacturer for support?

Or called your big national bank?

Or your health insurance provider?

Sucks. Sucks. And double-sucks.

Customer service today has become a lost art. Our service expectation for businesses has become so pathetic that we've been numbed to expect nothing positive: dismissed, disinterested, or worse, disregarded.

Down the block from my home, there is a strip mall with a corner restaurant that changes ownership every six months. Since I've lived in the neighborhood, four restaurants have opened and four have closed. While I can't comment on the first three failures, and I can on the last.

When I dined at the latest restaurant's incarnation, the food was decent but the service was deplorable. Drinks went unfilled. The silverware was dingy. The waitress was arrogant, as if our patronage was an inconvenience. After leaving, I thought, "That place ain't gonna last," and sure enough, a few months later the sign went up: "For Lease."

While bad customer service is frustrating while playing our consumer role, it gives us entrepreneurs a great opportunity.

Where customer service lacks unearths great opportunity.

You see, the beauty of expectation is that it works in reverse. While complaints of expectation are about the violation of expectations negatively, customer service that S-U-C-S is about violating expectations positively.

EXCHANGE "SUCKS" FOR "S-U-C-S"

You can explode your business into the stratosphere by deploying a customer service strategy that exceeds expectations: I call it SUCS, or "Superior Unexpected Customer Service."

We all expect a certain level of suckage when it comes to customer service. This is an advantage for Fastlaners. For example, if I discover a $10,000 fraudulent withdrawal on my bank statement, my first instinct is to freak out. My second instinct is to call the bank to resolve the problem. At that point, my brain immediately creates a smorgasbord of expectations for the bank call.

Here is my "expectation profile," or what I expect:

- I expect to hear a recorded message or an automated attendant.
- I expect to press a never-ending menu of buttons: press 1 for this, press 2 for that, press 3 for something else.
- I expect to be shuttled from one person to the next.
- I expect to speak with someone not fluent in English named "Steve" but sounding more like a Pradeep or Sanjay.

These are my expectations. No doubt, it isn't favorable. My bank, and hundreds of other banks like it, get away with crappy service because it is expected.

However, let's flip the scenario on its rear.

What if I call the bank and instead of the voicemail rat-maze, my call is immediately answered by an English-speaking person. No voice mail, no press 1, press 2, no automated attendant. I get a REAL PERSON answering the phone, like you answer your phone. After speaking five minutes to the customer service rep, my problem is resolved—and heck, I wasn't even transferred to another agent. I'd be like, "Holy Mother of God! Wow!"

This is a SUCS event: a Superior Unexpected Customer Service event.

It is a transformation from customer service that naturally sucks, to SUCS.

You see, when you violate your client's customer service expectation profile positively, you turn your customers into loyal, repeat buyers, and ultimately, disciples of your business.

LEVERAGE FREE HUMAN RESOURCE SYSTEMS

One passive income system is human resource systems—good old-fashioned people. Except that employees aren't cheap, so human resource systems typically need management. Wouldn't it be great if you could benefit from a FREE human resource system?

You can when you create disciples for your business.

Customer service that SUCS, service that violates your customer's low-expectation profile positively, turns customers into lifelong clients.

They become disciples of your business providing a never-ending stream of free advertising. Word of mouth, or social proof, is the best advertising there is. In effect, the mathematical equation behind social proof and discipleship is: 1 + 1 =3.

Because two customers creates one new one through word-of-mouth, the return on investment (ROI) on happy customers is infinite.

Your customer service strategy influences your company's growth more than advertising itself. Satisfaction isn't enough because it implies expectations are being met. To create raving customers, *you must exceed satisfaction.*

When I negotiated with potential buyers for my company, I was asked frequently: "How much do you spend to recruit advertisers?"

My unexpected answer?

Zero.

Incredulity and skepticism followed. Sure, I did it the old-fashioned way when I started: prospecting, marketing, advertising, and cold calling. But after awhile, my advertiser acquisition cost disappeared because my advertisers did it for me . . . for FREE!

When your clients love your business, they become disciples and advertise for you. They become unpaid human resource systems, evangelists who drop your name wherever necessary.

How do you create disciples for your business?

Provide customer service that SUCS—Superior Unexpected Customer Service. When you send an email to a corporation, how long does it take to get a real, human response? A day? Week? At my company, I answered my customer emails within minutes, not hours or weeks. People would email us just to test our response rate. I was in business to violate my customer's expectation profile, and it paid dividends.

I followed this up with live customer service. A call to my company got a real person that worked for the real company. No press 1, press 2. Support wasn't outsourced because I didn't want service outsourced.

Customer discipleship grows businesses exponentially because *human resource systems talk*. For example, my web-hosting provider is Liquid Web. The first time I contacted Liquid Web for technical support, I submitted a ticket and my expectation profile formed … I speculated it'd be a day or two before I heard back.

I was wrong. Within ten minutes, Liquid Web Support responded and fixed my issue within 20 minutes. They provided customer service that S-U-C-S and violated expectations.

The result?

I'm a disciple of Liquid Web. When someone asks me, "What hosting do you recommend?" I confidently respond with "Liquid Web." I am an evangelical customer. I pay Liquid Web in two forms of currency: 1) My money and 2) My frequent recommendation of their service. The effective value of this latter currency is priceless because I am now their FREE human resource system selling their product. Imagine the potency when you have not just one raving customer, but 10,000. Will your business grow 2% in one year? Or 200%?

To provide great customer service and explode your business, determine your customers' expectation profile. What are their expectations when they deal with your business? How do they relate to competitors and similar businesses in your industry? Make a subjective call on how your customers expect service. Then VIOLATE IT.

Any time you positively violate your customer's expectations, they buy from you again. Then they become unpaid human resource systems, liaisons, disciples, and free advertisers. All build speed. And speed builds wealth.

Great customer service costs more to provide, but the benefits should outweigh the costs. If more money were spent on pleasing existing clients rather than trying to find new ones, the average business would survive longer than five years.

Unfortunately, business owners who seek money first and needs last often spend their advertising budget on new customer acquisition, customers who aren't familiar with their uninspired and crappy customer service. It becomes a constant battle, like emptying a leaky boat with a bucket: Replace the old disgruntled customers with newer, oblivious ones.

Violate customer's expectations.

Create evangelists.

Create human resource systems that will work for you, for free.

Attract money.

WHERE ARE YOUR LOYALTIES?

The greatest myth of business ownership is "be your own boss." Owners who live by that mantra eventually find themselves bosses of nothing—dead, bankrupted businesses. Success in business comes from making your customer the boss and the No. 1 stakeholder to your business.

A stakeholder is defined as a "Person, group, or organization that has direct or indirect stake in an organization because it can affect or be affected by the organization's actions, objectives, and policies." Long-term business suicide occurs when you are your own selfish stakeholder and forsake your customer.

Want to really know why customer service sucks?

It's because business owners place their customers at the bottom of the stakeholder chain. Public companies are the worst offenders, as shareholders come first, Wall Street second, and executives third. Guess who sits at the bottom?

You and I.

My repeated, and often preached, motto to my employees was, "The customer pays your paycheck, not me—keep them happy."

You see, my stakeholder wasn't my selfish desires for fast cars and big houses. It was my customer, because I knew *they had the power.* My loyalty was with my customer. Yes, I had a boss, and the boss had the keys to everything I selfishly wanted.

LOOK BIG, ACT SMALL

In my high school gym class, my teacher had a knack for butchering the simplest of names: Henderson became Hankerson and Seagrams became Cegraves. No matter what your name was, he would shred it. I don't know if he was senile or just being funny.

So fast-forward more than a decade, and who is listed on my website as my chief technology officer? Mark Cegraves. Oh, and look who's my web developer—Gretchen Hankerson! Wow, so did I hire my friends from high school? No, I didn't, especially since their names were illusions of real people. None of these people worked for me. Yet if you visited my website's "Contact" or "About Us" page, they were listed as employees in high profile positions: CTO, business development, or Web Producer. These people weren't employees, but it looked like my staff was big, and growing.

This started as a harmless "inside joke" with my employees, but I eventually realized it had a benefit: it branded my operation to look big. Dominating. Well-funded. Growing. Of course depending on the person, an employee manifest featuring butchered names from a 1987 gym class tested ethical limits, but my purpose was clear: *I wanted to look big but act small.*

SETTING UP SUCS

Big companies notoriously provide poor service. Meanwhile, small companies are better apt to provide service with a personal touch. My objective was to look like I had the power of a big company, yet give personal service as if I were a one-person operation. When you receive detailed, exemplary service from a big company, you create a SUCS event and create loyal, evangelical customers.

Anywhere customer service is expected to suck, you have a business opportunity. Looking big and acting small is a setup for SUCS events. The customer expects mediocre service from the start. This tactic works well for any company that operates without a physical presence. Obviously, you can't look big if you own a small retail store, but for those of us with Internet companies, you can.

The trap that snares many business owners is the extreme opposite: *They look small and act big.*

"Joe Blow Enterprises." Does this give you confidence that you are dealing with a strong, reputable company? It screams "This is a one-man show!" and conveys amateur. Sorry, "Joe Blow Enterprises" is a monumental fail. I'm sure the logo is nonexistent, and, if there were one, it'd be bland, boring, or look like it was designed using some freeware paint program. This company's website is static, stale, and childlike. No, Comic Sans doesn't cut it for a professional image. This company sells to the world but doesn't have a toll-free number. Small. Small. Small.

The problem compounds when their smallish business operates with biggish company actions. Call their business and you get a long maze of buttons to press only to land at the bottom of a voice mail dump. Send an email? Forget it. Most emails are ignored, and the ones read are answered weeks later. "I'll get back to you" never happens. Customer service issues aren't resolved in hours, but in weeks.

If you insist on working 4 hours a week, your business won't grow because your selfishness is more important than growing a business meteorically. Look small and act big and you dig your own potholes.

BEAT COMPETITORS BEFORE THEY START

My other purpose for "looking big" was to beat my competition before they even started. When someone (or some company) wants to set up shop and compete with you, they investigate you first. They look at your website, see what you're doing and the prices you're charging. Then they decide if they want to invest time and money to enter the space. To the untrained entrepreneur, a big company will scare would-be entrepreneurs almost like it scared me . . . "Oh jeez, how can I compete when they have 12 employees against little me?"

If an entrepreneur thinks they can't compete because you're too big and too well-funded, you've won before they've even started. They either commit halfheartedly or defer to another industry with duller competition. *Look big, but act small.*

CHAPTER SUMMARY: FASTLANE DISTINCTIONS

- Complaints are valuable insights into your customers' minds.
- Complaints of change are difficult to decipher and often require additional data to validate or invalidate.
- Complaints of expectation expose operational problems in either your business, or in your marketing strategy.
- Complaints of void expose unmet needs, raise the value of your product or service, and expose new revenue opportunities.
- Great customer service is as simple as violating your customer's low expectation in the positive.
- Poor service gaps are Fastlane opportunities.
- Satisfied customers can be human resource systems who promote your business for free.
- Satisfied customers have a dual residual effect: Repeat business and new business via discipleship.
- Your customer's satisfaction holds the key to everything you selfishly want.
- Looking big but acting small sets up customer service expectation violations in the positive.
- Looking big can scare away potential competitors.

Throw Hijackers to the Curb!

People are definitely a company's greatest asset.
It doesn't make any difference whether the product is cars or cosmetics.
A company is only as good as the people it keeps.

~ MARY KAY ASH

YOUR CASTLE IS MISMANAGED

Your castle is your business. If you put crooks in the castle, expect trouble. Returning to our chess analogy, the rook—or the castle—represents the people you put in your business. This includes employees, partners and investors, and advisers.

THE BUSINESS MARRIAGE: PARTNERS

A business partner is like being married. It either works fabulously or it ends in fiery divorce.

Three years ago, Jim and Mike were drinking at a bar and a legendary idea was born that compelled them to start a business together. Their only consideration for the union was their excitement. They agreed to do a 50/50 profit split and promptly began. Mike finds their first client, while Jim finds the second. Within a few months, their client base expands to 28, enough for both to draw a profit and quit their daytime jobs.

After two years, Jim's time on the job and quality of work starts to suffer. Not that Mike knows what Jim is doing every minute of the day, but he notices something concerning. For every four clients Mike brings to the company, Jim brings one, and sometimes, none. He later learns that Jim read a book that advocates working four hours a week. And to make matters worse, Jim's clients are not supported well and Mike has to take up the slack; yet every Friday, like clockwork, Jim is there to get his 50/50 cut.

When Mike brings this to Jim's attention, Jim gets defensive, and tensions mount. This confrontation only decreases Jim's productivity to where he sometimes doesn't have new clients for months. Mike tries to dissolve the partnership, and Jim resists. Why should he? He's collecting 50% profits off Mike's efforts. Mike ultimately has to hire a lawyer and seek a legal remedy. A few years later, the partnership dissolves and, along with it, the friendship.

Partnerships are marriages. After the love affair and the lust wears off, they must survive on character, synergy, and complementary attributes. My early entrepreneurial ventures were all partnerships, and all miserable failures. Not that my partners were bad people, but our work ethics, values, and visions were not compatible. I remember one partner had a normal 9-5 job and was active in intramural sports; the business was number four or five on his priority list. The other partner was out working four other businesses, including ours. That left my business and me, which was priority *numero uno*. See the issue here?

Search the Fastlane Forum for "partnership" and you'll find a garden of complaints about partnerships gone bad. One partner wants to expand, the other wants to brand. One partner wants to advertise, the other wants to develop. One partner wants expensive cars and money yet arrives late and leaves early. Partnerships are like marriage—half the time they will fail because the partners just aren't compatible.

"They" say you should partner with people who have complementary skills to you. If I'm a marketing guy, I should partner with a technical guy. If you're a sales-and-people guy, you should partner with an analytical guy. While this is a great starting point, it's like marrying the first person you date simply because they like the same music as you. Many other personality characteristics will make or break a partnership.

- Do you have the same work ethic? Will your partner skate while you burn the midnight oil?
- Do you have the same vision? Or will they compete with each other?
- Do you want to grow slowly while your partner wants to own the world and do it fast?
- Do you want to sell franchises while your partner just wants one unit that pays the bills?
- Do you trust this person with your life?
- Do you have the same personality type?
- Do you have the same risk tolerance?

The fact is people get into partnerships for the wrong reasons. Like people start businesses under false premises (not need-oriented), they partner under a false premise: *Diversification.* The partners don't seek synergy; they seek diversification of risk, expense, and workload. Often, each partner looks to the other for the burden to bear, and when one bears more, resentment builds.

Partnerships can work, just like a lot of marriages work. Just make sure you know whom you're engaged to. A two-week honeymoon with your college roommate might not be enough courtship to determine compatibility. Would you marry someone after two weeks of dating?

GET A+ A'S

I've had many verbal negotiations with investors, and when the 90-page legalese document arrived on my desk, what was said and what was written were two different things. We discussed an amortized note at 10% over 5 years, so why does it say 5% over 10? Who exposed the incongruity buried in an avalanche of legal jargon? Not me. It was my attorney.

Then there was the time when a simple omission of a business expense can cost you thousands of dollars in taxes. Who knows that a $38,000 interactive voice response system is depreciable when you think it's just some overpriced telephone system? An accountant.

If I didn't have a good team of A's—*accountants* and *attorneys*—I'd be poorer. And yes, these people aren't easy to find because they're like partners under contract, another group of individuals who have the keys to your castle.

Don't be an idiot like me. Still green, I remember my first accountant, found right out of the Yellow Pages—not from referral, but blind hope. It didn't take long to see that she wasn't concerned with tax planning. No questions about my business or my concerns, just impatience to finish the forms and get it done. Additionally, most of her clients were Slowlaners who dabbled with W-2s and 401(k)s rather than corporations. Great pick, MJ. I needed someone with a Fastlane mindset, and I committed to finding one. After interviewing and investigating a half-dozen accountants, I found one whose clients were primarily business owners.

Be very careful with whom you trust with the keys to your castle because they can drive you to financial ruin. Remember Nicolas Cage; his manager allegedly drove him to the precipice of financial ruin. Investigate and interview. Get referrals from successful, established entrepreneurs. Treat your two A's like you would any partner, because they have unfettered access to your castle, and those with the keys have the potential to steer you wrong.

WOULD YOU LIKE A CHAINSAW WITH YOUR BEER?

When you blindly trust others to anything—business, financial investments, security—you're vulnerable to being conned.

There's an old beer commercial where a couple is driving down a dark country road and they spot a hitchhiker with a case of beer and a live chainsaw. The driver wants to pick up the hitchhiker because he advertises something he wants—the beer—but is blind to the chainsaw. Blind trust is like picking up a hitchhiker on a deserted road hoping to tap into his case of beer, but not seeing the torture device behind his back.

You must make your trust an asset to be earned by others. Let actions speak louder than words. When you allow words to disarm your trust or BS meter, you become vulnerable to attack.

One of the worst employees I ever hired was a pathological liar who stole from me. Why on earth did I hire her? She disarmed me with words. During the interview process she told me that she sang in the church choir and was a religious woman. While I didn't ask anything religious, I assigned honesty to religion. It dismantled my defenses and I hired her without verification. It took me several years (and hard lessons) to uncover the truth.

VERIFY FIRST, TRUST LATER

Former president Ronald Reagan once said, "Trust, but verify." When I hired the liar, I trusted but didn't verify. It took several robberies, video cameras, and public record searches to uncover the truth. I verified too late and it cost me.

The most egregious cases of trust are in our financial system. Bernard Madoff perpetrated the largest Ponzi scheme ever, and billions of dollars were lost. How does one man siphon billions from millions? Unverified trust. Thousands trusted Madoff and thousands failed to verify. Those who did verify didn't invest and some even blew the whistle. We are a trusting people and we want to believe the best. We want to believe in fairy tales and happily ever after. We want to believe we can make millions on Facebook ads, just as long as we PayPal that guru $97.

When I started my entrepreneurial career fresh out of college, I trusted everyone. I bought all kinds of crazy schemes that promised wealth. What happens when you trust everyone? You get burned. You get lazy. You hire criminals. When you trust everyone, you chase business opportunities that violate the Commandment of Control. Others get to dictate your financial road trip. And when that happens, you crash and burn. There is only one person you can blindly trust in this world, and that is YOU.

Why so cynical? If you don't understand now, you will later. *When you serve millions, you come in contact with millions.* Only then will you understand the truth of the consumer/producer equation. Your eyes will be opened to how many people will go the extra mile to try to screw you. There is no place safe from liars, con artists, and crooks. These people commiserate in the least likely of places: your community church, that harmonic dating website, and at your posh country club.

If I lose $10,000 on an investment that I meticulously investigated, I can deal with it. Easy come, easy go. Yet, if I have $10,000 stolen from me because I blindly trusted someone who I let into my vehicle, it's different. Today I trust no one but give everyone the opportunity to prove trust. There are a lot of good people in this world, and they do outnumber the bad by a wide margin. It just takes a mild effort to find them and keep them in your life. Just be careful who you pick up on the side of the road. Don't be tempted by a cold brew, but be blinded to the chainsaw.

FIRE RECKLESS CHAUFFEURS

Are inmates running the asylum? When you're not home, who runs your castle? Who chauffeurs your business?

Providing great customer service is one thing; getting employees to deliver it is another. When you shift your focus to the bottom line, often the frontline is sacrificed. How much is that untrained $10/hr. front desk person with a bad attitude really costing you? To make customers disciples of your business, employees must share your customer service philosophy. You can't let any employee ruin a multimillion dollar investment. *All the intangibles in the world can't change a poor customer service experience.*

After a nine-day stay in Las Vegas I learned how robotic service is the ultimate of business liabilities, regardless of poshness. Most people vacation in Vegas to escape from coworkers, incompetent employees, dirty houses, traffic, and your typical menagerie of life's dramas. Compliments of my friend's company convention, my Vegas stay started at the Rio Hotel. I had never stayed at the Rio and normally wouldn't consider this hotel. The place was hoary and dated; the bed was stiff and the accommodations worn. Nonetheless, I found the staff very nice. The dealers were friendly and the casino staff was accommodating to our minor requests. I enjoyed my stay.

After three days at the Rio, my hotel stay transferred over to the Venetian Hotel, a hotel that my American Express concierge arranged. For those unfamiliar with the Venetian, it is a newer hotel with opulent architecture: ornate columns and corbels, lavish chandeliers, and other affluent appointments that scream royalty. My stay at the Venetian was for six days.

Unfortunately, after six days, I will never return.

Loved the fancy Italian architecture, but their people suck. Our nightmare started on day one and continued every single day, marred by poor human experiences: unresponsive housekeeping, unacceptable hold times to hotel services, failure to deliver promises, robotic staff, overcharging, and, overall, a failure to provide an escape. There are two critical lessons in this experience:

1) A SUCS customer service philosophy must be delivered by your employees.
2) Spectacular product features can't overcome poor service.

First, employees must deliver your customer service philosophy. Your people are ambassadors of your business and they communicate your vision. Essentially, they're business chauffeurs, and if they're reckless, your vision is destroyed.

Your employees drive the public's perception of your company.

Was it the Venetian's policy to treat me with such disrespect and disinterest? Doubtful. The failure was in the communication lines from management to employee. Not just one employee, but several. You can't be driving the ship all day. Your employees carry the water buckets, and if they aren't ordained in service, they hijack satisfaction and create liabilities. A customer centered policy is irrelevant if employees don't translate that policy into frontline action.

The second lesson is this: No amount of spectacular product features, such as great technology (snazzy websites) or great architecture (lavishly appointed hotels) can compensate for poor customer service. Despite the Venetian's billion-dollar appearance, the marble floors and the ornate columns, their customer service sucked. Yet, at the Rio Hotel, customer service was excellent, which translated into a great experience, despite the hotel's dated building.

This incongruity represents a one-way street: Fanatical customer service—service that SUCS—can help compensate for shortcomings, but fanatical features cannot compensate for poor customer service, or poor human interaction. The Venetian's floor could have been made of solid gold. It wouldn't have mattered.

Nothing overcomes poor human experiences!

You could own the best hotel located on the best beach, but if customers are treated like inconveniences and requests go unanswered, they won't return. Exponential business growth is fueled by fanatical customer service, and your frontline employees must share your vision. It doesn't come from boastful mission statements plastered on the CEO's office wall.

CHAPTER SUMMARY: FASTLANE DISTINCTIONS

- A business partnership is as important as a marriage.
- A good accountant and attorney will save you thousands, perhaps millions.
- Accountants and attorneys have the keys to your castle; make sure you trust them fully because they have the power to right or wrong you.
- Unmitigated trust exposes you to unmitigated risk.
- Unverified trust can lead to uncontrollable consequences.
- Your employees drive the public's perception of your company.
- Fanatical customer service can overcome shortcomings, but fanatical features can't overcome poor customer service.
- Customer service philosophy is delivered from human interactions—not ambitious mission statements on a wall plaque in the CEO's office.

Be Someone's Savior

A market is never saturated with a good product,
but it is very quickly saturated with a bad one.

~ HENRY FORD

YOUR KNIGHT IN SHINING ARMOR

Is your product or service someone's knight in shining armor? Is it going to save the day? Or is your knight cut from selfishness, fueled by your hopes that it will gallop in on a black stallion and make you rich while simultaneously allowing you to be your own boss?

THE CROWDED WORLD OF "ME TOO!"

"Me-too" businesses make "me-too" incomes. It isn't hard to find businesses founded on something other than a need. They have no differentiation or uniqueness, and they sink into a crowded abyss of me-too and make their owners crazy once the illusion of "be your own boss" fades. Businesses founded on false premises will rocket to the bin of *commoditization* and force you to do the inevitable: To play checkers.

What is commoditization?

Commoditization is a product or service that appears homogeneous among providers. For example, a heavily commoditized service is air travel. Most people aren't loyal to any airline; they're loyal to the best price. The product becomes commoditized.

Another example is gas. I get gas at any of seven different gas stations because the product is commoditized.

People tend to make buying decisions for commoditized goods and services based on one metric: PRICE. If you don't, it's because the business has done a good job differentiating its product from the alternatives. If your product isn't unique, it doesn't stand a chance and you're forced into the strategy of "cutting prices to stand out from the crowd."

GET IN BUSINESS FOR THE RIGHT REASON

Why are you in business? Most likely for the wrong reason.

A perfect example is the limo industry, where new companies recirculate like turnstiles at the train station. What compels someone to open a limousine business? Rarely because of need. Nope, people get into the business because they are fulfilling their own selfish need—because they just want to, just like I wanted to years ago. In fact, the limo business appears to be some sort of graduation from taxi driver. Did the market need a new limousine company? Was there intent to deliver a superior product that stands above the competition?

Nope.

The intent was selfish: *I want to own a limo company so I'm going to start one.*

This creates excess supply and weak demand—too many limos running around and not enough customers. When supply exceeds demand, prices must drop; suddenly, the product becomes commoditized.

Disregarding market needs leads to commoditization where your soul is sold to the buyer who wants the cheapest price. Where does this insanity start? People start businesses they have no business starting. People start businesses "doing what they love" or "doing what they know."

A gentleman who owns a carpet-cleaning business posted a similar story at the Fastlane Forum. He wrote:

> *The problem is that although I provide incredible value for what I do, it is something that people don't want to buy. People avoid cleaning their carpets for as long as possible. So in reality, I'm providing something that is of little value. Thus, I can conclude that I need to change my business premise. So what values do I change my business premise to target? What do people value today? I think I'm in a business that is based on a bad premise.*

I feel bad for this man.

Why is he in the carpet-cleaning business? Because there was a need? Or because *he needed a job and wanted his own business*?

Regardless of the reason, he operates in an industry where the service is commoditized. Business owners fight over every customer while they earn fewer and fewer dollars for each. If he wants to grow, he has to cut his price.

My response was that you can't change your business premise because you are already in the business. The right business premise would have steered you clear of the industry or got you in the industry to attack a unfilled need. When hundreds of people get into a business solely because they know how or want to (not need based), you get put into commoditization position: price wars haggling over a few dollars. There is limited need (limited demand) and too many providers (supply). The point of having a need-based premise *is to avoid the industry entirely*, or to get in it to solve a specific problems and skew value, not to change it after the fact. If your product isn't someone's knight, standing out from the crowd and skewing value, it stands to be commoditized.

GET YOUR EYES OFF THE COMPETITION'S BUTT

Although my Internet service was for consumers, my paying customers were small-business owners. When you interact daily with hundreds of small-business owners, you get a keen insight into how they approach business. I mistakenly assumed that all business owners thought like I did, when often it was the opposite. I learned fast that *most business owners paid more attention to their competition than to their own business.* Instead of minding their own business, they had their noses into everything that everyone else was doing. This means you neglect your own product and become reactive instead of proactive.

Are your eyes on your vehicle and the road ahead? Or are you rubbernecking at the cars all around you?

Oh no! Excel Limousine dropped its hourly rate by five bucks! Mercy, call out the price police! Heavens! Godfrey Limousine is advertising its limousine as a 2017 model when it's a 2011 model! I'm calling my attorney!

If your eyes are glued to the competition's butt, guess what?

Your eyes aren't on the road ahead. If you're following, you aren't leading, and if you aren't leading, you're not innovating.

If Company X does something and you react, you are being reactive, not proactive. Why aren't they following *your* lead?

If your preoccupation is with every single thing your competition does, you're cheating your business and your customers.

HOW TO USE YOUR COMPETITION

Another "dead professor" moment: Forget about your competition 95% of the time. The other 5% should be used to exploit their weaknesses and differentiate your business. If you forget about your competition, you're forced to focus on *your* business, which is to innovate, skew value, and win over the minds of your customers. And when you fill needs and your army of customers grows, something suddenly happens: *Everyone follows you.*

In my industry, I lead the pack. I innovated and many followed. If I instituted a new feature, my competition would add the same thing months later. I was the first company to use the lead generation revenue model, and it was later copied dozens of times. My eyes weren't affixed to everyone else because I was preoccupied with my own success and the satisfaction of my customers.

On the rare occasions you peek in at your competition, do so for exploitation. *Mine their weaknesses and add value where they aren't.*

Uncover the need. Exploit their customer service gaffes. Is it impossible to receive good service? Do dissatisfied customers litter the web with their displeasure?

When I launched my first company, my competition consisted of existing websites and the traditional Yellow Pages. The weakness of both was *risk*. To advertise, you had to pay a big upfront fee regardless of benefit. If you spent $5,000 and acquired one new customer, you just spent $5,000 for one client. Scary risk proposition, huh? I thought this was too risky for business owners, so I sought to solve it.

For mature companies, competition can exploit what you shouldn't be doing, versus what you should be doing. My closest competitor was known never to answer their email. This gave me an advantage.

If you are going to take your eye off the road and spy your competitors, do so for finding value opportunities.

Exploited weaknesses are where brands are born.

What are they doing wrong?

Where's the inefficiency?

Within the gray area of unsatisfied customers lies the opportunity to improve value and ramp up differentiation. *Differentiation is a defense to commoditization.* Gloating over your competition should serve only one purpose: To find weaknesses and then be better at that weakness within your own operation. To the customer, this difference will be interpreted as better value. And better value equals more buyers won.

CHAPTER SUMMARY: FASTLANE DISTINCTIONS

- Commoditization occurs when you get into business based on a false premise—"I want to own a business" or "I know how to do this, so I'll start a business doing it."
- If you are too busy copying or watching your competition, you're not innovating.
- Use your competition to exploit their weaknesses, differentiate, and skew value.

Build Brands, Not Businesses

Everyone has an invisible sign hanging from their neck saying,
'Make me feel important.'
Never forget that message when working with people.

~ MARY KAY ASH

QUEEN ME: MARKETING AND BRANDING

In chess, lose your queen you lose the game. In business, most entrepreneurs play the game without their captured queen.

Have you ever bought a product from television, and when you used it, it sucked and didn't perform as advertised? Then, in dissatisfaction, you tried to return it and got the runaround from a guy who sounded like he had a double-digit IQ? That is the power of marketing: bad people, bad service, and bad product, but AWESOME MARKETING.

If you have an OK product (a weak knight), poor customer service (drunk bishops), and incompetent people (a castle full of idiots), you can survive with a powerful queen.

The queen is the most powerful piece in chess and it is also in business. Marketing can convince people to buy mediocre products. Marketing can hide or disguise service flaws. It can shadow incompetence, and it can keep convicted felons disparate from their product. The power of marketing is that an effective ad campaign can move products, regardless of the cockroaches hiding underneath. Marketing is a game of perceptions, and whatever the perception is, that's the reality.

BUILD A BRAND, NOT A BUSINESS

Businesses survive. Brands thrive. A brand is the best defense to commoditization. When your business just pays the bills for the month, you're playing checkers and being one-dimensional. People are loyal to brands and relationships, not corporations or businesses.

When you think about a Volvo, what do you think of? I think safety. Porsche? I think speed. How about Ferrari? Rich. Volkswagen? Practical... which then mutated untrustworthy with their 2015 diesel technology scandal. Toyota? Reliability. Yet, when someone mentions Chevrolet, nothing clear comes to mind other than bankruptcy, union squabbles, and unpredictable reliability. Some auto manufacturers have carved out strong brands, while the others fortify a business.

Our friend with the carpet-cleaning business also has a business and not a brand. Brands don't have identity crises, businesses do. If our friend wants to excel in an industry saturated with me-toos, he's going to have to brand and differentiate himself. He needs to be a Lamborghini in a traffic jam of Chevys. What will make his carpet cleaning business different from the rest? Why should people hire him even though his prices might be 20% higher?

These tough questions have tough answers, especially since his entry into the industry was based on a faulty premise. However, upon further investigation, most of his unscrupulous competitors use bait-and-switch advertising tactics gummed down with fine print. Perhaps this industry weakness is exploitable? My challenge to him was to leverage that nuisance. Perhaps he can brand himself as a "no-nonsense" carpet cleaner—fixed prices, no surcharges, and no fine print.

Apple, the computer maker, is a great example of building a brand based on a need, or a nuisance. People hate viruses, spyware, and the constant "Your updates are ready" messages that are associated with PC computers. Apple exploited PC's weaknesses and solved their problems. It has built itself into one of the most successful brands in history. Apple isn't the cheapest because they've engineered a brand and they can demand a higher price. Say "Apple," and many images come to mind: creative, trendy, easy, and hip. When I think of PC, I think of blue screens, illegal operations, and "you must reboot your computer 17 times before this update takes effect." One is a business. The other is a brand.

GET UNIQUE: THE USP

The first step at building a brand is to have a Unique Selling Proposition or a USP. As a business without one, you're adrift in a sea of me-too businesses without a rudder, unmoored to the tradewinds of the marketplace. USP-less businesses offer nothing distinct or unique, no benefit or logical reasons why someone should buy other than hope or circumstance wrapped around a cheap price.

Your USP is your brand anchor and is typically your lead value skew.

What makes your company different from the rest?

What will compel a customer to buy from you over someone else?

My USP was powerful: "No-risk advertising: If we send you nothing, you pay nothing."

Advertisers joined by the truckload because they were tired of expensive advertising options which offered this risk proposition: "Pay us $5,000 upfront, then hope and pray." I exposed a pain-point, fixed it, and then advertised it.

Our carpet cleaner had no USP. Nothing set him apart, as he might as well just been a lonely grain of rice in a 50-pound bag of feed.

USPs are the building blocks to brands and can compensate for higher prices or even an inferior product. FedEx was introduced to the world when it said, "When your package absolutely positively has to be there overnight." M&M's said, "The milk chocolate melts in your mouth, not in your hand."

Notice how these USPs target benefits. I don't like Domino's Pizza (despite once being employed by them), and yet that didn't stop them from building a pizza empire based on the USP of "delivered to your door in 30 minutes or less—or it's free." Domino's identified the need: Pizza delivery was a long ordeal. They solved it, branded it, and the rest is history. More recently, Dominos became the first major fast pizza chain to offer vegan cheese as an option. This uniqueness broadens their market to a swath of new consumers who never before considered the chain.

DEVELOPING YOUR USP

How do you develop a solid USP for your company? There are five steps.

Step 1: Uncover the Benefit(s)

Get into business for the right reason: to add or create value, solve problems or fill a need. That creates your first USP. If you are already in business, find your greatest product benefit, one that sets it apart from the competition. If you don't have a distinct benefit that's obvious to your potential buyer, you're operating without a USP.

Step 2: Be Unique

The objective of a USP is to be unique when compared to the alternatives. This plants a logical argument into your customer for choosing your company, because, without your company, they are forgoing the benefit.

USPs should use powerful action verbs that create desire and urgency.

"Lose weight" should be changed to "Obliterate fat" or "Shred pounds."

"Grow your business" should be dropped in favor of "Explode revenues" or "Shatter sales records."

Your USP's uniqueness creates a consumer divergence when it comes to their buying decision. If you pick a Mac over a PC, you are choosing safety, speed, and reliability over viruses and bloatware.

Step 3: Be Specific and Give Evidence

Noise is everywhere, and if you are going to rise above it, you have to alleviate natural consumer skepticism. Do so by being specific, and if possible, offer evidence.

WEB SITE: "Your car sold in 20 days or less or it's free."
PRODUCT: "Drop 20 pounds or you don't pay a dime."
SERVICE: "Your home sold in 30 days or I own it."

Domino's Pizza didn't say "Delivered on time," they said, "Delivered within 30 minutes or it's free." It was a specific action and evidence of that action. (Your pizza is free if we don't perform!) In my case, the onus was on me to send my advertisers leads. If I didn't, I didn't get paid. "We send you business or you don't pay a dime."

Step 4: Keep it Short, Clear, and Concise

The best USPs are short, clear, and powerful. Long phrases get skipped over.

Step 5: Integrate Your USP into ALL Marketing Materials

A USP is worthless if it isn't conveyed throughout every aspect of your business. Include your USP on all your public communications:

- Your trucks, vehicles, and buildings
- Your advertising, promotional materials, and social media accounts
- Business cards, letterheads, signs, brochures, and flyers
- Your website and your email signature
- Your voice mail system, receptionist/sales scripts, etc.

Step 6: Make It Real

A USP has to be convincing, enough so that people buy or, even better, switch brands. If it doesn't capture your audience's attention, or the benefit/hook is too weak, it won't work. And then make your USP real. You must deliver on what you say. A pizza delivered in 40 minutes makes the 30-minute guarantee a fraud. Fraudulent USPs get exposed and create "human resource systems" ready to rick-roll your company on social media.

GET NOISY

Next time you're stuck in traffic, look around. Every car looks the same. Nothing commands any significant attention. It's a sea of sameness. Born a marketer, this is why outrageous cars not found at every street light intrigue me. They rise above the noise, and optimally, we'd like our brand to do the same.

Face it. We seek to be different. Unique. The average teenager strives for uniqueness, which is why we have nipple rings, eye piercings, Goth, and tattoos—all expressions of "I'm different!"

Successful companies take the same approach with their branding and marketing.

Writing this book, while challenging, wasn't the real challenge. Getting it into the hands of people will be the real challenge. Why? Because the topic of finance and moneymaking is crowded and saturated with me-toos. In other words, the noise is deafening. While this book is the realization of my dream, to succeed as a best-selling author I need to get my brand above the noise.

One look on YouTube and all I see is noise.

College dropout earns $2,000 in one day trading penny stocks. Find out how!
See how I make $15,000 a month with this crypto blockchain opportunity!
New startup with a forced-matrix plan guarantees you a six-figure income!
I just joined this awesome affiliate program and made $300 today!

I recently used an Internet calculator that tabulated my "wealth percentile," which ranked my net worth in comparison to all of my peers in the United States. I was ranked in the top .05%. While I'm flattered, it exposes my challenge. My net worth is indicative of "unique" and "extraordinary" but in the world of perception, it's lost in the noise. On Instagram, you'd never guess that everyone is near broke. Nope, everyone is a multimillionaire, a success coach, a guru, or a model. Everyone is in the top 1% of his or her game, including the real top 1%. You see, we all are marketers and some of us are marketers of an illusion. What this does is creates an abundance of noise and makes it harder for the real value-providers to be heard. Your marketing efforts must rise above the noise.

HOW TO RISE ABOVE THE NOISE

There are five ways to get your message above the noise: 1) Polarize 2) Arouse emotions 3) Be risqué 4) Encourage interaction and 5) Be unconventional

Polarize

Polarization probably isn't the best business strategy for a mass-market brand, because polarization involves extreme viewpoints or messages. You don't want to piss off half your customer base! However, polarization works fabulously for websites in need of traffic or books in need of readers.

Polarization works because it involves an extreme viewpoint, which forces people to either *love* or *hate* you. Donald Trump is polarizing. You either love him or want to toss him off a boat in the alligator-infested Everglades. Political pundits use polarization to sell books, because readers want to rally for a cause, or furiously refute it. websites that polarize attract visitors as people defend their cause while others attack it. If you're a rabid Yankees fan and start a website that viciously attacks the ineptness of the Mets, you can expect a polarized audience—people who agree and concur and people who oppose and defend.

This book itself can be classified as polarizing. Many people will castigate my viewpoints as extreme since it goes against conventional wisdom. OMG he said the cutting coupons won't make me rich! He castigated my 401(k) Opposition to "normal" will always be considered polarizing.

Be Risqué

Sex sells, and it is the most used get-above-the-noise technique. Sex is a powerful noise disruptor because sex never goes out of style. You can overuse it, but people will always respond to it. In 2005, GoDaddy aired its first Super Bowl ad by using sex as weapon to get above the noise. The now-infamous GoDaddy Girl ads followed in subsequent years. I never thought the ads were that good, yet they got above the noise and got people's attention. The result? Increased sales and GoDaddy's market share surged to 32% after 2006.

Social media marketers use the risqué technique on Facebook and YouTube with glaring obviousness. Ever notice YouTube videos with sexual thumbnails always have ten times the views? In another case, one woman does video lectures on marketing techniques in her bikini. When she does, her bikini video receives *five times* the viewership and comments. Why do the bikini lectures do better than the normal ones? Simple: Sex gets above the noise. Men see the woman's busty chest in the video preview and think, "Oooh, I gotta check that out," while women are curious—"OMG, who is doing a video in a bikini top?" It's almost a mix of polarization and sex.

But be careful: leveraging sex as an attention grabber can also tarnish your brand if it isn't tasteful or within a reasonable spectrum of cultural sensitivity. "Great message" and "tacky" is in the eye of the beholder. And no, I won't be doing shirtless videos anytime soon. :-)

Arouse Emotion

Most consumer buying decisions are driven by emotions. You and I buy stuff because we want to feel something. I don't buy a Lamborghini to go from point A to point B; that's practicality. I buy to *feel* something—pride, achievement, uniqueness, adrenaline, and fame.

Another example of using emotions to move your audience comes from the nonprofit organization the American Society for the Prevention of Cruelty for Animals (ASPCA.org). This organization was founded over a century ago and I had never heard of it until recently. How did they break above the noise? They launched a powerful marketing campaign that unleashed emotions; their commercials featured caged, abused animals combined with a tender, heartfelt soundtrack.

If you can move your audience's emotions and *make them care*, they will buy. Exhilarate people, make them cry and make them laugh. Your message will rise from the ashes of noise and compel buyers.

Be Interactive

It's one thing to watch, it's another to do it. They say if you want to boil your passions, test drive the car of your dreams. Interactivity increases response for anything. If you can taste it, feel it, or use it, you will be more likely to buy it.

Interaction is like hearing your name. It's your favorite. On Facebook, the most popular applications are "surveys" and "questionnaires" because people love narcissism. My favorite movie is *The Usual Suspects*! I love pizza! I own a poodle! People love to talk about themselves, and if you entwine that into your marketing plan, you will improve the response to your product or service.

For example, if I launch a survey "Are you speeding the Fastlane or stuck in the Slowlane? Find out now." I am using an interactive campaign designed to involve people and get them to talk about themselves. When your potential customers break down their personal barriers and expose pieces of themselves, a relationship builds making it easier to sell. A relationship sells more than an anonymous corporate entity.

"Find out what happens next . . ." Some corporations are using traditional media and the Internet to foster interaction. I recently saw a commercial for an automobile manufacturer that filmed a story with a high-speed chase, except the story never concludes and we are left with "Find out what happens next . . . visit [website]." By teasing audiences with incomplete messages or stories, potential customers are left with an open loop that needs closing. They visit the website seeking closure.

The revolution of social media, blogs, and "Web 2.0" is founded on interaction. You just don't want to read an article; you want to comment on it! Your two cents must be heard!

And finally, video gaming and the "freemium" business model is another example of interaction. When you download a free video game and get addicted to its gameplay, you're more likely to "upgrade" and pay for the premium features.

Be Unconventional

Convention breeds familiarity. If you've seen it three dozen times in the last month, do you think it will work? For example, "Be your own boss" is such an overused phrase its power has been neutered. Yet, I still see advertising from so-called gurus using "Be your own boss," as if the phrase wielded power. Its been pulverized into flaccidity, so why the heck are you using it?

What's unconventional? Have you ever seen a Lamborghini sold for a dollar? I haven't and if I did, I'd remember. The campaign would arouse curiosity because it's unconventional. What crazy person would sell an exotic car for a buck? Is it a scam? What's the catch? I've got to see!

Another example of unconventional is to break convention by mocking it, or interrupting it. Remember the Energizer bunny? It's still going and going. These commercials built a brand based on unconvention—the advertiser created a series of standard, boring marketing messages and shattered them with sudden interruptions of the Energizer bunny. The marketer anticipated your familiarity with convention (ugh, another boring commercial) and shocked the audience by interrupting that boredom with a pink rabbit. AdAge.com recognized these commercials as one of the top 100 campaigns of all time.

On the internet, mocking convention works fabulously when combined with political incorrectness and humor. The Dollar Shave Club launched their company with a hilarious YouTube video and several years later, PooPourri did the same thing. The viral videos where shared millions of times, creating a swath of media attention and more importantly, customers.

Another mocker of convention is the Geico Insurance Company, which took typical situations and shattered them with the surprise punch line: "I just saved a bunch of money on my car insurance." Another Geico spot mocked convention when they aired a promo for a new reality TV series called "Tiny House." The promo featured a newlywed couple in a midget-sized apartment who endure cramped quarters and rising marital tensions. The couple is shown hitting their heads on low ceilings and struggling for a good night's sleep in a tiny bed. But wait, this expected convention of reality is only a ruse that bursts into unconvention when the announcer voices: "The drama will be real, but it won't save you any money on car insurance."

If you get someone's attention, half the battle is won. The other half is letting selfishness take over your audience and tailor your messages to self-interest. In other words, the good old "What's in it for me?" How about saving 15% or more on your car insurance?

WHAT'S IN IT FOR ME?

It's ironic: To succeed a Fastlane we must forsake selfishness yet satisfy the selfishness of others. Did I say this would be a cozy stroll down the beach?

The first human behavior you can count on is selfishness. People want what they want. People don't care about you, your business, your product or your dreams; they want to help themselves and their family. It's human nature. Therefore, our marketing messages must focus on benefits, not features.

People need to be told exactly what's in it for them.

How will your product or service help them?

What's the benefit?

In marketing speak, it's called the "What's In It For Me?" (WIIFM) principle.

My customers were small-business owners and yet I served millions of consumers, too. This intermediary relationship allowed me to study the behavior of both consumers and producers in a powerful, accelerated fashion. I learned things in weeks that would take educators months to learn. I noticed that small-business owners fall into their own selfish trap and love singing the praises of their company. They sell features, not realizing that people rent convenience and events, not limousines.

As consumers, we buy things to solve needs. We participate in transactions to fill voids.

You don't buy a drill; you buy a hole.

You don't buy a dress; you buy an image.

You don't buy a Toyota; you buy reliability.

You don't buy a vacation; you buy an experience.

We must become problem solvers and align our business as a savior to someone. Features must be translated into benefits. Does the fact you are the largest limousine company in Colorado solve my problem? It doesn't until you translate that feature into a benefit.

TRANSLATING FEATURES INTO BENEFITS

If you want to sell anything, translate features to benefits. A four-step process accomplishes this.

1) Switch places.
2) Identify features.
3) Identify advantages.
4) Translate advantages into benefits.

First, trade places with your typical buyer. Be them. Who are they? What is their *modus operandi*? Are they affluent CEO types? Or price-sensitive Wal-Mart shoppers? Cash-strapped students? Or single moms? If you can't identify your typical buyer, your results will be flawed and your benefit hidden. Once you identify your buyer, ask: What do they want? What do they fear? What problem do they need solved? Or do they just want to "feel" something?

For example, two brands of the same product could have two different buyers. A person who buys a Corvette has different psychological motives than someone who buys a Volvo. Both are cars, yet the Vette buyer isn't buying basic transportation. He's most likely a risk-taker, self-employed, independent, outspoken, and assertive. The Volvo buyer is probably more concerned with family and safety, likely conservative and analytical. Two totally different buyer profiles means each marketing message must be specifically targeted to the desires of each group.

After you switch places with your customer and grasp what they want, your next step is to isolate the product features. For my web service, I let my customers schedule their vehicles and target leads for each, by both date and service type. While these features were great, it was my responsibility to translate them to benefits. What makes them so great? What advantages do they offer my client?

After you isolate the features, translate those features into benefits, or a specific result. Extrapolate forward the benefit of that certain feature. This is where you drive home why someone should buy from you, versus the other guy.

For my web service, the seemingly simplistic feature of "upload pictures" translated to: "Quit wasting time with client meetings at garages. Upload photos of your fleet and show your clients your product!" The "target" feature translated to: "Target the clients you want—right down to the day, service, and vehicle type." Schedule vehicles translated to: "Maximize your fleet's road time and receive leads based on your vehicle availability!" Each feature transcribed to a specific benefit that would compel my buyer to join. I didn't let them fill in the blanks; I filled in the blanks for them.

USING PRICE AS A BRANDING WEAPON

Price is like a paint job for your product or service.

My first taste of "paint" and its implications came young. I wasn't much older than six or seven. Mom staged a two-day garage sale, and she permitted me to sell some toys and keep the money. One item I offered for sale was a "football clock," a timekeeping monstrosity. I vividly remember its sale price—$2.55. A steal, I reasoned.

On the first day of the sale, my football clock gathered many looks, but no sale. My young mind plotted. How can I get $2.55 for my clock? I didn't want to budge on my price, surely because $2.55 was the cost of some gadget I wanted to buy at the corner store. Then I had an idea.

I grabbed the masking tape Mom used for labeling prices. I tore four small pieces of tape and stuck them above the current price. Then on the first piece of tape, I boldly wrote $5.55 and crossed it out. The next piece of tape I wrote $4.50 and crossed it out. Then, $3.95, and the next $2.95. Each piece of tape successively had a lower price, clearly crossed out so buyers could see the "price reduction," leaving the same old price of $2.55.

Now my clock was priced exactly the same, except it was presented differently. The taped higher prices, visibly slashed, conveyed two things: 1) A higher value and 2) A smoking deal.

And guess what? The second person to look at the clock bought it. I succeeded at reframing price in the mind of my buyer. Of course, at seven years old, I had no clue what "marketing" was, and I certainly didn't know that my pricing scheme was indeed, a scheme. Yet this was my first marketing exposure and price's implication to value.

PRICE CONVEYS MORE THAN JUST COST

Price is a brand-builder because *price implies value.* The more expensive your price, the higher its perceived value. The cheaper your price, well, the cheaper it will be perceived. Price isn't just a number that tells someone cost. It conveys value and worth.

There's an old story about how price equates to value. Cleaning his basement, a man found an old dresser and decided to give it away. He moved the dresser to the street corner and placed a sign atop it: FREE. Shockingly, the dresser stood there all day, and for several days thereafter. This confused the man because the dresser, albeit old, was in decent shape and just needed a quick wood stain for perfection. The man decided a new strategy was warranted. He went to the street corner and replaced the "FREE" sign with "$50." Not an hour later, the dresser was stolen.

Same objective, different pricing strategy.

Unless price is your brand (Wal-Mart, Southwest Airlines), don't let price steal your brand when it should be defining it. Price is more than just a competitive metric that slides up and down to sell goods faster. It also indirectly conveys the value of your product or service.

I had multiple competitors who undercut me by 10%, sometimes even 20%. Yet I continued to prosper. I wasn't the cheapest, so why did I do well? My service had better value, and I kept my price correlated to that value. My leads were better targeted. I had better joint venture partners. I had great support. I was running a brand while my competitors were running businesses.

My artist friend, who painted the most exquisite, beautiful paintings, priced her work through her own limited price filter. She was a single mom living paycheck to paycheck. For her, $500 was an extraordinary amount, and because of that, she priced her works far below their true value. Her own corrupted vision of price distorted her earning power and degraded the perceived value of her work. I suggested a price increase. Take that $90 painting, make it $300, and see what happens. Sure enough, she sold just as much art at the higher price, because price implies value and defines brands.

Even in the Slowlane, pricing can play a role, in the form of a salary you're willing to take. For example, this was posted at the Fastlane Forum:

> *A company placed two ads for only one web programmer position in the paper. One listed the salary as $120K a year. The other ad listed it for $32K a year. The first, higher paying ad received only about four responses. The second ad for MUCH less pay got over 100 responses. Most people have a lack of confidence in themselves and their ability and are willing to settle for so much less.*

Are you settling for less in business? Is your warped frame of value corrupting your unrealized potential? The right pricing strategy is crucial to brand building and marketing. The wrong price conveys the wrong meaning. For industries with heavy commoditization, price is crucial. A public relations consultant can charge 30% higher than their competitors, but a gas station can't.

While I'm not feminine or metrosexual, I have a fascination with designer purses because I admire their pricing strategy. How does a handbag sell for $4,000 when it probably costs them less than $100 to produce? Branding and marketing. Price is a part of the brand build.

Premium pricing is one of the many ways to get into the consumer's head. But only if you can convince them of value beyond the cost of its practicality. What makes you different from the rest? Why should someone pay you more? As a marketer you have to drill into your buyer's mind and get your brand differentiated. Own the consumer's mind and you own the consumer.

CHAPTER SUMMARY: FASTLANE DISTINCTIONS

- Marketing and branding (the queen) is the most powerful Fastlane tool.
- Businesses survive. Brands thrive.
- Businesses have identity crises, brands don't. Identity crises force business owners into price commoditization.
- Unique Selling Propositions (USPs) is a brand key and differentiates your company from the rest.
- People have a natural desire to be unique and different.
- Marketing success requires messages to break above the noise, or advertising clutter.
- Polarization is a great above-the-noise tool if your product targets a polarized audience—usually politics, minority opinions, and even sports teams.
- Sex sells and always draws eyeballs. (But can tarnish your brand image.)
- Consumers make buying decisions based on emotions before practicality.
- If you can arouse audience emotions, convincing customers to buy is easier.
- People like talking about themselves. If you can incorporate interaction or "try before you buy" into your campaigns, you will have better success.
- To be unconventional means to first isolate and identify what is conventional, then doing the opposite, or interrupting that convention.
- Consumers are selfishly motivated. Always target your messages toward the predisposition of "What's in it for me?"
- Features are translated to benefits when you switch positions from producer to consumer, identify the feature's advantages, and extrapolate those advantages into a specific result.
- Price implicitly conveys value and worth.
- Don't allow your own perception of price lead your brand to mediocrity.

Choose Monogamy Over Polygamy

No horse gets anywhere until he is harnessed.
No steam or gas ever drives anything until it is confined.
No Niagara is ever turned into light and power until it is tunneled.
No life ever grows great until it is focused, dedicated, disciplined.

~ HARRY EMERSON FOSDICK

CHEATING SPOUSES AREN'T GOOD PARTNERS

As we near the end of our conversation; I must address the Fastlane's need for faithfulness . . . monogamy.

In college, my friend Mark Tekel was quite the ambitious entrepreneur. And Mark, if you're reading this, I apologize for the call out. But what the hell were you thinking?

Mark would get involved in a different business every week. One week it was some moronic MLM program, the next it was some turnkey ad scheme found in the back of an entrepreneur magazine, and the next it was some classified ad program. Different week, different opportunity. My friends eventually coined this opportunity-hopping neurosis the "Tekel Syndrome."

The Tekel Syndrome is a compulsion to scatter your focus across different projects and opportunities. It's also a symptom of money chasing versus need filling. When you invest your time into five different businesses, you become a polygamist-opportunist. The idea is to toss as much shit on the wall as possible because something's gotta stick. Something's gotta make me some money!

A scattered focus leads to scattered results.

Instead of one business that thrives, the polygamist-opportunist has 20 businesses that suck. Ten businesses earning $10,000 cumulatively are not better than one business that does it single-handedly.

When you segregate your effort among assets, you build weak assets.

Weak assets don't do heavy lifting, and they don't build strong pyramids.

Weak assets do not generate speed.

Weak assets do not scale to multimillion-dollar valuations.

Weak assets do not accelerate wealth; they build income to pay the month's bills only to start again next month.

I dabbled into polygamy when I started another web business that mimicked my current company. Once launched, the new web business siphoned time from my core breadwinning company. In effect, I cheated on my spouse and it showed. Time once allocated to my thriving company now went to my infant company.

The results were not good, and I had four options: 1) Continue cheating on my existing business, 2) Hire someone to manage the existing business, 3) Hire someone to manage the new business, 4) Discontinue the new business.

Ultimately, I discontinued the new company, because I reasoned that hiring additional employees would inject management time into my life.

MONOGAMY LEADS TO CRAZY FUN POLYGAMY!

I don't know any highly successful polygamist-opportunists unless they were monogamous first.

Seriously, think about it.

The richest people in the world got rich by focusing on one core purpose, not by diverting focus. Lebron James wouldn't be any good at basketball if he spread his interests around. He focused on one thing and one thing only: basketball. He ate, slept, and shit hoops. Now, with his legendary status and millions in net worth, he can afford to be polygamous with his interests.

To hit the top of your game, business or otherwise, you have to eat, live, and shit your thing. If you're dabbling in 10 different things, your results will be dabbling and unimpressive. Focus on one thing and do it in the most excellent way.

Some of the greatest tech entrepreneurs built impressive companies by 100% committed focus, not diverted attentions into other ventures. After successful entrepreneurs hit the mother lode of wealth, then, and only then, do they divert into other ventures that deviate from their core business.

In other words, *their monogamy led to polygamy.*

What's usually the first thing an entrepreneur does after they sell their company for $100 million? They go out and invest in multiple companies, get involved in philanthropy, and spread out their passions.

Why is polygamy now possible?

Money.

Money buys systems, like human resource systems, and money systems that buy time.

Fastlane success comes from monogamy; not split attentions among wives and mistresses. It's marriage. Yes, good old-fashioned monogamy. Focus on one Fastlane business and kick ass at it.

CHAPTER SUMMARY: FASTLANE DISTINCTIONS

- Tekel Syndrome sufferers are polygamist-opportunists who opportunity-hop.
- A weak business commitment commits you to weak assets. Weak assets do not accelerate wealth.
- The most successful entrepreneurs lived and breathed their business with 100% commitment.
- Successful business monogamy can lead to successful business polygamy, a diversification into many passionate interests and investments.
- Save the "I have ten businesses" until after you sell one company for millions.

Put It Together: Supercharge Your Wealth Plan!

Your choices are made in a moment, but their consequences will transcend a lifetime.

~ MJ DEMARCO

GIVE WEALTH A SUPERCHARGER

The journey of a thousand miles begins with one step. I've spun a lot of information your way and it's time to put it together and take your first step. It's time to unfold your process with concerted action. You now have the necessary psychological and mathematical framework that will give you better probabilities for wealth. To start your Fastlane financial road trip bolt on the **F-A-S-T-L-A-N-E S-U-P-E-R-C-H-A-R-G-E-R**, which is an acronym for the Fastlane process.

1. Formula (Fastlane supercharger)

Wealth is a **F**ormula and a systematic process of beliefs, choices, actions, and habits that form a lifestyle. Wealth is a process, not an event.

2. Admit (fAstlane supercharger)

Admit that the preordained path to wealth, "Get Rich Slow," is fundamentally flawed because of Uncontrollable Limited Leverage, weak mathematics predicated on time (Wealth = Job + Markets). Admit that "Get Rich Quick" exists. Admit that "no plan" is not a good plan. Admit that luck is the residue of engagement.

3. Stop and Swap (faStlane supercharger)

Stop following the wrong roadmaps. Stop doing what you've been doing. Stop selling your soul for a weekend. Stop thinking that 401(K)s and indexed-funds will make you rich. Swap ineffective roadmaps for the Fastlane roadmap. Swap your allegiances from consumer to producer.

4. Time (fasTlane supercharger)

Time is the king asset of the Fastlane—specifically, free time. Invest in activities that pay more than money, they pay free time. Avoid time thieves, such as parasitic debt that converts free time into indentured time. Invest time into a business system that can transform indentured time into free time. Make decisions with time as a key decision factor.

5. Leverage (fastLane supercharger)

Leverage controllable and unlimited mathematics to create wealth. There is no leverage within the Slowlane wealth equation, an equation predicated on time (hourly pay, annual salary, annualized return, years invested). If you can't control the mathematics that underscore your wealth, nor accelerate them into large numbers, you can't control your financial plan. Leverage is harnessed by a system that does the work for you.

6. Assets and Income (fastlAne supercharger)

Wealth is accelerated by exploding income and **A**sset value via a business that can be systemized and eventually sold in a liquidation event. Live below your means but seek to expand your means by focusing on income while simultaneously controlling expenses. Exponential growth of income and asset value, not slashing expenses, creates millionaires.

7. Number (fastlaNe supercharger)

What's your **N**umber? How much money will you need to live your dream lifestyle? Determine your number, break it down by the penny, and make it real today. Start saving your loose change, open a brokerage account, and put a chart on your wall that continually monitors your number's progress. Make your dream lifestyle real by posting photos of that life at your workspace. For example, if you want a cabin on a mountain creek, find a picture of that vision and put it on computer so you have to see it every day. Make your future visions real and force them into your psyche so you're constantly reminded. Make those dreams tangible and inescapable!

8. Effection (fastlanE supercharger)

Grace **E**ffection and you shall be graced with wealth. The Law of Effection states, "The more people whose lives you affect in an environment you control, the more money you will make." Impact millions and you will make millions. When you solve needs on a massive scale, money flows into your life. Money reflects value.

9. Steer (fastlane Supercharger)

Life's **S**teering is choice. At some point, you must commit to the Fastlane ideology, and that commitment forms your process. Wealth is not one choice (event), just like you cannot choose to lose 100 pounds and suddenly wake up 100 pounds lighter. How you steer determines whether the Fastlane is a lifestyle, a hobby, or a lottery ticket. To enforce good decisions at the extremes, deploy WCCA and WADM. Decision horsepower is strongest in youth and bleeds with age. Examine your past choices. Why are you where you are? What has been treasonous to your life? Why are you drowning in debt? If you don't rectify the mistakes of your past choices you will be destined to repeat them. Behavior change begins with a reflection of your past decisions and modifying them for the Fastlane mindset. Become responsible, followed by accountable.

10. Uncouple (fastlane sUpercharger)

Officially **U**ncouple from the Slowlane wealth equation by creating your business structure in a favorable Fastlane entity: a C- or S-Corporation, or an LLC. Thereafter, your entity is the body of your surrogate business system. It "pays itself first" and the government last. It survives time separate from your time. It is your first step at creating an asset.

11. Passion & Purpose (fastlane suPercharger)

With a business entity and a dollar figure that outlines your dream life, you will need a **P**assion and a **P**urpose to fuel you into habitual action. Don't confuse "passion" with "do what you love." Passion burns your soul and drives you to do whatever it takes. Passion revs you with excitement and enrages you with discontent. Some passions are selfish (I want a Lamborghini) and other passions are selfless (I want to help orphaned children). It doesn't matter what it is, as long as the passion burns hot enough to burn a hole in your pants and gets you stoked for process.

12. Educate (fastlane supErcharger)

Education begins at graduation. Pledge to never stop learning. What you know now is not enough to become the person you need to be tomorrow. Seek Fastlane knowledge that fosters the construction and operation of business systems in an environment that you control. Get to the library and get on the Internet. Information is the oil on your financial journey. Ensure daily reading in short bursts by leveraging existing time blocks often squandered: the train, the plane, while exercising, on lunch break, an hour in the morning before work, or while waiting at the post office.

13. Road (fastlane supeRcharger)

Get onto a Fastlane **R**oad. But don't worry if you can't decide which road; the road can pick you. Train your mind to see needs, problems, and ways to improve things. Observe your thoughts and language, because they expose unmet needs, or needs met poorly. You don't have to find the next breakthrough; just find an improvement opportunity, a pain-point, or a service gap, and solve it. Many of the best businesses in the world are based on products that already existed; the owners solved the problem better or more efficiently. When you focus on market gaps, roads open. Yes, the road chooses you.

14. Control (fastlane superCharger)

Control your financial plan as this refers to the Commandment of Control. Engage in an organization that you fully control, from pricing to marketing to operations. Fastlane entrepreneurs don't cede control over critical business functions to hierarchical control structures, because they are the control structure. Swim as a shark, not a guppy.

15. Have (fastlane supercHarger)

HAVE what others NEED and money will flow into your life. This reflects the Commandment of Need. You can't explode your income by chasing money. Stop chasing money, because it eludes those who try. Instead, focus on what attracts money, and that is a business that solves needs. Money comes from providing value. Cast aside selfishness and seek to HAVE what your fellow man WANTS. When you do, money flows into your life because money is attracted to those who have what others want, desire, crave, or need.

16. Automate (fastlane superchArger)

Automate your business and honor the Commandment of Time. Get your time detached from your business. The best passive-income money-tree seedlings are money systems, rental systems, computer systems, content systems, distribution systems, and human resource systems. The key to automation in any business lies in these seedlings.

17. Replicate (fastlane superchaRger)

Replicate your system and honor the Commandment of Scale. Get on a playing field where home runs can be hit. To make millions, you must impact millions. To impact millions, you must be on a field capable of affecting millions! Can your product, service, process be replicated on a global scale to tap the Law of Effection?

18. Grow (fastlane superchar**G**er)

Grow your business by treating it multi-dimensionally, like a game of chess. Build a brand, not a business. Treat customers like your boss and reposition complaints to opportunities. Listen to the world as they offer the best directional clues. Resist commoditization. Differentiate yourself from the competition. Get above the noise. Focus on one business and one business only.

19. Exit (fastlane supercharg**E**r)

Have an **E**xit strategy. Full passivity accomplished by a money system is one Fastlane destination. Money systems are best funded by liquidation events of massive asset values. Know when it's time to liquidate your assets, transforming paper money into real money. Know when it's time to get off the horse and learn to ride a new one.

20. Retire, Reward, or Repeat (fastlane supercharge**R**)

After liquidating your asset(s), **R**etire or **R**epeat. Regardless of which, **R**eward yourself for milestones met along the journey. Sell your first product? Celebrate! Go to dinner, buy a cigar, drink a beer. Break $100,000 in net worth? Treat yourself to something nice. Book a joint-venture deal? Celebrate with an indulgence. Go over $1 million? Take a nice vacation. Break $10 million? Buy a Lamborghini.

"UHH, SIR . . . WE'RE CLOSING . . ."

The Fastlane isn't a destination.

It isn't something you try, it's something you live.

It's a mindset and it all starts in your head.

If you're already looking at business opportunities and asking "Is this Fastlane?" you still don't get it. The Fastlane is a seed that starts in your brain, and grows from there. You can nurture the seed. It is there NOW. Question is, will it grow? Be fed sunshine and water? Or will it wither and die once life's drama takes over?

Fight through Slowlane dogma and you will find that the Fastlane journey is one of discovery and incredible self-growth. And more importantly, your dreams will be resurrected and teeming with probability.

It doesn't matter where you start, but how you proceed. The garage door to an exceptional life is open—leave behind the past that keeps you grounded and take the road. All Fastlaners start in similar straits of life turbulence.

But MJ, I have a mountain of credit card debt!
But MJ, I have a job stocking shelves at the supermarket!
But MJ, I have no time after work!
But MJ, my wife hates my business ideas!
But MJ, you don't have two kids to support!

Beware of the "buts," because they do just that: They grind your butt into the couch, doing nothing. Excuses never made anyone rich, and we all have them. Stop being like everyone and start taking action. Make a choice this year that can change your life forever.

Wow . . . we've been here a long time, the sun has set, and the coffee shop attendant has flipped the closing sign. I want to thank you for trusting me with your time. I hope it was helpful to your dreams, your life, and your goals.

If you want to discuss the Fastlane strategy further with over 40,000 entrepreneurs from around the world, join the community at TheFastlaneForum.com. It's FREE and yes, I say "hello" to my readers and contribute there nearly every day. Also, I've written a newer book (Unscripted © 2017) which lays out the entire blueprint for turning the Fastlane into a total life strategy—why just build a business, when you can build a life?

If this book has inspired, changed you, or help set you free, please tell a friend or let me know at the forum. I hope *The Millionaire Fastlane* has awakened your dreams and given them a chance to breathe. Always remember, if your dream is alive, you're *already living the dream!*

I hope everything for you, and perhaps someday, your impact on the world will reverberate through the years when you can reflect on that simple choice made long ago . . . that choice to pick up a book and read it.

To your dreams, your life, and your happiness. . . good luck and God bless.

~ MJ DeMarco

APPENDIX A
Reader Reflections

MJ, I'm a high school teacher . . . how do I go Fastlane?
Can you address any problems in your world? What if you invented a product that every school needed for their curriculum? What if you wrote a book that was targeted to teachers? Could you start your own private school? Can you create an education program and sell a subscription to it? A video education has legacy. Once you create it, it exists through time, separate from your time.

If you can't identify a need near your existing road, can you identify other problems on a different road? Perhaps a student has insight into a problem that needs a solution. Do you hear their complaints? Their issues, trials, and problems? Needs are everywhere, and they don't have to be viewed from your current road. Roads are opened only when you knock on their doors.

Additionally, as a teacher you have unprecedented access to time that most others don't. The off summer months could serve as great Fastlane launch point.

MJ, my neighbor has owned a business for 19 years. He's never home and he has time for nothing. And he certainly isn't rich. Owning a business doesn't guarantee wealth!
I agree. Your neighbor's problem is his business likely fails the Commandment of Time. If your business cannot divorce from your time through a money-tree seedling, your business is probably just a bill-paying job.

MJ, I owe $22,000 in debt and am barely making ends meet. Where do I start?
Start by understanding the source of that debt. Why does it exist? How did you accumulate $22,000? Your debt accumulation wasn't an event, *but a process* that happened over many years. You don't just wake up one morning and have $22K in debt! Your choices led the way—the many choices to buy on credit over paying cash. You chose to buy those trendy clothes. You chose the fancy car. You chose to run with the Joneses and charge everything on your credit card. Or perhaps you live in a house that's just too expensive.

Escaping debt requires a commitment to process over event, except in the reverse. Repent from the Sidewalk and make new choices that keep the debt from growing, or better, get it declining. Pay cash for everything. If you can't pay cash, you can't afford it.

Second, focus on your income. Face it. You need to make more money. If you owned a business that profited $15,000 every single month, would that debt suddenly seem like such a burden? No, it wouldn't. You'd have it paid off in weeks, not decades. *Income is the answer*, with a temporary mandate at expense reduction to curb debt growth. Start by looking at a side-hustle; sell on eBay, do odd jobs, sell your art on Etsy. At some point, commit to starting a need-based business that you can use to expand income and expose yourself to the Fastlane wealth equation. Yes, you might need to get your hands dirty doing something others would find repulsive. Do what others won't. You either want it bad, or not at all.

MJ, my wife and I are traveling two different roads. She is a lifelong Slowlaner consumed with saving every dime and living a life of frugality, and I am a serial entrepreneur who wants a little more from life. My problem is my "serialness" hasn't produced success other than turmoil in my relationship.

Has your wife read this book? If so, and she doesn't agree, you might have tough decisions for your future. Your spouse is your lifelong partner, and if your roads don't run parallel, it could be rough riding ahead. Like our choices and their horsepower, relationships also have trajectory. Today's road that diverges one degree from your partner's road will be divergent 90 degrees years from now.

Personally, I'm not interested in relationships that are "good enough" but relationships that empower both individuals to be their best. I can't speculate on your relationship's strength; only you can. Can you and your spouse compromise on some common tenets that can bridge your divide? Like the value of time? The importance of financial literacy? The need to divorce your income from time? The ruinous effects of parasitic debt? Perhaps these common grounds are strong enough to keep your roads bound for a common goal.

And finally, your "serialness" might be a problem. Are you a polygamist opportunist balancing 10 different opportunities? Your business is a spouse. Quit cheating and give one business all of your attention. You will get out what you put in, and rationing your time among mistresses is a slow roll to lackluster incomes and asset values.

MJ, what about real estate? You don't mention it a lot . . . is it Fastlane?

For real estate to "be Fastlane" requires effort and manipulation of the Five Commandments. Namely, are you a real estate investor because of need or because it's just something you know? A successful real estate investor flips a house because it needs rehab. A successful real estate investor develops an apartment complex because the neighborhood needs it.

Additionally, real estate possesses magnitude but lacks reach. That means multiple successes, or intentional iteration is required. One tiny property isn't going to make you rich, but 200 accumulated over the years might. Accumulation doesn't happen in a few short years, but many. I never met a 22-year-old multimillionaire real estate investor simply because it is a slower Fastlane with asset values that cannot be manipulated as easily as your own self-created business. Asset value is limited by magnitude, which is why the richest real estate investors are not only older, but they focus on high-dollar properties. Real estate possesses an excellent detachment component that survives time.

MJ, is affiliate marketing "Fastlane"? I know some guys who are killing it!

Affiliate marketing (AM) violates the Commandments of Entry and Control, and if you can subvert those restrictions, it can be Fastlane. Unfortunately, by the strictest of definitions, AM is not Fastlane. Nonetheless, it can be a great strategy for income and serve as a digital marketing education. It also can be a great place to get started in business. Sometimes you just need to start doing something, anything! Remember, "Fastlane" starts in the head.

As for the big money marketers, sure they exist. Likewise, lottery winners do too. And yes, there are some career network marketers who are millionaires. My viewpoint is not about absolutes but about *probabilities*. Whenever you violate control, you relinquish control. Whenever you violate entry, you must be exceptional.

For every affiliate marketer earning $30,000 a month there are 300,000 earning less than $100. For every network marketer who earns $50,000 a month there are 500,000 making less than $100. For every lottery winner who wins $1 million, there are one million losers. Probabilities!

If you think you can defy probability and be exceptional, go for it. And congratulations! I can think of several exceptional affiliate marketers worth millions. If they can succeed in that field, I have no doubts they can kill it in the Fastlane!

Experience in non-Fastlane disciplines doesn't mean that the discipline is worthless or to be avoided. I am about mathematics and probabilities—that's why my bread isn't in someone else's basket. Affiliate marketing is a powerful mechanism to grow your business; that's why I advocate *creating* affiliate programs that the masses will want to join, not *joining* them.

MJ, should I skip college?

I can't make your life decisions, especially when I know nothing about you, your culture, or your background. For me, it all depends on its cost, your maturity, your goals, and its marginal benefits. If you want to be a doctor, engineer, or a nurse, yes, you need school! If you want to invent a product that needs significant engineering, you're probably going to need college! Just be careful of education servitude and know that a college degree is not a prerequisite to wealth. The velocity of any education varies by its intended purpose and cost. I went to college and I have no regrets, although today, I wouldn't pay $50,000 for it.

MJ, my upline sponsor said you're a dream stealer and that your viewpoint on network marketing is flawed.
Great, then keep taking advice from him. Let me know how that goes in five years.

I have a wife and two children to support and I can't afford to quit my job. Where can I find time to go Fastlane?
Time isn't the issue—desire and passion are. Without burning passion, your desire manifests as interest, not commitment. Committed Fastlaners build wealth, while interested Fastlaners build excuses. You are deep in the trap because you have responsibilities. This is how the Slowlane wins and keeps you amenable to its plan. To break free, you need to commit and draw from an insatiable passion personal to you and your family. That passion will find you the time, whether it's early mornings, late evenings, or on the weekends. Remember, the average American watches 9 years of TV in a lifetime. Start there.

MJ, you're pathetic. Lamborghini's and flashy cars don't make people happy.
LOL. I agree. Cars and expensive toys won't make you happy. I was already happy when I bought my first Lambo, and it reflected my reward (fastlane SuperchargeR). Happiness evolved from the achievement's process, while the purchase was the reward and the event. Achievement is the cake, the reward is the frosting. Your repeated action toward specified goals will make you happy, not a car! And when that happens, you might be shocked that the ostentatious car is no longer desired.

Additionally, scientific studies have proven that autonomy (freedom) represents 50% of a person's happiness equation. I am free and the sports car symbolized that freedom. Are you free or just a hater hating?

I'm a single mom and a dental hygienist. How do I go Fastlane?
Ugh. Again, "Fastlane" starts in your head. Then it grows. You could be mopping floors and "be Fastlane". Going "Fastlane" in business lies in the commandments CENTS (Control, Entry, Need, Time, and Scale). Can you create a business that solves a need on a massive scale? On your existing road (dental), is there a dental need that could help thousands? If you can't expose value opportunities or solutions respective to your industry, you have to open your mind to the world. Remember, you aren't just a dental hygienist; you're a mother, a woman, and a daughter. There are hundreds of roads in those subsets. What are you passionate about? Politics? Natural living? Gardening? Are there unmet needs therein? If you can't figure out a new road, let a problem that needs a solution uncover your road.

Starting a business is risky. Is there any way to minimize that risk?
Yes. Get in business for the right reason, and the right reason is to fill a void in the marketplace or to do something better than anyone else. Business becomes risky when entrepreneurs start companies based on flawed, selfish motives. Remember, strangers don't care about your dreams and we're inherently selfish.

Risk is escalated when you get into business without a defined need, brand, or purpose. Risk is escalated when you get into business *doing what you love* versus *doing what needs to be done*. Risk is escalated when you cede control over major business functions to someone else. Yes, business is a risk because entrepreneurs lose perspective on the fundamental purpose of business, and that is to solve problems, skew value, and help your fellow man. Profit follows—it doesn't lead.

MJ, it's clear that you are a control freak. Since the Fastlane is predicated on passive income from interest, how do you deal with interest rates since you cannot control them? If interest rates are zero, doesn't that invalidate the Fastlane?

Yes, when it comes to my financial plan I'm a control freak, and you should as well. If you aren't in control, then you're dependent on someone else for your comfort and security. Not for me. Second, yes, I cannot control interest rates. However, your number (Chapter 37) should be large enough to accommodate interest rate variances. Even in this low-interest-rate environment, I still can find safe, predictable 5% returns because I think globally, not locally. Also, income is not limited to interest, but corporate dividends and partnership income. If your nest-egg number is predicated on a 10% yearly return, you are fooling yourself and will feel interest rate pains. Set your number high enough to expect variance.

MJ, can't a good mentor be a form of a wealth chauffeur?
Mentors are excellent resources if they're sought for guidance and not as personal escorts. I've mentored some individuals who weren't genuinely interested in hard work or sacrifice; they wanted someone to absorb risk and hand hold process. Mentorship is not about outsourcing process, but about providing guidance as you forge your own journey. Good mentors are accelerative tailwinds!

MJ, aren't you being hypocritical by scourging "material extravagance" and yet describing the Fastlane by material items like Lamborghinis and big houses?

No, because the Fastlane isn't about buying stuff but about *freedom*, and the freedom to afford whatever you want. There's a difference between being imprisoned by your stuff and buying what you can afford. If you can drop $300,000 for a car and not be a shackled to the purchase, go for it. See my answer above with respect to autonomy.

MJ, why should I listen to you? You got lucky.

Fact: the larger the outcome, the more likely "luck" will be perceived and/or felt. Luck is merely a function of probability and I strive to manipulate probability. Some people don't manipulate probability and their wealth chances amounts to calling a coin flip 10 times in a row. I work to put myself in a position where I only need to correctly call the coin flip once. Both scenarios are functions of probability.

MJ, I can't come up with any ideas. Every time I think of a problem or find a need I discover someone else is solving it. It's impossible to find legitimate ideas!

You're thinking about it too esoterically. As long as the world is imperfect, there will always be ideas. To profit in business, you only need to skew value on a couple of value attributes. A skewed value attribute could be better ingredients, better delivery, better customer service, better packaging, better user interface, better website, better functionality, better this, better that. Skew two or three value attributes and you have yourself a business. I detail this process in my newer book, Unscripted.

MJ, aren't you being a hypocrite because you're getting rich selling books?

Writing is my passion and I can do it without the confirmation of money. Most of my net worth (over 90%) comes from activities not related to authorship. Yet, If I "get rich" selling millions of books, it's only because the mathematics (CUL) of the Fastlane work. The equations that made me rich, continue to make me rich. Isn't that what I'm teaching here?

MJ, I'm in a rut and can't seem to break free. I stock shelves during the day and wash dishes at night. I can't seem to make headway.

Change starts with your beliefs, because they dictate your future choices. If you want to make headway, you have to BELIEVE you can make headway. Starting your process starts with a simple choice. Make better choices and your first choice should be an examination of your past choices.

Why are you where you are?

What has been treasonous to your life that has put you at a stainless steel sink washing dishes?

Second, you need to reflect on how you can help others within your talents. If you lack talent, you need to acquire it. You can become an expert at anything with enough study and application. This is fact. Unfortunately, such dedication comes with a price and often involves turning off the TV and making a sacrifice of immediate pleasures in lieu of a more favorable future.

I don't care if you're scrubbing toilets; if you solve the needs of many, you will solve the needs of one.

And that one person? THAT ONE PERSON IS YOU.

APPENDIX B
The 40 Fastlane Lifestyle Guidelines

I SHALL . . .

1. Not dismiss "Get Rich Quick" as improbable.
2. Not allow the Slowlane to bury my dreams.
3. Not allow Slowlane prognosticators to contaminate my truth with their dogma.
4. Not ordain the Slowlane as *the* plan, but let it be *a part* of the plan.
5. Not sell my soul for a weekend.
6. Not expect nor seek a chauffeur to wealth.
7. Not trade my time for money.
8. Not put time in control over my financial plan.
9. Not forsake control over my financial plan.
10. Not demote time as abundant and effervescent.
11. Not assign faith to events, but to process.
12. Not take advice from gurus who preach one roadmap, while getting rich using another.
13. Not use compound interest for wealth, but for income.
14. Not disrespect the passivity of a dollar.
15. Not cease learning at graduation, but start it.
16. Not impose the burdens of parasitic debt into my life.
17. Not play on Team Consumer, but switch to Team Producer.
18. Not dismiss the plausibility of my dreams.
19. Not chase a path of money, but a path of need.
20. Not fuel my motivation by love, but by passion, purpose, and why.
21. Not focus on my expenses, but on my income.
22. Not pay myself last, but first.
23. Not do what everyone does.
24. Not trust everyone, but allow trust to be proven.

25. Not relinquish control over my business.
26. Not hitchhike, but seek to drive.
27. Not operate within limited scales and in tiny habitats.
28. Not dishonor the horsepower of my choices.
29. Not swim as a guppy in a pool, but as a shark in the oceans.
30. Not consume first, but produce first, and consume later.
31. Not partake in barrier-free or entry-weak businesses.
32. Not invest in other people's brands, but in my own.
33. Not give credence to ideas, but to execution.
34. Not forsake my customer for other stakeholders.
35. Not build a business, but a brand.
36. Not focus my marketing messages on features, but benefits.
37. Not be a polygamist opportunist: Focus!
38. Not operate my business like checkers, but chess.
39. Not live above my means, but seek to expand my means.
40. Not live without the insurance of financial literacy.